The Macintosh Bible
"What Do I Do Now?" Book

What to Do Instead of Panicking

B

The Macintosh Bible
"What Do I Do Now?"™ Book

What to Do Instead of Panicking

Charles Rubin

PEACHPIT PRESS
Berkeley, CA

A Goldstein & Blair book

The Macintosh Bible "What Do I Do Now?" Book
Charles Rubin
A Goldstein & Blair Book

Peachpit Press, Inc.
2414 Sixth Street
Berkeley, CA 94710
(800) 283-9444
(510) 548-4393
(510) 548-5991 (fax)

Technical editing: Randall Slafsky, John Kadyk
Copy-editing: Lyn Cordell, Dashka Slater, John Kadyk
Proofreading: Dashka Slater, Jan Brenner, Karen Faria
Index: Stephen E. Bach
Word processing: Jan Brenner, Louis Benainous
Cover: Charles Fuhrman Design   Cover concept: Arthur Naiman
Inside design: Connie Torii, Byron Brown
Page layout (using QuarkXpress 3.0): Byron Brown
Fonts: Univers, Palatino, Brush Script (from Adobe), PIXymbols from Page Studio Graphics
Printing: Consolidated Printers, Berkeley CA

Library of Congress Cataloging-in-Publication Data

Rubin Charles, 1953-
    The Macintosh Bible "what do I do now" book : what to do instead
of panicking / Charles Rubin -- 2nd ed.
        p.   cm.
    Includes index.
    ISBN 0-940235-23-4 : $15.00
    1. Macintosh (Computer) I. Title
QA76.8.M3R82 1991
004.165--dc20   91-42658
                                                                CIP

printed in the United States of America   printing #   2 3 4 5 6 7 8 9

Table of Contents

Acknowledgements

This book would not have been possible without a lot of help. I'd like to thank Randall Slafsky for his painstaking technical review of the manuscript. Despite a rather hectic work schedule and home life, Randy read every word and made dozens of helpful suggestions and corrections, all under a fairly tight deadline. I'd also like to thank Lee Hinde of the MacNexus user group in Sacramento, California for his comments on the book's technical content.

I'm grateful to the Developer Technical Support group at Apple Computer. My questions via AppleLink were always dealt with promptly, and in most cases the person fielding my questions went out of his or her way to expand upon the subject, giving me much more help than I'd asked for.

My editors, who always do their best to make a book as good as it can be, outdid themselves this time with their thoroughness and insight. Many thanks to Lyn Cordell and Dashka Slater (who edited sections of the manuscript) and particularly to John Kadyk, who put it all together and without whom this book (and probably most of the books that come out of G&B) would never have made it into print.

Another member of the Goldstein & Blair team who helped me more than anyone was Jan Brenner, schlepper, word processor and copy editor extraordinaire, who went beyond the call of duty in keeping the editing and production schedules on track and was always there with a sympathetic ear.

Finally, I'd like to thank the many readers of the first edition of this book who wrote in with suggestions for improving it. Some of these people helped point out typos, and others offered new problems (and often solutions) that have been added in this edition. Keep those letters coming, folks.

We've made every effort to make this book as helpful and accurate as it can be. Any mistakes that remain are my responsibility alone.

Charles Rubin
Oakland, California
October 10, 1991

Introduction

One nice thing about the Macintosh is that you don't have to know a lot about computers before you start using it—you just insert a disk, turn the Mac on, point, click and get on with your life. Sure, you have to learn enough to tell a mouse from a menu, but if you're like most of us, you want to spend as little time as possible reading a manual before you get down to computing.

That's exactly why a lot of people like the Mac—it lets you start by doing instead of reading; but beneath its appliance-like exterior, the Mac is a computer all the same, and, like any other computer, it will occasionally do something unexpected. Perhaps you'll just see an unfamiliar message on the screen, or maybe the Mac won't even start. Maybe the screen will freeze and the Mac will refuse to accept commands, or it might suddenly forget how to print a document. Whatever the problem, you can't continue working until you fix it, but you're not anxious to thumb through page after page of the Mac manual trying to figure out what to do. That's where this book comes in. It's a reference guide that shows you how to respond to basic Mac alert messages and fix common Mac operating problems quickly. When something happens that you don't understand, you can look it up here, follow a few simple steps and—most of the time—get back to work without further ado.

How to use this book

This book describes specific Mac alerts, problems and solutions. As you can see from the table of contents, the alerts and problems are grouped into chapters based on activities you perform with the Mac.

The first three chapters cover basic Mac hardware and software concepts like the System Folder, the Chooser, the Finder and its menus, icons, pointing and selecting. You'll need to understand these basic terms and concepts (if you don't already) to apply the solutions presented in the chapters that follow. After all, if the solution to a problem involves using the Chooser, it's important that you know what the Chooser is and how it works.

Chapter 4 is a brief guide to preventive maintenance and troubleshooting. By reading and following the suggestions in this chapter, you'll avoid a lot of potential headaches, and learn the techniques you'll use in later chapters to recover from problems that do occur.

Chapters 5 through 14 describe specific alert messages, problems and solutions. If you understand the basics covered in the first four chapters, you should be able to turn to these chapters when problems arise, and find a quick solution.

Because networking is a separate and somewhat complex topic, we've reserved our final chapter for a discussion of the issues and problems specific to networks. Once you've read the introductory section to Chapter 15, you'll be equipped to handle the alerts and messages pertaining to networks which are covered in the rest of that chapter.

The best strategy is to read—or at least skim—Chapters 1 through 4 so you'll be familiar with basic Mac operations, maintenance and troubleshooting techniques. This shouldn't take very long, and it will save you a lot of head-scratching later when you're actually trying to solve a problem. If your Mac is attached to a network, you should also read the introductory section to Chapter 15. After that, keep the book near your computer. Use the table of contents and the index to find discussions of particular problem areas, or zero in on specific problems using the *Alert message locator* at the end of the book.

What the book covers

This book covers technical basics and common alert messages and problems for any Mac you're likely to be using now, running any version of the system software from 4.2 through 7.0. Since System 7 has many new features and in some cases operates significantly differently from previous versions, sections that deal specifically with System 7 are identified by special margin icons like the one next to this paragraph. If you're using System 7, these markers will save you time by guiding you directly to sections that deal with the latest version of the system software. If you're using an earlier version, you'll be able to skip material that doesn't apply to you. Sections that deal specifically with System 6 are identified in the section head.

In case you're wondering whether this book will have you pulling chips out of your Mac's insides, rest assured that it won't. Most of the problems you're likely to have with your Mac are software-related and will respond to software solutions. If faulty hardware is the culprit, this book will help you identify the problem so you can either fix it yourself (using a repair guide like *The Dead Mac Scrolls* from Goldstein & Blair) or take your Mac in for service.

As a rule, System 7 is much better than System 6 at explaining problems and suggesting what you should do when they occur. System 7's alert messages are more detailed, and some even offer to help you fix problems automatically. Nonetheless, all those alert boxes, beeps and exclamation points are enough to make anyone a little nervous, and this book's mission is to put you at ease.

In Chapters 5 through 15, the book follows a consistent format for presenting Mac problems and solutions. First, there's a heading or an actual alert box that identifies the problem. In cases where the alert is significantly different in System 7 than it is in earlier versions of the system software, the System 7 version comes first, and the System 6 or older version follows. In some cases, several different alert boxes signal what is essentially the same problem, so sometimes this book groups several alerts to identify one problem and solution.

After the problem heading or alert box, there's a brief section explaining why the problem may have occurred. Finally, the solution section tells you exactly what steps you should follow to recover from the problem. Follow the steps in order until your problem is solved—you may not need to use them all.

Computers are very complicated devices, and the Mac is no exception. A truly amazing variety of specific problems can occur as you use a Mac, including cosmic rays (seriously!) that can cause errors in memory chips, and random voltage surges that can cause a file to be saved in a corrupted form so it can't be opened again. Nobody—not me, not your local computer guru, not even the people who designed the Mac and its software— can always pinpoint the precise problem at a given time. But fortunately, most of the Mac's symptoms present a relatively limited number of ailments, and a few dozen simple remedies will cover just about any situation you're likely to encounter.

This book focuses on solving Mac problems rather than belaboring all the curious technical reasons why they occur. After all, if your goal is to spend as much time computing and as little time reading about computing as possible, windy technical explanations will just get in the way. This is one case where what you don't know won't hurt you.

1 | Basic Mac hardware and software

All computers work through the interaction of *hardware*—the physical components—and *software*, the magnetically or optically recorded instructions that tell the hardware what to do. Like a cassette player and a cassette tape, the hardware and software in your Mac are a team—each needs the other in order to accomplish anything. In this chapter, we'll look at the Mac's hardware and software components.

Hardware basics

Every Mac consists of at least a CPU (defined below), disk drive(s), a monitor or display screen, a keyboard and a mouse. Most Mac systems also include one or more *peripheral hardware devices,* such as a printer or an external hard disk drive. Here's a short course on how each of these components helps make the Mac work.

The CPU

CPU stands for *central processing unit* and technically refers to a specific portion of a computer's microprocessor chip. However, Apple uses the term CPU more broadly to mean *the box that holds all the computer's brains,* so we will too. This box also contains a power supply, one or two floppy disk drives, various *ports* for connecting printers or other devices, and (depending on the Mac model) a display screen, a hard disk drive, and one or more expansion slots.

The main feature of the CPU is the *logic board,* a printed circuit board that contains a couple of dozen semiconductor chips, some other electronic components, and circuits connecting them all. It isn't necessary to know about every device on this board, but we'll refer to certain devices, chips, and groups of chips later, so we'll go over them here.

- The *microprocessor* is the brains of the Mac—it executes the instructions that come from the software you run.

Different Mac models have different microprocessors, and the specific microprocessor determines how fast a Mac performs its work and how much memory it can use. Some Macs have additional microprocessors that speed up certain functions, like mathematical calculations or data transfer between the CPU and disk drives or printers.

- RAM *(random access memory)* temporarily holds programs and data. When someone refers to the Mac's memory, they're talking about its RAM. Different Mac models can contain different amounts of RAM, from less than a megabyte (one million bytes) to over 100 megabytes. Under the control of its microprocessor, the Mac can change the contents of its RAM easily by replacing the data that's stored there with something new. When you open a program, the Mac loads some of that program's instructions into its RAM. When you quit the program, those instructions are removed from RAM, and the space they occupied becomes available for other programs or data. RAM can only retain data while the computer is turned on, so any programs or other data stored in RAM are lost when you turn the computer off.

- The *PRAM (parameter RAM)* is a separate area of RAM used for storing information that may change from time to time, but that must be retained by your Mac even when it's turned off. This special RAM is powered by a small battery so it can store data even when the Mac itself is not on. Some of the things stored in the PRAM are the current date and time and the name of the current startup disk.

- The *ROM (read-only memory)* contains permanent information that can't be changed by the Mac. Instructions in ROM are physically etched into chips, so they're always available for the Mac to use whenever you turn it on. For example, every Mac's ROM contains instructions that govern the way objects are drawn on the screen.

If you have an LC, SE, SE/30 or any of the Mac IIs (si, cx, ci, etc.) your machine's logic board also contains one or more *expansion slots* into which you can plug various *expansion or interface cards.* Among other things, expansion cards can make your Mac run faster, allow it to communicate over Ethernet or Token-Ring networks, to communicate with mainframe computer networks, or to display text and graphics on external monitors (some Mac IIs also have a video port for this purpose—see the next section).

Other than the logic board, your Mac CPU contains one or two floppy disk drives, which is where you insert floppy disks to start up the Mac, feed it data or run a program. These days, most Mac CPUs also contain internal hard disk drives. Hard disks work like floppy disks except they hold a lot more information on a disk that ordinarily can't be removed, and they give you much faster access to your data.

Plugging in peripheral hardware devices

You could just plug in the Mac's CPU and turn it on, but you couldn't command it without a keyboard, you wouldn't see the effects of your commands without a monitor, and you couldn't print anything without a printer. Just as you do with a component stereo system, you have to set up all these peripheral devices and connect them together before your Mac will work.

Most of the peripheral hardware components that make up a basic Macintosh system plug into the CPU, sometimes through an expansion card in a slot on the logic board, but more commonly through a *port.* Every Mac has several ports on the back of the CPU case; above each port is an icon that identifies its purpose. You won't find all these ports on every Mac, but you may see several of these icons:

The *external floppy disk drive port* is for connecting an external floppy disk drive. Some Macintosh II models don't have this port—they have two internal floppy disk drives instead.

The *mouse* or *ADB port* is for hooking up the mouse or keyboard. The type of port you have depends on your Mac. The Mac Classic, LC, SE and II models have one or two identical ports, called ADB *(Apple desktop bus)* ports. If your Mac has two ADB ports, you can use one for the keyboard and one for the mouse, or you can daisy-chain these devices, plugging the keyboard into the Mac and the mouse into the keyboard.

Mac Plus and older models have only one mouse port on the back of the CPU; the keyboard port is on the front of the machine and uses a completely different connector.

 The *video port* on some Mac II models lets you connect a video monitor to the Mac. (Other Mac II models require you to connect a monitor via a video display card plugged into an internal slot, as mentioned in the previous section.)

 The *printer port* is where you connect the Mac to a local printer (that is, a printer used by just one Mac) or to an AppleTalk network. If you're connected to an AppleTalk network, your Mac can communicate with the devices on that network, including printers, modems, file servers and other Macs.

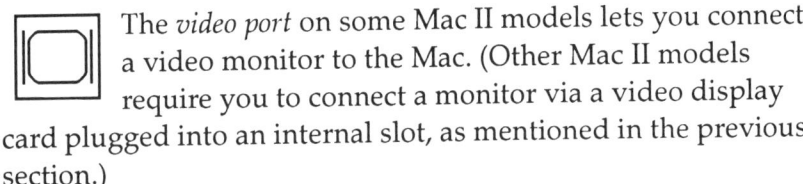 The *modem port* is where you connect modems or direct-connect data cables so your Mac can transmit data to other computers. A modem lets your Mac transmit or receive data over a standard telephone line, and a direct-connect cable transmits data directly to another computer at the other end of the cable.

The printer and modem ports can be used interchangeably to hook up local printers or modems. You can connect a modem to the printer port and a printer to the modem port, if you like, as long as you let your Mac's software know you've done that by using the Chooser DA (see Chapter 3, page 69). However, each of these ports works best if you use it for its stated purpose.

And, if you're attaching to an AppleTalk network, you must *always* connect it to the printer port.

 The *sound output port* is where you connect external speakers or headphones to the Macintosh, so that sounds play through them instead of through the Mac's built-in speaker.

 The *sound input port* is where you connect a microphone so you can record sounds and play them on your Macintosh. Only newer Macs such as the LC or IIsi have a sound input port; however, you can use a special adapter to record sounds through another port on older Macs.

 The *SCSI (small computer systems interface) port* is usually where you connect the Mac to an external hard disk drive. In addition to hard disks, most scanners, CD-ROM drives and tape backup units are also SCSI devices that must be connected to this port. Some printers are SCSI devices, too.

You can connect up to seven hard disks or other SCSI devices through this port by hooking the first device to the Mac's SCSI port, the second device to the first device, the third device to the second device and so on, in what is called a *SCSI chain*.

Each device in the SCSI chain must have a unique address, numbered from 0 to 6, so that your Mac knows which device it's talking to at any given time. Your Macintosh itself has SCSI address 7; therefore, if you plug in an external SCSI hard disk, it must have an address other than 7. If your Mac has an internal hard disk, that disk's SCSI address is always set to 0.

Software basics

As mentioned earlier, all this hardware needs software—that is, instructions—to do anything useful. The Mac's ROM permanently stores some of the instructions the Mac needs, but most of the Mac's software is stored on floppy disks or on a hard disk. Three types of software are essential to the Mac: system software, applications and data files.

System software is the collection of files and programs the Mac needs to recognize and use its various hardware components, to understand and run the applications you use and the data files you create, and to perform other fundamental tasks.

Applications are programs that let you use your Mac to perform specific functions, like creating written documents (word processing programs), drawing graphics (graphics programs), calculating numbers (spreadsheet programs), or communicating with other computers (communications programs). Some applications combine two or more of these basic functions, or offer even more specialized functions (such as accounting programs).

As mentioned above, the system software relays information between the applications and the Mac's hardware. Whether you're running the Finder, a DA or control panel, or a standard application like a word processor or spreadsheet, all applications rely on the system software for information about the current date and time, which printers or disks are available, and other aspects of the Mac's hardware. In effect, an application requests information from the system software, which the system software obtains from the hardware and passes back to the application, as shown at the top of the next page:

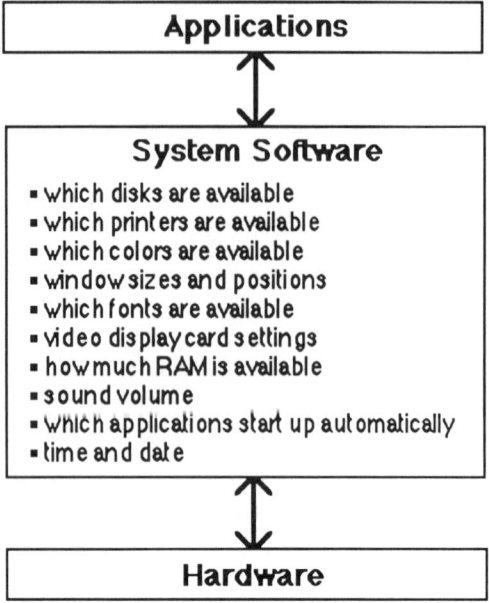

Depending on which version of the system software you're running, there are three kinds programs that work like applications:

- standard applications, like word processors or spreadsheets

- *desk accessories (DAs)*, which can be small productivity tools like the Alarm Clock or Calculator, or utilities like the Chooser, which lets you adjust certain features of the system software

- *control panel* programs (System 7 only), which let you adjust various features of your Mac's operation

Originally, DAs and control panels were distinguished from standard applications by the way you installed and used them, but this distinction has blurred since the release of System 7. So although they're not generally considered applications, we're calling them that here because you use them like regular applications. For more information on how the role of DAs and control panels has changed, see Chapter 3, page 56.

When you install system software on a Mac, it includes a small collection of DAs and control panel programs that are supplied by Apple. In Chapter 3, we'll see how to use some of these tools to change various settings in the Mac's system software. You can buy other DAs or control panels from third parties, just as you would buy standard applications.

Data files, or *documents,* are the third type of software the Mac needs. They're storage files created by applications or by the system software. When you write a letter with a word processing program and then save the letter to disk, you create a data file containing that letter.

Some parts of the Mac's system software can create and save data files automatically. When you copy something to the Scrapbook DA, for example, the item is automatically stored in the Scrapbook file. When you first enter text into the Note Book DA, a Note Book file is automatically created inside your System Folder. On the other hand, most applications require you to create and save data files using the program's *Open, New* and *Save* commands (see Chapter 2).

System software components

Many of the operating problems you'll run into with a Mac are related to the system software, so let's look more closely at the the various system software programs and what they do. You need at least three system software components to make the Mac operate:

- The *System* file contains instructions that tell the Mac how to manage its screen, memory, microprocessor(s), disk drives, keyboard, mouse and other devices. A Mac won't start unless it's connected to a disk drive that contains a System file and a Finder file.

- The *Finder* is a program that displays the Mac desktop's icons, windows, menu bar and menus, and that lets you

create, rename, copy, move, resize, delete and otherwise
manipulate your files.

- The *System Folder* is where the System, the Finder and
  other system software files are stored. When you install
  Mac system software with the Installer program, the
  Installer automatically creates a System Folder and puts
  the necessary files into it.

Other than the System and Finder, the files in the System
Folder aren't absolutely necessary for starting the Mac, but you
do need them to control the Mac's user-adjustable settings, to
select and use printers or other connected devices and to handle
a variety of other housekeeping chores.

The contents and organization of the System Folder vary,
depending on whether you're using System 7 or a previous
version of the Mac's system software. Since System 7 is now the
standard, we'll look at it first. If you're still using System 6 or an
earlier version, you should also read *The System Folder before
System 7*, on page 25.

The System Folder under System 7

Under System 7, the System Folder contains several other
folders, which hold most of the system software files. You can
see the contents of the System Folder here:

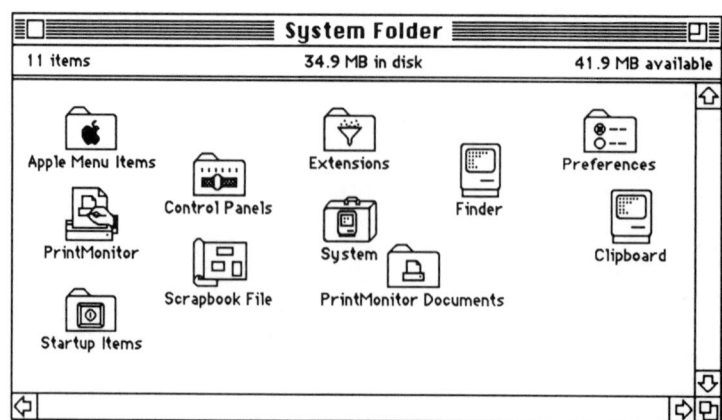

Not all of the folders within the System Folder contain system software files, but several of them do. Let's take a look at the contents of each folder to see how the Mac's system software files are distributed among them.

The *Apple Menu Items* contains the desk accessories that come with the Mac's system software. Under System 7, anything you place in this folder will appear on the menu when you display it. (See *Using DAs* in Chapter 2 for more information about the Apple Menu Items folder.)

The *Control Panels* folder contains *control panel programs*. Each of these programs controls an aspect of the system software, such as the networking setup or the way files are displayed in Finder windows. To use a control panel program, you just open it like any other application. They're only stored in a separate folder so you can locate and use them easily. Under System 6, control panels are called control panel devices, or *cdevs*, and you can only use them through the Control Panel DA. (See *Using control panels* in Chapter 3 for more information about System 7's control panel programs.)

The *Extensions* folder contains *Chooser extensions* and *system extensions*. Chooser extensions—called *device drivers* or *Chooser resources* under System 6—allow the Mac to communicate properly with printers, modems, scanners, network file servers and other devices. When you open the Chooser DA's window, for example, you'll see icons representing Chooser extensions called LaserWriter, ImageWriter and StyleWriter, which allow the Mac to communicate properly with these printers. Although you physically plug these devices into the Mac or an AppleTalk network, the Mac's system software doesn't realize they're there until you notify it. You must use the Chooser DA to specify the device that you want to use and tell the Mac where it's connected. (See Chapter 3 for more details on Chooser extensions.)

System extensions—called *inits* under System 6—are files that change the System file's standard settings. For example, one Apple-supplied system extension file allows the System file to recognize an Apple CD-ROM disk drive. The Mac loads these system extensions automatically each time it starts up, and they run unobtrusively in the background while you're doing other things with your Mac.

While Apple supplies a handful of system extensions, most are sold by other companies. For example, one third-party extension called Capture lets you select a portion of your Mac's screen and save it as a graphic file on disk by pressing a couple of keys. Another, called QuicKeys, modifies the System file so you can create macros (automated routines) that execute whole sequences of commands with a couple of keystrokes.

The *Preferences* folder contains files that store user-adjustable settings for the Finder, file sharing options and other system functions. You can also use it to store your own preference settings for various applications.

The *PrintMonitor Documents* folder doesn't contain any system software files. It's a temporary storage location for documents you've printed to a LaserWriter (or to another laser printer that uses the LaserWriter Chooser extension). This folder is automatically created the first time you print with the PrintMonitor program, which is also stored inside the System Folder. (For more information about the PrintMonitor program and this folder, see *Printing* in Chapter 2.)

The *Startup Items* folder doesn't contain any system software files. Under System 7, programs that you place inside this folder are opened automatically each time you start your Mac. If you want a certain program to start whenever you turn on your Mac, you would place it inside the Startup Items folder. (See *Setting startup items* in Chapter 3 for more information about this folder.)

Along with the System file, the Finder and these additional folders, the System Folder holds the *Clipboard* and *Scrapbook* files. These files store items that you copy to the Clipboard or the Scrapbook DA. If you use the Note Pad DA to store text, you'll have another storage file called *Note Pad File* in your System Folder.

The System Folder before System 7

In pre-System 7 versions of the system software, the programs and files are not grouped in separate folders; they're all placed directly inside the System Folder, like this:

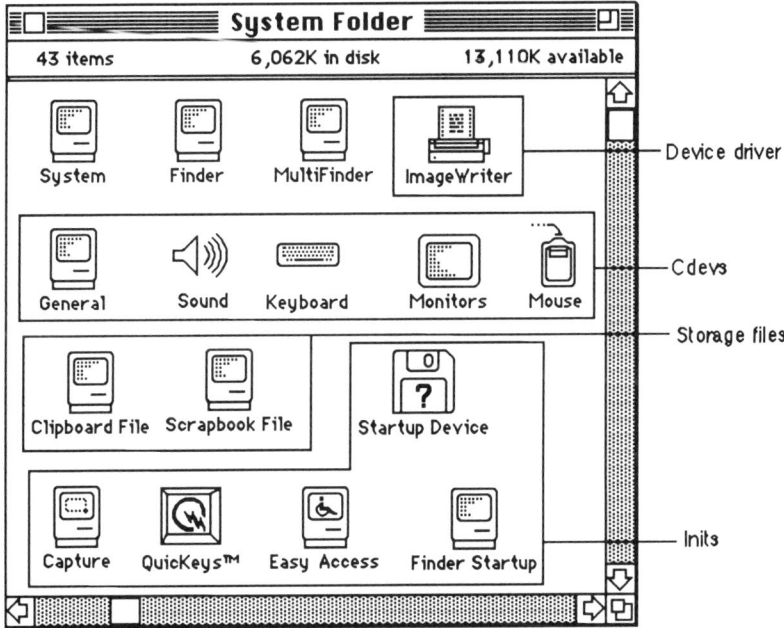

Although they aren't segregated, the items in the System Folder still fall into a few categories, which we've labeled in the previous illustration. Let's see how each of these categories works.

Device Drivers or *Chooser Resources* work exactly like Chooser extensions in System 7. (See the discussion of the Extensions folder on page 23.)

Cdevs, or *Control Panel Devices* are similar to control panel programs in System 7, except they don't work like individual applications. When you have cdevs in your System Folder, they're loaded automatically when you start your Mac; they appear inside the Control Panel DA's window, from which you can select them after you've chosen the Control Panel DA. Each cdev displays a set of options that let you perform various system functions. (See the section in Chapter 3 called *Using the Control Panel DA in System 6* for more details about cdevs.)

Inits are just like system extensions in System 7. The Mac looks for them and loads them automatically each time it starts.

If you're using a version of System 6, your System Folder will also contain a copy of the PrintMonitor program and storage files for the Clipboard, Scrapbook and Note Pad.

One additional file you'll find in the System Folder is *MultiFinder*. MultiFinder is an extension of the Finder that allows you to open and run more than one program at a time as long as your Mac has enough RAM. (In System 7, MultiFinder's features are included in the Finder.) Once you have two or more programs open, you can quickly switch between them, which is a lot faster than quitting one program and opening another each time you want to change applications. You could, for example, open a word processing program and a spreadsheet and then switch between them to view or copy data. To use MultiFinder, you must have the Finder file in your System Folder. Also, you'll find that it takes at least two megabytes of RAM to run more than one application at a time.

2 | Basic Mac operations

What Do I Do Now

In this chapter, we'll look at some basic Macintosh operations to see how the Mac's hardware, system software and applications interact. As we go through these operations, you'll learn the basics of starting a Mac, opening disks, working with applications and printing files. Then we'll discuss managing multiple applications with the Finder (System 7) or MultiFinder (System 6). Finally, we'll talk about using PrintMonitor to print documents in the background while you continue using the Mac for other tasks.

The startup sequence

Let's assume you've just set up your Mac for the first time. You have a StyleWriter connected to the printer port and an internal hard disk drive that contains a System Folder. When you turn on the Mac's power switch, here's what happens:

1. The instructions permanently etched in your Mac's ROM tell it to check all its chips, send a startup sound through the speaker, activate the screen and search for a disk with a System file on it.

2. The Mac checks for a floppy disk in its internal disk drive, but in this case, it doesn't find one.

3. Next, it checks for an external floppy disk drive, again without finding one.

4. Finally, the Mac checks for a hard disk and finds what it's after. It loads the System file located in the System Folder on the internal hard disk and—following the instructions in that file—displays a "happy Mac" icon onscreen:

5. As the System loads, the happy Mac is replaced by the *Welcome to Macintosh* box. (It's possible to replace this box with another screen, called a startup screen, and that may be what you see at this point.)

6. One at a time, the Mac loads any system extensions (or *inits*, under System 6) located in the System Folder. Generally, extensions are loaded in alphabetical order by name, although some have nonalphabetical characters in their names to ensure that they'll be loaded first. As the extensions load, most display an identifying icon in the lower-left corner of the screen; however, some extensions don't announce themselves with an icon.

7. Still following the instructions in the System file, the Mac locates and loads the Finder, and the familiar Mac desktop appears on the screen:

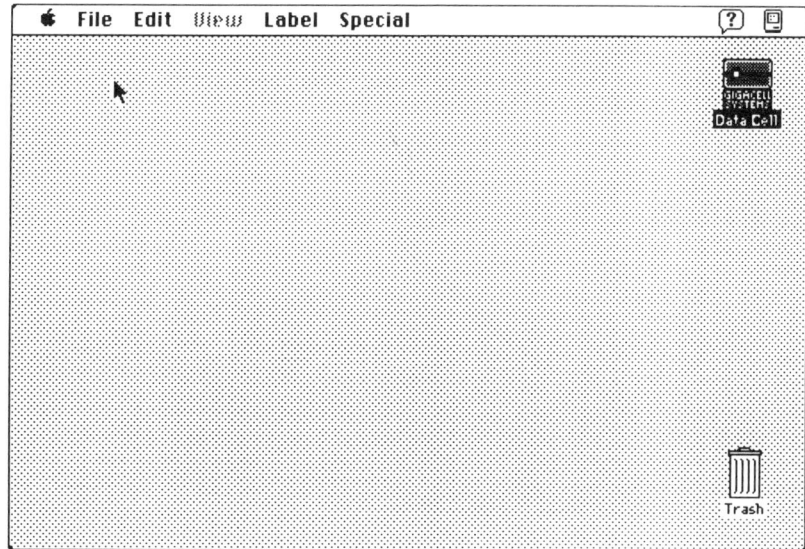

The Finder's desktop displays icons representing any hard disks you have connected to the Mac and any floppy disks you have inserted, along with each disk's name. At this point, the

Finder and your Mac are ready and waiting for further instructions or actions from you.

Selecting and opening objects on the desktop

Whether you're working with disks, files, programs or even with data inside programs, one basic principle for interacting with the Mac always applies:

SELECT FIRST, THEN EXECUTE.

The whole Macintosh interface is based on pointing to something with the mouse, clicking the mouse button to select the item, and then working with it. (In System 7, you can also select an item on the desktop by typing the first few characters of its name.) Before you can work with a disk, a file or a program, before you can execute a command, before you can choose a printer or network file server—before you can do anything—you must first select the item you want to work with. Failing to select an item is a common mistake for new Mac users; if you issue a command and nothing happens, this may be your problem.

When an icon, disk, command or file name is selected, it's displayed in reverse video—that is, whatever is normally white turns black and whatever is normally black turns white, like a film negative. If an item isn't darkened, it isn't selected. Once you've selected an item on the desktop, you can open it or drag it from one location to another.

To open an object on the desktop, you point to the item, click on it once to select it and then choose the *Open* command from the File menu. You can also use a shortcut called *double-clicking* to open items in the Finder: instead of clicking on an item once and then choosing the *Open* command, you double-click—click twice quickly—to open the object.

Viewing items on a disk

When you open a disk icon, you'll see a window that lists the disk's contents, its size, and the amount of free space it contains, like this:

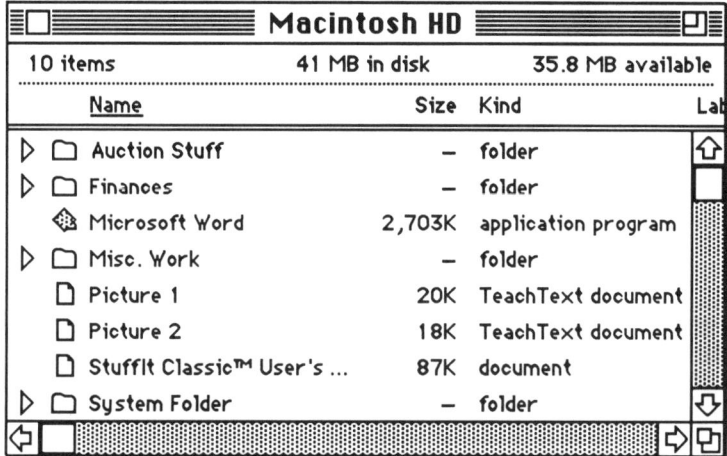

Disks are often divided into multiple levels, or hierarchies, of organization. The window above shows that this disk contains individual files (both data files and applications) and folders, which represent a second level of organization. Folders can be placed inside other folders, so a disk's organization can be several levels deep. To see what's inside a folder, double-click on it to open its window or—if you're using System 7—click on the triangle next to its name. The Kind column tells which items are folders, which are applications and which are documents.

All this information about the disk is maintained by the system software; the Finder is simply relaying it to you.

Working with applications

You can open an application in the same way you open a disk or folder, by double-clicking on it. If enough RAM is available, the program will load and its opening screen will appear.

If there isn't enough RAM to accommodate the program, the Mac will display a message telling you so.

Opening data files

Once an application is open, you can create new files or open existing ones by choosing *New* or *Open* from the program's File menu. If you choose the *New* command, a new, empty file will appear. If you choose the *Open* command, the Mac will display a *directory dialog box* that looks like this:

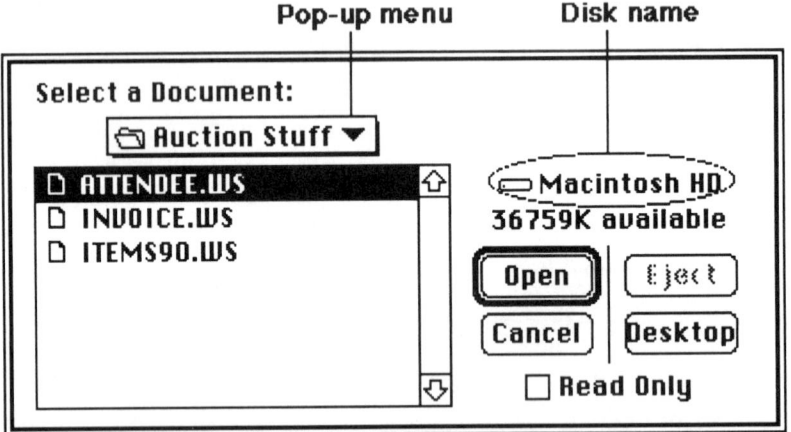

Depending on the program, the box may list all the files in a particular folder or only files that the current application can open. Each Mac application creates its own file type, and can open only a limited number of other applications' files. To open a file, you can either double-click on the file's name, or click once on its name and then click the *Open* button.

The directory dialog box lets you view the files in different folders on a disk or switch from one disk to another. The pop-up menu above the list of files tells you what folder you're looking at, and the name above the buttons at the right tells you which disk you're viewing. In the example above, the list shows the files inside the *Auction Stuff* folder on the disk named *Macintosh HD*.

When you use the *Open* command to access a directory dialog box, the box that appears always shows the last disk location from which you opened a file. If you open your program from a folder called *Applications* and immediately choose the *Open* command, you'll see the contents of the *Applications* folder in the directory dialog box. To view a different area of the disk, click on the pop-up menu to select another folder, or click the *Desktop* button at the right to access a list of all the disks that are currently available to your Mac. Then you can select a new disk and view its contents by double-clicking on its name.

In most cases, you can use a shortcut to open a particular file by opening the file and the program that created it together. Since each program's file type is unique and is stored with its files, the Mac's system software can usually tell what program created a file. When you double-click a file's icon in the disk window or on the desktop, the Mac finds the program that created the file, opens it, and then opens the file itself.

Occasionally file types aren't specified, so the Mac can't always tell which program created a file, and sometimes the program that created a file is not available. If the Mac doesn't know which program to load when you double-click a file or can't find the program it needs to open it, you'll see a message to that effect.

For example, in the disk window shown on page 31, *Picture 1* is identified as a TeachText document, so double-clicking it would automatically load the TeachText program. However, the *StuffIt Classic™ User's....* document is identified only by a generic document icon, so the Mac wouldn't know which program to load if you double-clicked this item.

Saving data files

Once you've created or opened a file with an application, you can save it quickly by choosing *Save* from the program's File menu. If you're saving a file that you originally opened from the disk, it will automatically be saved to the same folder and disk from which it was opened. If you're saving a new file, the directory dialog box will appear so you can name the file and choose a folder and disk location for it. If you want to save an existing file to a different location or under a different name, use the *Save As...* command on the program's File menu to display the directory dialog box, and then specify the new name or location.

A few applications (like FileMaker Pro) automatically save changes to files as you make them. These programs don't have a *Save* command because it isn't necessary; however, they still have a command like *Save As...* that lets you save a copy of the file with a different name or in a different location.

Printing

Now, suppose you've finished writing a memo in Microsoft Word and you want to print it on your StyleWriter printer. Let's assume you're using the Mac for the first time, so even though the printer is connected, the system software isn't aware of it. To tell the Mac you're using a StyleWriter, you use the Chooser DA:

1. Select the Chooser DA from the menu. You'll see a window similar to the one at the top of the next page:

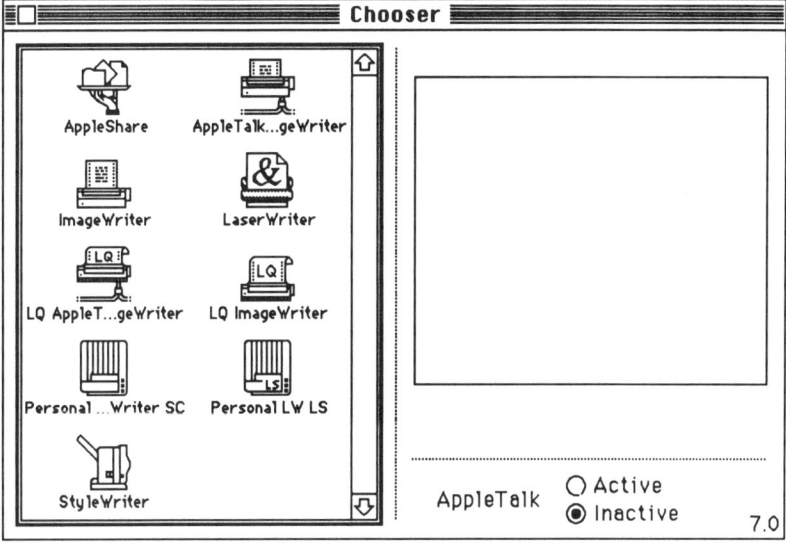

2. Click on the StyleWriter icon to select it. The icon will highlight and the large box at the right will display the icons of the two Mac serial ports, like this:

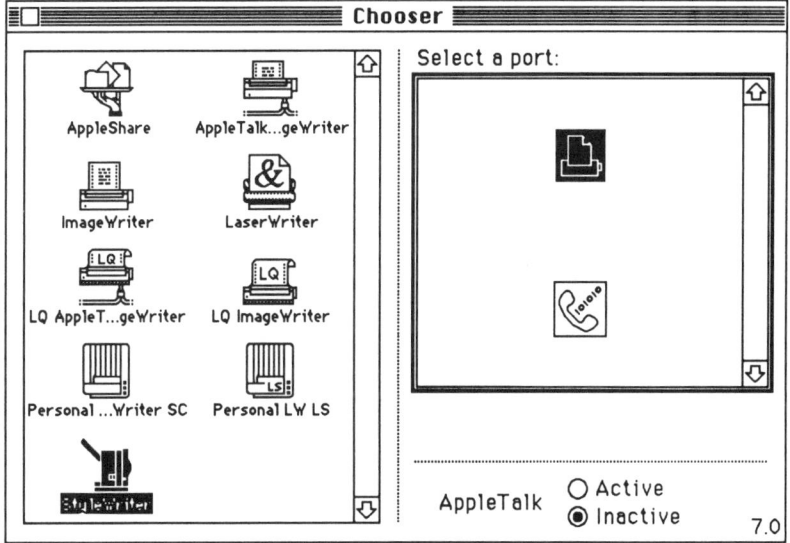

3. If it's not already selected, click on the printer port icon to tell the Mac that the StyleWriter is connected to that port.

4. Click the close box at the upper-left corner of the Chooser window to close the Chooser DA. Now the Mac knows it has a StyleWriter printer connected to its printer port, and can relay that information to your applications when you choose their *Page Setup...* and *Print* commands.

You can select only one device to print to at a time. If you ever want to print on a different device, you'll have to notify the Mac's system software by selecting that device in the Chooser.

Now that you've told the Mac which printer you want to use, you're ready to print your memo.

1. Choose *Page Setup...* from Word's File menu, and adjust or confirm any settings it displays. Because you've already selected the StyleWriter with the Chooser, Word knows you'll be printing on a StyleWriter and the page setup options will apply to that particular printer.

2. Choose the *Print* command from the File menu. Word displays the StyleWriter dialog box, which contains its printing options.

3. Select the options you want and print the file.

Managing multiple applications

Both versions 6 and 7 of the Mac's system software allow you to have several applications open at once; however, this feature works somewhat differently in the two versions. Under System 6, you must use a special program called MultiFinder to manage multiple applications. The System 6 Finder can manage files for only one application at a time. Under System 7, there is no MultiFinder, because the Finder itself is capable of managing as many applications as you wish, as long as you have enough

RAM to accommodate them. There are also differences in the way the two versions handle DAs, control panels (cdevs), and standard applications. In the next section, we'll look at the way things work under System 7. If you're using System 6, you can skip ahead one section.

Managing multiple programs under System 7

Under System 7, DAs, control panels and standard applications work in essentially the same way—the Mac treats them all as standard applications. To install these programs you simply drag them onto a disk, and to open them you just double-click their name or icon.

Again, you can open as many programs, DAs or control panels at once as you want, providing you have enough memory. Each program requires a specific amount of memory, and asks the system software to set that amount aside when you try to open the program. If you don't have enough, the system software will alert you and the application won't be opened. (See Chapter 3 for information about adjusting the amount of memory used by applications.)

When you first install System 7, you'll find a selection of DAs on the menu. This is simply a matter of convenience; normally DA names appear on the menu because the DAs themselves have been placed inside the Apple Menu Items folder in the System Folder. Once it's listed on the menu, you can choose a DA's name there to open it. Alternatively, you can open the Apple Menu Items folder and double-click individual DA icons. All control panels are stored inside the Control Panels folder. You can double-click them there to open them.

As you open different DAs or standard applications under System 7, their names appear on the Application menu, which is indicated by an icon at the far-right side of the menu bar. By pulling down this menu and choosing a program's name, you can activate any program listed there. As soon as you quit a program, its name is removed from the Application menu. You can always tell which program is currently active because its menus appear in the menu bar and its icon represents the Application menu icon.

Control panel program names don't appear on the Application menu—to activate an open control panel, you must select the Finder from the Application menu and click on the control panel program's window.

Managing multiple programs under System 6

Under System 6 and earlier versions of the system software, standard applications work differently from DAs and control panel devices (called *cdevs* in System 6).

DAs are a special kind of application that must be installed directly inside the System file using either Apple's Font/DA Mover or a third-party DA manager like Suitcase or MasterJuggler. Because they require special installation, DAs are stored in a distinct type of file called a *suitcase*.

Once they are installed in the System file, the DAs' names appear on the menu, and you must choose them there to open them. You can open more than one DA at a time under System 6, as long as you have enough memory.

You must install cdevs in the System Folder, and you can only access them by choosing *Control Panel* from the menu. (See the section in Chapter 3 called *Using the Control Panel DA in System 6* for more information.)

As mentioned earlier, System 6 lets you decide whether to run only one standard application at a time or as many as you have room for in RAM. Using the Finder alone limits you to running only one program at a time—if you're running a word processor and you want to open a spreadsheet program, you must quit the word processing program first. By switching to MultiFinder, you can run several application programs at once, just as you can under System 7.

To run MultiFinder, you must have the Finder program in your Mac's System Folder. When you're running MultiFinder, the Finder itself always runs along with any other programs you start up, so if necessary, you can always switch to the Finder to work with disks or files without having to quit other programs.

As you open programs under MultiFinder, their names are added to the bottom of the menu, and you activate different programs by choosing their names there. The program that's currently active is the one whose menus and icon appear in the menu bar.

As with System 7, you need at least two megabytes of memory to run multiple programs under System 6. Although it's possible to run MultiFinder on a Mac with only one megabyte of memory, that amount won't allow you to launch and manage multiple programs.

Background printing with PrintMonitor

Background printing, or *print spooling*, allows you to continue using your Mac for other tasks while it prints a file. Both System 7 and System 6 add a print spooling capability to your Mac when you use a LaserWriter (or any other printer that uses the LaserWriter Chooser extension or printer driver). The Print-Monitor application inside the System Folder provides this capability.

When you first select the LaserWriter Chooser extension in the Chooser DA, the Mac automatically turns on background printing and activates AppleTalk (if it isn't active already). Once background printing is turned on, the Mac automatically loads the PrintMonitor program whenever you issue a *Print...* command from any application. If you're running System 7, the PrintMonitor program's name is added to the Application menu. If you're running MultiFinder under System 6, PrintMonitor's name appears at the bottom of the ⬤ menu.

When you tell the Mac to print something, it opens PrintMonitor and transfers your document to the PrintMonitor Documents folder inside the System Folder. From there, the document is fed to your printer, page by page. You can instruct the Mac to print several documents one after the other, and they'll be saved in the PrintMonitor Documents folder until their turn comes up. Meanwhile, you retain control of your Mac so you can continue with other work while the printing is handled in the background.

Activating PrintMonitor displays its window and menus; you can use the window to change the order of the print jobs that are waiting to be handled, or to pause or cancel printing of a particular document or documents.

Because it prints in the background, PrintMonitor usually does its job invisibly. When a problem (such as a paper jam) does crop up, PrintMonitor notifies you. (See Chapter 14 for more information about PrintMonitor.)

3 | Communicating with the system software

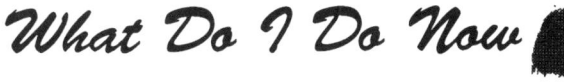

Communication is all that's required to solve some problems, and the Mac's system software includes many features designed to assist the flow of information between you and your Mac. Dialog boxes are the Mac's way of obtaining additional input from you, and various kinds of alerts let the Mac tell you when something goes wrong. Other features allow you to adjust the system so it works the way you want it to. In this chapter, we'll see how your Mac's software communicates with you, and how you can tailor the system to suit your needs.

How the Mac tells you what it wants

The Mac has several ways of asking you questions or telling you something is wrong. These messages and indicators vary in urgency and seriousness from simple requests for information to hard system crashes that annihilate whatever work you were doing at the time.

Dialog boxes

Dialog boxes are the Mac's way of asking for further information. When you select any menu command that has an ellipsis (...) after it, a dialog box something like this one will appear:

```
LaserWriter  "Personal LaserWriter NT"          7.0    [ Print ]

Copies:[1]          Pages: ⦿ All ○ From:[   ] To:[   ]   [ Cancel ]

Cover Page: ⦿ No ○ First Page  ○ Last Page

Paper Source: ⦿ Paper Cassette  ○ Manual Feed

Print:          ⦿ Black & White  ○ Color/Grayscale

Destination: ⦿ Printer          ○ PostScript® File
```

Most dialog boxes present options that you can specify (like how many copies of a document to print) and a button that you must click to execute the command with those options in effect.

The system beep

The system beep (or boing, or clank, or whatever sound has been substituted for the beep) is the Mac's main way of getting your attention. Either the Mac's system software or an application or DA you're running can trigger a beep when you do something that isn't permitted in a given situation, like clicking outside a dialog box on the screen.

The system beep is just a reminder that something won't work—a gentle nudge that tells you you've made an operator error, rather than a sign that something's wrong with your Mac. Since most people commit these small transgressions quite regularly, the system beep can become annoying. If it bothers you, you can eliminate it by lowering your Mac's speaker volume to 0 in the Sound control panel, discussed later in this chapter. (You can also use this control panel to select from a variety of sounds that you may find more amusing than the humble beep.)

Alerts

Alerts are similar to dialog boxes, but they aren't linked to commands; they simply appear on the screen in certain situations. Some alerts—like the *Printing In Progress* message that pops up during a print job—just let you know what's going on. Others warn you of a problem, and these are always announced by one or more system beeps and a flashing menu bar or menu bar icon. In addition, a brief message attempts to describe the problem and—sometimes—tells you what to do about it. You may even be given a chance to do something immediately by clicking one of several buttons in the alert box. In other cases, your only option will be to click an *OK* or *Continue* button that puts the alert box away. In general, System 7's alerts are much more specific and helpful than those in System 6.

Many alerts point out a problem you can fix (like your printer being out of paper), but some are the Mac's way of letting you know you're in big trouble. In any case, you should consider your options carefully before you click any of the buttons in an alert box, because some of the options can be destructive, like the one that erases a disk the Mac considers unreadable. Chapters 5 through 15 explain all the common alerts and how best to deal with them.

System errors

System errors are special alerts distinguished by the dreaded bomb icon, which is a sure sign that you're out of luck for the moment. These messages can be extremely frustrating because while your Mac is still functional enough to display an alert box, the alert's only purpose is to tell you that your program is dead and your data is history.

System error alert boxes always contain an official-looking *ID* number in the lower-right corner, but these error codes may not help you fix a problem or avoid it in the future. Once in a while you'll see a system error message that includes a *Resume* or *Continue* button, but clicking the button rarely does any good. If your Mac is hurting badly enough to display a system error, your best—and often only—option is to restart the machine and hope the problem doesn't recur. Chapters 5 through 15 deal with some specific system error situations.

Hard system crashes

A hard system crash is only a warning in the sense that a blowout is a warning of a tire problem. It means your Mac is so screwed up, it can't even display a system error message. Instead, the screen may dance and jitter, your current program may be replaced by a random pattern of wavy lines, or everything may simply lock up. Sometimes these symptoms are also accompanied by a buzzing or crackling noise. Believe it or not, these dramas are often software induced (any bizarre sounds you hear are a sort of electronic funeral march played through the Mac speaker, not the sound of your logic board going up in smoke). Again, the best remedy is to restart your Mac.

How you tell the Mac what you want

The rest of this chapter focuses on the methods and commands you use to adjust or communicate with your system software. You'll need these basic techniques to solve many of the problems covered in later chapters of this book.

Although some of this material may be familiar to you, at least skim this part of the chapter. If you do get stuck in the middle of a problem-solving session and can't remember how to use a particular system software tool, you can always refer back to these pages.

The methods of controlling the Mac's system software fall into four general categories:

- Finder commands, which you select from menus in the Finder

- control panels, which are utilities that you can use to adjust various aspects of the system software

- the Chooser DA, with which you specify any peripheral devices you want to use

- System Folder folders, which help you organize your system software files

If you're using System 6, the sections on control panels and System Folder folders don't apply to you—read *Using the Control Panel DA in System 6* and *System Folder operations under System 6* instead. Some aspects of the other sections are also System 7-specific—watch for the System 7 icon in the margin next to this material. (The section heading will tell you when a section is specific to System 6.)

Finder commands

Among the Finder's commands, these five allow you to control the Mac's hardware or to adjust various characteristics of the system software:

- the *Get Info* command
- the *Sharing* command (System 7 only)
- the *Make Alias* command (System 7 only)
- the *Restart* command
- the *Shut Down* command

In this section we'll look at each of these commands in turn.

The Get Info command

When you select an item on the desktop and choose the *Get Info* command (or press ⌃⌘Ⅰ), the Mac displays a window containing information about that item.

The information you see in this window depends on the type of item you've selected. Disk and folder information windows only tell you the kind of item, its size, location, and when it was created and last modified. In addition to this information, application, DA, document, alias and Trash windows include options for changing the characteristics of the item. Two options are common to almost all of these information windows: changing the item's icon and locking the item.

In every information window (including disk and folder windows), you can select the item's icon and change it by pasting in a different icon from the Clipboard. For example, you might design your own special icon using a paint or draw program and then use it to replace your hard disk's icon. To do this:

1. Select the new icon in the drawing program or the Scrapbook (wherever you have it stored) and press ⌃⌘C

(or choose *Copy* from the Edit menu) to copy it to the Clipboard.

2. On the desktop, select the item whose icon you want to change and press ⌘I (or choose *Get Info* from the File menu). That item's information window will be displayed.

3. Click on the item's icon in the information window. A selection box will appear around it.

4. Press ⌘V (or choose *Paste* from the Edit menu). The copied icon will replace the current icon in the information window.

5. Close the information window. The item will now be represented by its new icon on the desktop.

Except for disk and folder windows, all information windows also have a *Locked* checkbox in the lower-left corner. When you check the *Locked* box, the item is locked on the disk so that you can't delete it, rename it or alter it in any way. You can open a locked item, but when you do, an alert will appear telling you the item can't be changed. If you try to delete a locked item, an alert will tell you that it can't be thrown away.

Typically, you'll lock documents to prevent others from changing their contents. Although you can lock applications, it's usually not a good idea to do so because some don't work properly when they're locked.

In DA information windows, the *Locked* checkbox is the only option; however, information windows for applications, documents, aliases, and the Trash present a number of additional choices.

Application information windows

When you select an application and choose the *Get Info* command, the information window that appears contains the usual information about the item's size, location, and modification and creation dates, as well as the *Locked* checkbox in the lower-left corner. At the lower-right, however, you'll see a feature that only appears in application information windows: a box displaying the suggested and current amount of memory set aside for the application. (In System 6, the current size is called the *Application Memory Size*.)

When you run System 7 (or MultiFinder under System 6), you can have more than one application running at a time. For this scheme to work, your Mac needs to know how much of its total memory it should assign for use by each program. Every new application that you launch asks the Mac for a certain amount of memory. If that much memory isn't available, your Mac displays a message saying so. If enough memory is available, your Mac sets it aside for that particular program.

Applications tend to be conservative when asking the system software for memory. A program will ask for enough memory to let you work with a small or moderately sized file, but if you try to work with a large file, you may run short. If an application ends up needing more memory than it originally asked for, the application will quit—often unexpectedly.

Fortunately, although DA and control panel memory allocations are fixed, you can change the amount of memory a standard application asks for by using the Memory box in the application's information window. The suggested size is the amount of memory the program automatically asks for. If the program's memory size has never been reset, the current size will match the suggested size, as it does in the information window for the Microsoft Works application, as shown at the top of the next page:

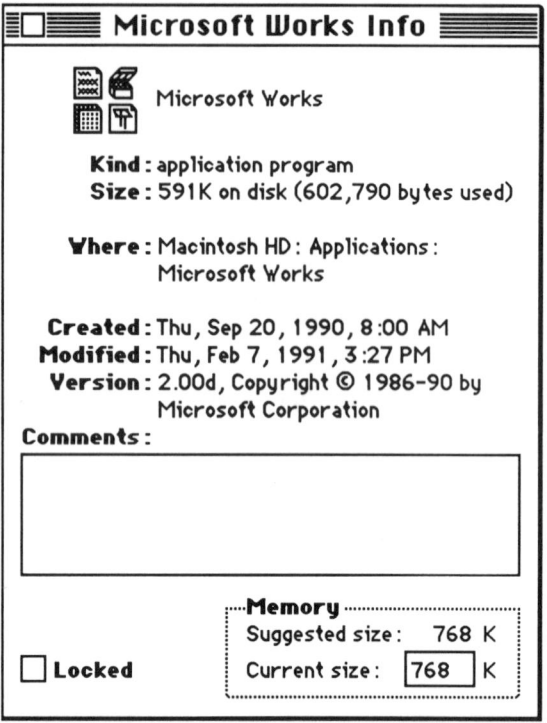

If a standard application keeps quitting spontaneously, you probably need to enlarge its current memory size. To reset a program's memory size:

1. Select the program's icon on the desktop and choose *Get Info* from the File menu. The Mac displays an information window for the application.

2. Double-click on the number inside the Current size box and type the amount of memory you want to use. It's best to increase the size by at least twenty percent.

3. Close the window. The next time you run it, the program will ask the system for the new current size you've set.

    Note that you can't change the current memory size of a program while it's running. If you get a message that says your program is running out of memory, you must quit the program before you can reset its memory size.

Although it's possible to reset a program's memory size to less than the suggested size, it's a bad idea. Doing so may make it impossible to run the program at all, or may cause it to crash unexpectedly.

Document information windows (System 7 only)

In System 7, a document information window looks like this:

Receivables Info

Receivables

Kind : Microsoft Works document
Size : 3K on disk (2,976 bytes used)

Where : Macintosh HD : Finances :

Created : Oct 25, 1990, 9:48 AM
Modified : Jun 24, 1991, 11:58 AM
Version : n/a

Comments :

☐ **Locked**   ☐ **Stationery pad**

Although a document window for System 6 is similar, it lacks one important component that appears here: the *Stationery pad* checkbox in the lower-right corner. By checking this box, you can turn any document into a *stationery pad*, a special type of document that always opens as an untitled document when you double-click on it, even though it contains information and has a unique name on the desktop.

By making a document into a stationery pad, you can store standard formatting or text that you want to appear on all new documents when you first open them. For example, you could add your name and return address to the top of a Word document and save it with the name *Letterhead*; then you could use the *Get Info* command to change the *Letterhead* document into a stationery pad. After that, your name and address would appear at the top of an untitled document whenever you double-clicked on the *Letterhead* document on the desktop.

To turn a stationery pad back into a standard document (which opens with its own name), just remove the check from the *stationery pad* box in the document's information window.

Alias information windows (System 7 only)

An *alias* is a proxy; it lets you open a file, disk or folder that's stored in another location. Alias names always appear in italics. When you select an alias and choose the *Get Info* command, you'll see an information window that looks like this:

```
▤▢▐▬▬▬▬ Word Info ▬▬▬▬▬▬

  ◈W◈  Word

  Kind : alias
  Size : 2K on disk (553 bytes used)

  Where : Macintosh HD : Word


  Created : Wed, Feb 13, 1991 , 5 :36 PM
  Modified : Wed, Feb 13, 1991 , 5 :36 PM
  Original : Macintosh
            HD : Applications :Microsoft Word

  Comments :
  ┌──────────────────────────────┐
  │                              │
  │                              │
  │                              │
  └──────────────────────────────┘

  ☐ Locked            ( Find Original )
```

As you can see, in addition to the usual *Locked* checkbox, this window also contains a *Find Original* button. When you click this button, the Mac searches your disk for the original program, document, disk or folder that the alias represents. (See *The Make Alias command* on page 54 for more information on aliases.)

The Trash information window (System 7 only)

In System 7, the Trash information window looks like this:

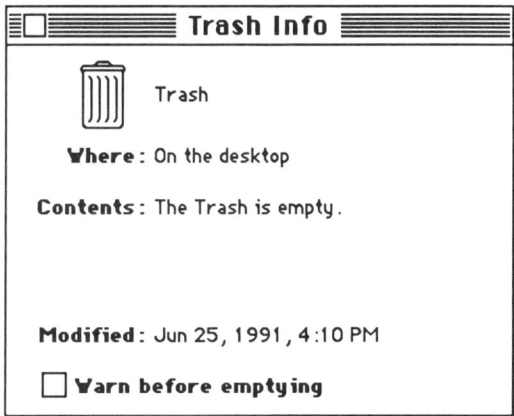

The *Warn before emptying* checkbox at the bottom of the window lets you choose whether or not the Mac will display a warning about the contents of the Trash when you choose the *Empty Trash* command from the Finder's Special menu. By default this checkbox is checked and the Mac alerts you before it empties the Trash. You can uncheck the *Warn before emptying* checkbox to disable the warning, and the contents of the Trash will be discarded immediately when you choose the *Empty Trash* command.

Notes on the Get Info command for System 6

Aliases, icons that can be selected and replaced, the *Warn before emptying* checkbox in the Trash information window, and the *Stationery pad* checkbox in document information windows are features exclusive to System 7; System 6 users won't have these options. You can bypass the Trash warning in System 6 by holding down the Ⓞ Option key when dragging items to the Trash, however.

The Sharing command (System 7 only)

System 7 offers built-in file-sharing capabilities for Mac users who are connected to each other on a network. The *Sharing* command lets you share selected disks or folders with other users on a network, control exactly who can access those shared items, and view the current sharing information for any item you can select on the desktop. In Chapter 15, which covers networking, we'll go over these activities in detail.

If you're running your Mac under System 6, the *Sharing* command isn't available, and you can't share your files with other Macs on the network. However, you can still access other shared files on the network from your Mac. For more information about accessing shared files under System 6, see Chapter 15.

The Make Alias command (System 7 only)

An *alias* is a stand-in for a folder, document or program on your disk that acts just like the original item when you select it or open it, but takes up only a fraction of the space of the original. By using aliases, you can access programs, DAs, control panels, folders or shared items that you use frequently from many different places on your disk. For example, the *Control Panels* item on the menu is an alias for the real Control Panels folder which is located inside the System Folder; when you choose the *Control Panels* alias from the menu, the real Control Panels folder opens.

To make an alias:

1. Select the item for which you want to make an alias.

2. Choose *Make Alias* from the File menu. A copy of the original item appears next to it with the name *<item*

name> alias in italics. Here, for example, the alias for Microsoft Works has been named *Microsoft Works alias*:

3. Once you've created an alias, you can move it anywhere you want on your disk and it will give you access to the original item when you open it. With the Microsoft Works alias above, for example, you could drag the alias onto the desktop. Then, whenever you double-clicked on the alias, the Microsoft Works program itself would start up.

You can make as many aliases for an item as you like and place them in different locations on your disk. If you need to access a certain folder frequently, you can put an alias for it on the desktop, and also place one inside every other folder on your disk.

For an alias to work properly, the alias and its original item must both be on disks that are currently available to your Mac. If the original for an alias is damaged or deleted from your disk, you'll get an alert message when you try to open the alias.

To remove an alias, just select it and drag it to the Trash. Deleting an alias has no effect on the original file. (You can also rename an alias without affecting the name of the original; however you should make the new name descriptive enough that you won't forget what the alias represents.)

The Restart command

The *Restart* command is the software version of shutting your Mac off with the power switch and then turning it on again, but it's a lot easier on your Mac's power supply and disk drives. Restarting is usually the first thing you do when your

Mac crashes and its screen locks up. Most of the time, a restart solves the software problem that caused your Mac to crash and puts you back in business.

You must also use the *Restart* command when you want to activate new system extension files or inits you've added to your disk, because these only become active during the Mac's startup sequence.

The Shut Down command

The *Shut Down* command purges everything from your Mac's memory and—depending on the Mac—either turns it off or clears the screen except for a dialog box that says it's OK for you to turn it off. The dialog box has a *Restart* button on it that you can click if you change your mind and want to start up again instead.

You should always use the *Shut Down* command before turning off your Mac, because it quits any programs you have running and closes down the system software in an orderly way. If you have files open that haven't been saved or have changed since you last saved them, the *Shut Down* command gives you a chance to save them. Also, if you don't use the *Shut Down* command, not only will your Mac take longer to start the next time you use it, but some of your system software files could be damaged in the process.

Using control panels (System 7 only)

In System 7, you can adjust several aspects of the system software using control panel programs. Control panels work like standard applications and DAs—you just double-click on them to open them and a screenful of options appears.

Control panel programs are usually located in the Control Panels folder inside the System Folder. You can access them there or, as a shortcut, you can select the Control Panels alias on the menu to open the Control Panels folder.

Over a dozen control panel programs come with System 7. Some offer convenience features like a world time map or allow you to check or adjust minor items such as the sensitivity of the mouse. In this section, we'll focus on the control panels and options that you'll use to solve the problems described later in this book. For a complete description of all the standard Mac control panels and what they do, consult a general guide to System 7 such as *The Macintosh Bible Guide to System 7*.

The control panels we'll be discussing fall into four functional areas:

- adjusting the Mac's look and feel
- changing the startup disk
- adjusting memory options
- adjusting file-sharing options

The control panels you use to adjust the look and feel of the Mac are General Controls, Views, Monitors and Sound.

The General Controls control panel

The General Controls control panel is shown at the top of the next page:

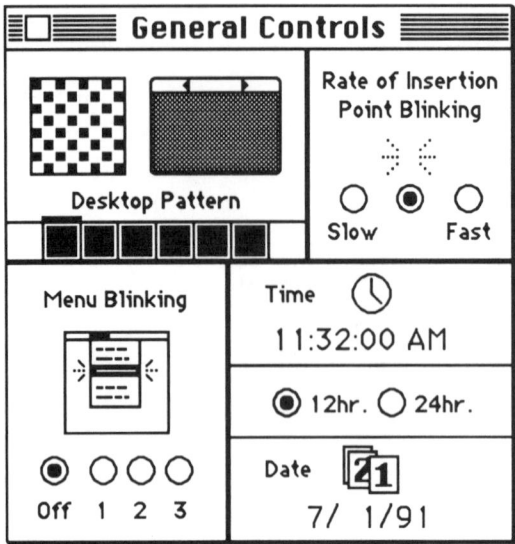

For our purposes, the important options on this control panel are the Time and Date. If your Mac's clock or calendar is wrong, this is where you reset it. To reset the time or date, click directly on the digit(s) for the hour, minute, second, day, month or year you want to change. A pair of arrows will appear to the right of the date or time. You can click the up or down arrows to choose a new number or just type the numbers you want from the keyboard. When you're finished, click on the clock or calendar icon above the time or date to reset the Mac's internal clock/calendar.

Date and time changes take effect immediately, although any items that were date- or time-stamped before you reset the clock will bear their old dates and times until you open and modify them; then the Mac will update these items.

The Views control panel

The Views control panel, which lets you change the way information appears in windows, looks like this:

At the top of the control panel are options you can use to change the font and size of the text that identifies items in list view windows. For our purposes, however, the important options are in the Icon Views and List Views areas at the center and bottom of the control panel.

The Icon Views buttons let you choose either a straight grid or a staggered grid for displaying icons in icon view windows. Examples of these styles appear to the left of the buttons. The *Always snap to grid* checkbox forces the Mac to align icons along the current grid. If you're trying to position the icons in a window and they keep snapping to a grid, you need to uncheck this checkbox. (You can always use the *Clean up* command on the Special menu to realign items to a grid.)

Among the List Views options at the bottom of the Views control panel are buttons that let you choose the size of the icon that identifies each type of item in a window. At the right, there are checkboxes that tell the Mac which categories (or columns) of information to show in list view windows. If, for example, you're looking for Kind information about a document in a list view window and it isn't showing, you need to open this control panel and click the *Show kind* checkbox to display that column of information. The default settings for these options appear in the illustration on page 59.

When you check the *Calculate folder sizes* checkbox, the Mac automatically calculates and displays the total size of items inside any folder and shows this information in every folder's Size column. (Normally, folder sizes are not shown.) Note that checking this box will make your Mac display windows a little more slowly, because calculating folder sizes takes time. The sizes are calculated one at a time, from the top of the window to the bottom, and appear individually as they're calculated, in place of the dashes that normally appear.

Finally, the *Show disk info in header* checkbox causes your Mac to show the total amount of used and free space on a disk in all window headers. The information appears just below a window's title bar, like this:

Macintosh HD		
8 items	41.1 MB in disk	35.7 MB available
Name	Size Kind	Label

Normally, information about the number of items in the window and the total space used and available on the disk appears only in icon view windows; checking this checkbox makes it available in list view windows as well.

Any changes you make in the Views control panel take effect as soon as you close the control panel.

The Monitors control panel

The Monitors control panel automatically records which monitor (or monitors) you have connected to your Mac. In this example, only one monitor is connected, and its icon appears in the center of the control panel with a number *1* on it:

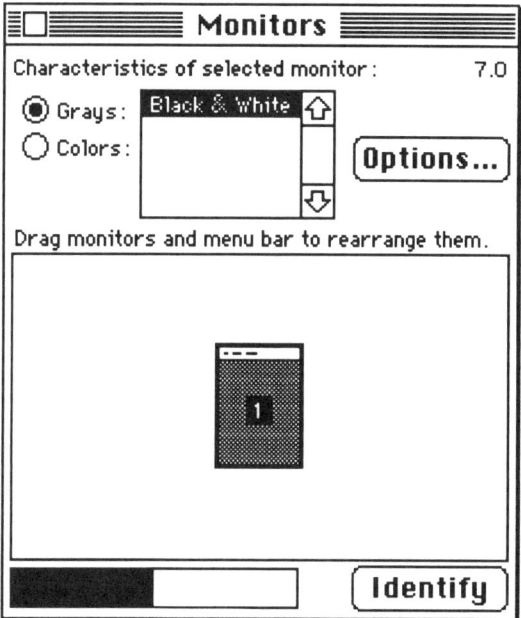

If you have more than one monitor connected to your Mac, you'll see a numbered icon for each monitor in the center of this control panel. One icon will have a menu bar on it, and the actual menu bar will be located on the monitor that icon represents. You can move the menu bar by dragging it from one icon to another.

When you have two or more monitors connected, the pointer will jump from one monitor to another when you drag it to the edge of the current monitor's screen. The arrangement of icons on the Monitors control panel determines which way the pointer jumps. For example, if monitor number 2 were to the right of monitor number 1 in the control panel, you would drag the pointer off the right edge of monitor 1's screen to make it jump to monitor 2's screen. If monitor 2 were to the left of monitor 1, you would drag the pointer off the left side of monitor 1's screen to make it jump to monitor 2. You can also drag the icons around to change the way the pointer moves from one monitor to the next.

Clicking on the *Identify* button at the bottom-right of the control panel displays a number on your screen to show you which monitor you're currently viewing, so you can always tell which monitor is number 1, which is number 2, and so on.

When you drag the menu bar or rearrange the icons in the Monitors control panel, these changes don't take effect until you restart your Mac.

The buttons at the top of the Monitors control panel let you choose whether to display grays or colors on the current monitor (assuming it's capable of showing colors). If the monitor is displaying colors and you want it to display only grays, you need to click the *Grays* button in this control panel. If it's showing only shades of gray and you want it to show colors, click the *Colors* button.

The *Options* button is for Macs that have built-in video display capabilities, like the Mac IIsi and the Mac IIci. This button lets you choose how much RAM you want set aside for video operations. The more memory you set aside, the more shades of gray or colors you can display, but setting a lot of memory aside for video tends to slow down your Mac. Changes to the amount of video memory don't take effect until you restart the Mac (you'll see a message to that effect when you make such a change). Once you've chosen how much memory to set aside, options for selecting different numbers of colors or grays appear in the scrolling list to the left of the *Options* button.

If a monitor connects to the Mac through an add-in video card, the card itself will have its own RAM, and you'll automatically see options for selecting the number of colors or grays you want in the scrolling list—you won't have to click the *Options* button. In this case, the number of colors or grays on your screen will change as soon as you make your selection and close the control panel.

The Sound control panel

Depending on which Mac model you have, you may not see the complete Sound control panel, which looks like this:

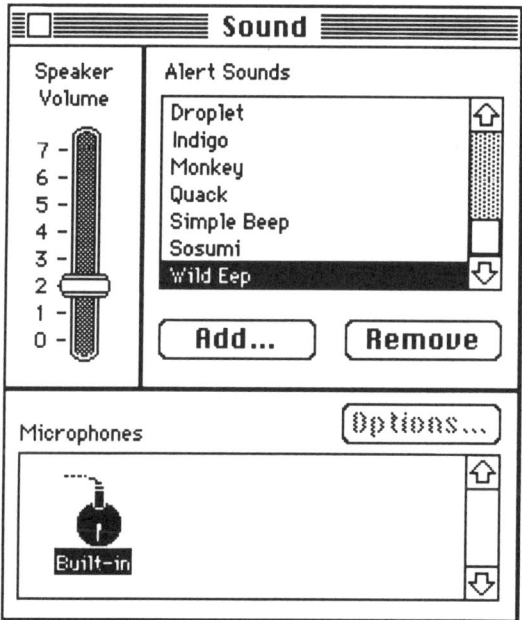

The slide bar at the left of the control panel lets you change the volume of sounds coming through the Mac's speaker. Just drag the slide to the setting you want (0 turns the sound off). In the scrolling list, you can select a different sound to replace the usual beep.

The Microphones box at the bottom of the control panel only appears if your Mac model has a built-in sound input port. This box lets you select different microphones for recording sounds, assuming you have more than one microphone connected.

Any changes you make to the Sound control panel take effect immediately.

Changing the startup disk

As explained in Chapter 2, when you turn on your Mac, it automatically looks for a System Folder, first on a floppy disk and then on its internal hard disk. The first disk it finds that contains a System Folder becomes the startup disk. The Startup Disk control panel lets you specify an alternate startup disk if you have one connected to your Mac. The Startup Disk control panel looks like this:

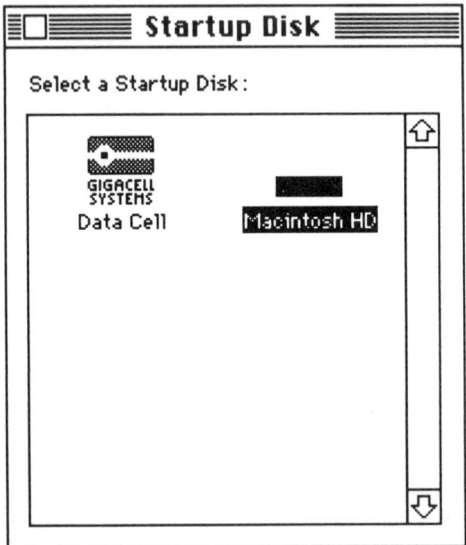

Any hard disk that you have running and connected to your Mac will appear in this control panel. To specify a startup disk other than the one your Mac normally uses, just select its icon here and then close the control panel. The next time you turn on the Mac, it will start from the disk you've chosen, provided that disk contains a System Folder.

Adjusting memory options

The Memory control panel lets you adjust the way your Mac uses its RAM to handle file storage and system-related functions. Depending on which Mac model you're using, your Memory control panel may be missing some of the options on the full control panel, which looks like this:

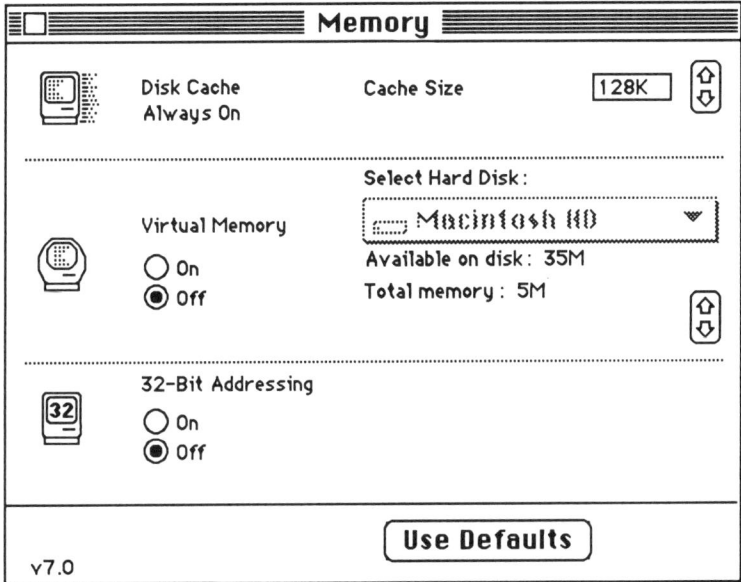

The Disk Cache section at the top of the Memory control panel lets you adjust the size of the disk cache, a special, discrete section of memory that's used to hold frequently used instructions so they can be quickly swapped into and out of RAM without being read from disk every time.

Under System 7, the disk cache must be at least 16K. You can use the arrows at the right of the Cache Size box to change the size of the cache. If you use applications that frequently swap instructions from disk, enlarging the cache will make those programs run a little faster.

On Macs using a 68030 processor, Mac LCs, or Mac IIs using a 68020 processor and an optional paged memory management (PMMU) chip, you can set aside part of your hard disk as *virtual memory*, which is disk space that your Mac uses like extra RAM. The Virtual Memory area in the middle of the Memory control panel is where you turn this feature on and specify how much disk space you want assigned to it. If your Mac can't take advantage of virtual memory, this area won't appear in your Memory control panel.

Like virtual memory, 32-bit addressing is only available on certain Macs that use 68020 or 68030 processors. This feature lets your Mac use far more physical RAM than it could under System 6—up to 128 megabytes on some models. If your Mac can't use 32-bit addressing, this area won't appear in the Memory control panel.

Adjusting file-sharing options

Three control panel programs are used to turn on file sharing and adjust its various options: Sharing Setup, Users & Groups, and File Sharing Monitor. The Sharing Setup control panel lets you set up your Mac for file sharing and turn file sharing on. This control panel is the first tool you use to begin sharing files from your Macintosh with others on your network.

If you want to share your Mac's files with specific people on your network and assign specific access privileges to those people, you must use the Users & Groups control panel to register those people by name. The File Sharing Monitor control panel tells you which other users on a network are currently connected to your Mac. You'll learn how to use these control panels in Chapter 15.

Using the Control Panel DA in System 6

If you're using System 6, control panels aren't double-clickable programs as they are in System 7. Instead, functions such as controlling the sound or the number of colors displayed on a monitor are handled with the Control Panel DA, which looks something like this:

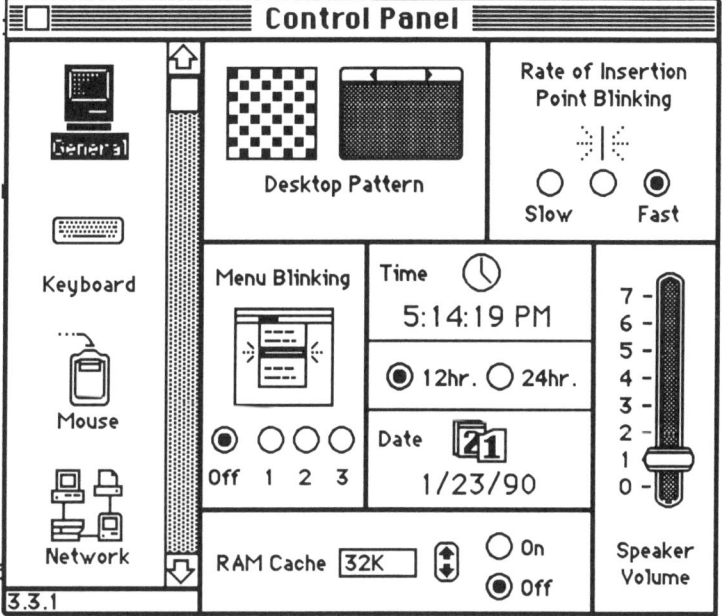

The far-left section of this window contains icons representing various cdevs (control panel devices), each of which controls some aspect of your Mac's performance. The icons for some init files, like QuicKeys, also appear in the Control Panel DA, but for the sake of simplicity we'll limit our discussion to cdevs. Each cdev icon in the Control Panel DA corresponds to a file in your Mac's System Folder. Your Control Panel may look different than the one shown here, because your System Folder may contain a different collection of cdevs. Apple supplies a number of cdevs with its system software, but many others (like the Network cdev shown above) are available from third-party software vendors.

When you select an icon from the cdev list, the settings controlled by that cdev are displayed in the rest of the window. In the above illustration, the General icon is selected, so its settings are displayed.

Cdev icons generally appear in the Control Panel in alphabetical order from top to bottom, but no matter which cdevs you have in your System Folder, the General icon is always at the top of the list. In addition, it is always selected automatically when you open the Control Panel DA, because it contains most of the system settings you'll typically want to change.

To use the Control Panel DA:

1. Choose the Control Panel DA from the menu. The Mac displays the Control Panel window, shown on page 67.

2. Click on the buttons or icons at the right to change the General settings, or click on a different cdev icon at the left to view another group of settings. If the icon you want to select isn't in view, you can scroll the column of icons until it appears.

3. Once you've selected a new icon, make whatever changes you wish to its settings.

4. When you've finished making changes, click the close box to put the Control Panel away. Most changes you make in the Control Panel DA take effect immediately after you close its window.

The General cdev's options are much like those in System 7's General Controls control panel, described on page 58; however, the General cdev also includes the option for adjusting the size of the RAM cache, which is a separate control panel under System 7. *Adjusting memory options* on page 64 explains how the RAM cache works. The only thing that's different about the RAM cache in System 6 is that you can turn it on and off.

System 6 also includes cdevs that correspond to System 7's Monitors, Sound, and Startup Disk control panels (except that the Startup Disk control panel is called the Startup Device cdev in System 6). For more information about these features, see page 60 (Monitors), page 63 (Sound) and page 64 (Startup Disk).

Using the Chooser DA

As you'll recall from Chapters 1 and 2, the Chooser DA is where you tell the system software which peripheral or network devices you want to use. All Macintosh models come with a Chooser DA. When you start your Mac, the System file determines which Chooser extensions (or *device drivers*) are present in the System Folder, and those icons appear in the Chooser window when you display it. If you haven't copied a device's Chooser extension file into the System Folder, your System file won't detect that device, and its icon won't show up in the Chooser. Most new Chooser extensions you copy into your System Folder automatically appear in the Chooser window the next time you display it, but some don't appear until you restart the Mac.

To use the Chooser, select its name on the menu. The Mac displays the Chooser window, which looks like this:

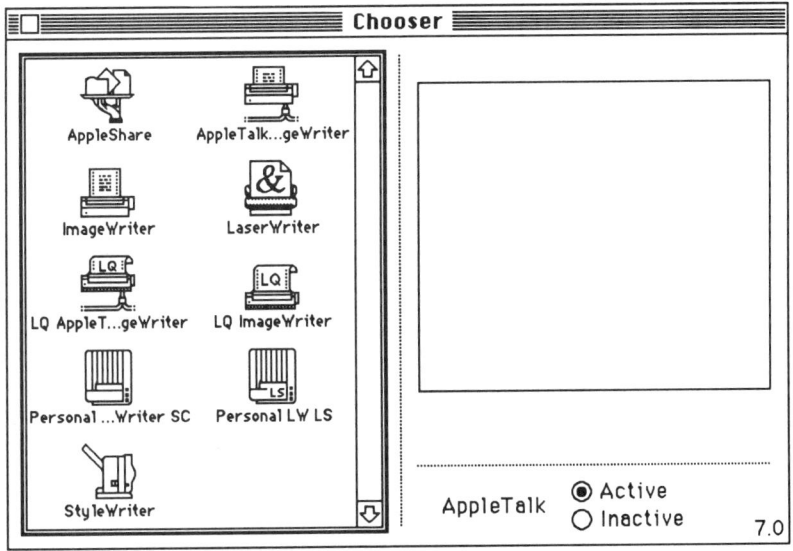

The icons on the left side of the window indicate which Chooser extensions or device drivers you currently have installed in your System Folder. (Under System 7, these extensions are grouped in the Extensions folder inside the System Folder.)

There are two distinct procedures for choosing devices to work with, depending on whether you're choosing a network file server for file sharing or another peripheral device. The procedure for choosing a network file server is covered in Chapter 15, page 277. When you're choosing a printer, a modem or any peripheral other than a file server, you can handle the whole procedure with the Chooser window itself. With the Chooser window open:

1. Select the icon that represents the type of device you want to use. If there's only one device of that type, its exact name will appear in the list at the right, and that name will be selected. If more than one device of that type is connected to your network, you'll see several names. (For example, if you're on a network that has three LaserWriters, you'll see a name for each of them.)

2. Select the name of the device you want to use. If you don't click on the actual device name, your Mac won't know which device you want, or may assume you want the device at the top of the list because that one may be automatically selected.

3. Click the close box to quit the Chooser. Any selections you make with the Chooser take effect immediately, so your Mac's system software now knows which printer or other device you want to use.

Remember, your Mac's system software only knows which printers, scanners or other devices to use when you select them with the Chooser. When you hook up a printer or other network device for the first time, you must select it with the Chooser or your Mac won't realize it's there. (By the way, you should *never* connect or disconnect devices while your Mac is turned on.)

The System Folder folders (System 7 only)

Under System 7, you can use three of the folders inside the System Folder to adjust the system software: the Apple Menu Items folder, the Extensions folder, and the Startup Items folder. Items that belong in these folders are placed in them automatically when you install System 7 with the Installer program or when you drag new items onto the System Folder icon on the desktop.

The Apple Menu Items folder

The Apple Menu Items folder contains the programs, DAs, control panels, folders and documents that appear on the menu.

If you want an item to appear on the menu, just drag it (or an alias for it) onto this folder. Placing individual DAs, control panels, folders, documents, programs or aliases on the menu gives you easy access to them at any time. To remove an item from the menu, simply drag it out of the Apple Menu Items folder.

The Extensions folder

The Extensions folder is where you store all your Chooser and system extension files. If you drag any Chooser extension, device driver, init file or system extension file onto the System Folder icon, your Mac will automatically place it inside the Extensions folder.

Some system extensions or Chooser extensions may work properly even if they're not inside the Extensions folder, but it's best to keep all these files in their proper place.

The Startup Items folder

The Startup Items folder is where you place any program, document or alias that you want to open automatically when you start your Mac. Once an item is inside this folder, the Mac will attempt to open it along with the Finder at startup.

The Mac opens the items in the Startup Items folder one at a time in alphabetical order. It will fail to open an item in only two situations: when there isn't enough memory available, and when the Mac doesn't know which program was used to create a document because the document's Kind designation doesn't say.

System Folder operations under System 6

Under System 6, there aren't any folders inside the System Folder. To add items to the Apple menu, you must use Apple's Font/DA Mover program or a third-party DA manager like Suitcase or MasterJuggler. To install system extensions (which are called *inits* under System 6), you simply drag them into the System Folder and restart your Mac.

You can set different startup items in System 6 with the *Set Startup* command on the Special menu in the Finder. This command lets you modify your System file so it looks for an application other than the Finder and loads it along with the Finder at startup. If you always work with Microsoft Word, for example, you can make it the startup application; then Word will load automatically when you start your Mac, saving you the extra steps of waiting for the Finder to load and then launching your program.

You also use the *Set Startup* command to switch between the Finder and MultiFinder. Under the Finder, you can only set one startup application, because the Finder only allows the Mac to run one application at a time; under MultiFinder, however, you can set several startup applications or DAs, because MultiFinder lets you open several applications at once. Whether you're setting one startup application or several, the procedure is pretty much the same:

1. Make sure you're on the desktop (look for the Trash icon in the lower-right corner).

2. Select the application or applications that you want to open automatically at startup.

3. Choose the *Set Startup* command from the Special menu. The Mac will display a dialog box like this one:

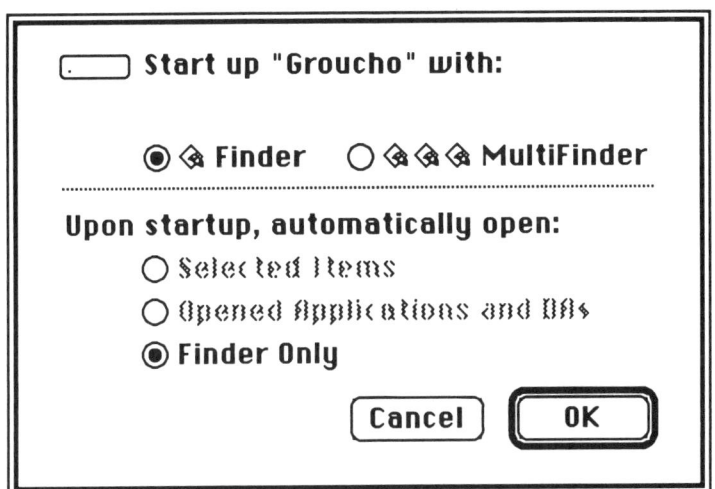

The disk name is at the top of the dialog box and your options are controlled with the radio buttons below.

4. Click on the options you want to select, and then click the *OK* button to reset the startup application. Your Mac will automatically load the applications you've chosen the next time you start or restart it.

Changes you make with the *Set Startup* command don't take effect until the next time you start your Mac.

4 | Keeping your Mac out of trouble

What Do I Do Now

Most common Mac problems arise from mistakes you've made rather than from some diabolical streak in your hardware or software. Even when your hardware or software is at fault, something about the way you use the Mac is often at the root of—or has at least aggravated—the problem.

In this chapter, we'll look at some daily and periodic things you can do to minimize the occurrence of problems with your Mac. Then we'll explain the basic repair techniques you'll use in later chapters to recover from Mac problems when they do occur.

Fourteen ways to avoid problems

In this section we'll recommend some general operating procedures that will help you prevent hardware and software failures. Although some of these may seem obvious, it's amazing how many people overlook them at exactly the wrong time.

1. **Make sure everything is plugged in securely before you start your Mac.**

Everyone checks the plugs when setting up or moving the Mac or its peripherals, but people often sit helpless in front of a dead Mac because the janitor knocked the power cord out of the wall with a vacuum cleaner the night before. You don't need to hand-tighten every connection each day, but you should definitely try this simple solution first if your Mac doesn't start up, or if you can't locate your network printer or file server with the Chooser.

2. **Never plug or unplug anything from the Mac while the Mac or the other component is turned on.**

This basic rule is the best way to prevent serious electrical problems with your equipment. Realistically though, you're probably not going to shut down your whole system just to check a loose modem cable, so here are the specific components you can and can't unplug while the Mac is turned on:

- Don't *ever* unplug anything connected to the SCSI port, the external disk drive port, the ADB (keyboard/mouse) port, any Mac II or SE expansion cards, or the electrical power cord from the Mac, a hard disk, a tape backup system or any other storage device while it's turned on.

- If you insist, you can unplug anything connected to the printer or modem ports or the audio port with the Mac running.

These guidelines will probably keep you safe, but again, it's best not to unplug anything while your Mac is turned on.

3. Don't cover up any of the cooling vents on a Mac, hard disk, monitor, printer or other component.

It's tempting to treat the Mac as furniture, perhaps using it as a bookend or stacking papers on top of it. Remember though, the Mac, its monitor and other components generate a lot of internal heat, and unless that heat is dissipated through unobstructed cooling vents, it will eventually shorten the life of semiconductor chips or other electric components inside the machine. Giving your Mac and other components enough breathing space is an easy way to avoid expensive repairs.

4. Don't place liquids near your Mac.

Lots of Macs have been put out of action at least temporarily because someone set a can of soda or a coffee cup within spilling distance. Spilled liquids can cause everything from a sticky keyboard to electrical shorts in the CPU that ruin your Mac's logic board. Make a habit of keeping liquids off the table that holds your Mac.

5. Allow plenty of room for your Mac's cables.

Lots of Macs are bristling with cables in the back, and this can make it hard to fit a Mac comfortably on a workstation that's set against a wall. People usually try to fix this problem by shoving the Mac as far back as they can in order to free up space in front for papers and the keyboard. If you push a Mac to the wall though, you usually end up squashing the cables, and that can cause problems.

Every cable coming out of your Mac is filled with smaller wires, and every wire can only be bent so far. Past a certain point (or *bend radius,* as the techies would say), wires begin to break. In a SCSI cable linking an external hard disk with your Mac for example, a few broken wires inside the cable can cause intermittent disk problems that are maddeningly difficult to diagnose.

The simplest way to avoid cable problems is to allow cables to bend naturally. Don't squash a cable against the wall, wrap excess cable into a tight bundle, stretch a cable to make it span too big a gap or otherwise force it to assume shapes that it wouldn't normally take on.

6. Don't quit programs or the Finder by turning off the power switch.

Always use the *Shut Down* command before you turn off the power. Choosing *Shut Down* may seem like an extra step when you're just going to turn off the computer anyway, but this command does more than empty the Mac's memory and black out the screen.

During the shut down sequence, the Mac quits all the programs it's currently running, gives you a chance to save any documents you may have forgotten to save since the last change and stores information about the current state of the Finder desktop so the Mac knows what to display the next time you start up from the same disk. If you simply turn off your Mac, it will take longer to start the next time (because it will have to determine how the Finder should look, instead of knowing that in advance). What's more, you could damage some system software files by hitting the switch without using *Shut Down.*

If your Mac is locked up so you can't use the *Shut Down* command, you'll probably have to use the power switch to turn the machine off so you can restart it; however, the Mac IIsi model has a keyboard shortcut ($\boxed{\circlearrowleft\mathbb{\#}}\boxed{Control}\boxed{\triangleleft}$) that will restart the machine if it's locked up. (There's also a system extension called Programmer's Switch by Paul Mercer that will let you restart any Mac II or SE model by pressing $\boxed{\circlearrowleft\mathbb{\#}}\boxed{Option}\boxed{\triangleleft}$. This program is available on electronic bulletin boards and from user groups.)

7. Don't move, hit or shake the Mac, a hard disk or a laser printer while it is turned on.

This one is really obvious, but it's easy to get careless and toss a book down on the desk so it hits an external hard disk. If you do this, you're risking a hard disk crash and the loss of your data.

Moving a running Mac is like moving a television set while it's on, except you're not only jiggling a tube that's generating thousands of volts, you're also in danger of disconnecting SCSI devices or external floppy drives. Moving a laser printer is even worse—you could end up spilling toner all over the inside, causing everything you print afterwards to have polka dots.

8. Don't restart, shut down or turn off your Mac while it's reading from or writing to a floppy or hard disk or any other storage device or while it's printing.

This trespass is sort of like driving away from a gas station with the fuel hose still pumping gas into your tank: you're cutting off the flow of data from its source, which can damage (or at least thoroughly confuse) the peripheral that's left in the lurch. Doing this with a hard disk could cause a head crash, which can destroy data on the disk.

9. Don't store more than one copy of the System, Finder or System Folder on the disk you use to start the Mac.

As explained in Chapter 2, the Mac looks for a System file and a System Folder on startup. If it finds more than one, it will load the first System file it locates, but it may then become confused about which System file is in charge, resulting in unexpected system crashes and other unpleasantries.

It's not difficult to see how this problem occurs: when you copy a new application to your hard disk from the original floppy, it's easiest to copy the whole disk, which sometimes contains its own System Folder. To keep extra System Folders off your hard disk, make sure you copy only program files from original application disks and periodically use the *Find* command on the File menu in the Finder (if you're running System 6, use the Find File DA or another file-finding utility) to search for duplicate System or Finder files or for System Folders.

If you do end up with more than one System Folder on your startup disk, you can tell which ones are extraneous by checking the icon that represents each of them. When it locates a System Folder and uses its files to start up, the Mac identifies that System Folder as the one that's in charge and places a small Mac on its icon, like this:

System Folder

To determine which of your multiple System Folders you should keep, select the window that contains each one, choose *Icon* from the View menu in the Finder and look for the System Folder icon that has a Mac on it.

10. When you connect more than one SCSI device to your Mac, make sure each device has a different SCSI address number before you start the system.

You can have up to seven SCSI devices connected to your Mac's SCSI port, but each device must have a different address (from 0 to 6). If two devices have the same address, your Mac won't be able to use either of them properly. Usually you set the address either with software that comes with the device, or by using a wheel or button on the back of the device itself. Check the device's manual for instructions.

11. Never turn any SCSI device on or off while the Mac is running.

Turn SCSI devices on before you start the Mac and turn them off after you turn off the Mac. The Mac always scans its SCSI port during the startup sequence. If you have a SCSI device connected but not turned on, the Mac won't recognize it.

You may get into the habit of turning on your hard disk and your Mac at the same time. That's probably OK with a small-capacity hard disk (under 100 megabytes), because the drive warms up so fast that it's ready to go by the time the Mac has scanned the SCSI bus. If you have a large hard disk or a removable cartridge hard disk, you'll have to wait until the drive's Ready light comes on to turn on the Mac.

If you turn off a SCSI device while the Mac is still running, the Mac may continue to think the device is available. This is especially problematic with storage devices: if you try to save to a SCSI device that is no longer turned on, you'll cause a system crash.

12. Minimize the System file (for System 6 users only).

The System file in a basic Macintosh running under System 6 contains over 300,000 bytes of complex instructions. As you use the Mac, parts of the System file are read and modified by the Chooser, the Control Panel DA, the Finder and by various other DAs and applications. It's like having fifteen editors working on a manuscript at the same time and expecting the result to be perfectly consistent.

The System file's size and the complexity of its interactions with other Mac software are responsible for many software errors; there's no sense in aggravating the situation by making the System file any larger than necessary. Each time you add a font, sound or DA to your System file, it gets more cumbersome. Adding extra inits to your System Folder also increases the amount of memory the System file requires to run. When your System file's size reaches about a megabyte, it's pushing the limit of memory set aside for it under System 6 and you'll begin to have problems printing or starting up.

The next time you feel an urge to load up the System file with all sorts of fonts, sounds and DAs you'll rarely use, or to enhance it by adding lots of dubious inits to your System Folder, remember that you're only making it harder for the Mac to manage something that's already tricky.

If you want to use lots of fonts and DAs, use a DA manager like Suitcase or MasterJuggler to install them. That way, those programs and fonts will be stored outside the System file.

When you use a DA manager, be sure to open the System file with the Font/DA Mover and remove any duplicate copies of desk accessories or fonts that you'll be installing with the DA manager program.

This problem has been eliminated in System 7, which manages fonts, sounds and DAs more efficiently than System 6, but that doesn't mean it's OK to clutter your System file with unnecessary fonts and sounds. Remember, a lean Mac is a happy Mac.

13. Minimize the System Folder.

Don't use the System Folder to store any files except those essential to the operation of the System file. The Installer program you use to install System files will put important files into the appropriate folders in the System Folder. Other programs you install may also place system-related files (like preferences files) in the System Folder.

But don't store any files in the System Folder that don't have to be there, such as data files or applications. The more cluttered the System Folder becomes, the longer it takes the System file to locate and load the resources it needs.

Remember, anything you can do to make the Mac's system-related tasks easier and faster will cut down on system errors.

14. Don't do more than one thing at a time. Wait for an operation to finish before you begin the next operation.

Everybody becomes a speed freak once they master the basics of computing. As soon as you've mastered the steps for printing a document or performing some other procedure, somehow your Mac—once such a marvel of technology—becomes slower than a pack mule. Then, instead of calmly waiting those agonizing milliseconds while the Mac obeys each command, you pile them on top of one another in the hope that the Mac will remember and execute them all in the proper order.

Most of the time your Mac can keep up, but sometimes it can't and then you'll have a problem. C'mon, give the Mac a break. How would *you* like it if your boss gave you a full week's orders in two seconds and expected you to follow them all flawlessly?

Periodic maintenance

The activities outlined in this section are on the order of a regular oil change or tune-up for your car. They won't necessarily keep your Mac from breaking, but they'll keep it running more smoothly, help eliminate some potential problems before they occur and make it easier to recover from problems that do crop up.

Make backup copies of everything.

There's one thing you can be certain of: sometime, somehow, you'll have a problem with your Mac that will cause you to lose some data. If you make regular backup copies and save an extra copy of your work to a second disk several times a day, you'll protect yourself against potential disaster. The more often you back up your data, the less work you'll lose when trouble strikes.

You should also make at least one backup copy of every program you have, including all the system utilities and setup programs that came with your Mac, your hard disk or any other components. You'll need working copies of these utilities to perform many of the repair techniques used in this book.

Sometimes, one of the system software installation disks or your hard disk setup program becomes damaged and the only remedy is to use another copy that works properly. You won't be able to do that if you haven't made at least one backup copy.

Rebuild the desktop file.

The desktop file is an invisible file found on every disk. It contains information about the files and programs on the disk and how you view them in the Finder. As a disk is inserted (or as the System file recognizes it at startup time), its desktop file is read into the Mac's memory. As you work with the disk (adding and deleting files), the desktop file grows because it stores information about files even after they've been deleted. This can create two problems:

- First, all that reading and writing of information makes a file increasingly prone to minor disk errors, which can cause data to be written incorrectly. This may show up when you try to open a file and can't, when a disk's icon doesn't look right or when the Mac tells you a disk is damaged or unreadable.

- Second, after several weeks or months, you end up with a desktop file that contains all sorts of information your Mac no longer needs because it concerns files that have been deleted. An extra-large desktop file takes longer to read, so you have to wait longer and longer for your Mac to display disk icons and windows in the Finder.

You can keep your disks in optimum shape by periodically rebuilding the desktop file on each disk. How frequently you need to do this depends on how many changes you make to the files you store on your hard disk, and on how often you change them. If you add or change a few files a day, you only need to rebuild the desktop file every month or so. (See *Rebuilding the desktop file* on page 90 later in this chapter for complete instructions.)

Replace the System file.

As explained earlier, the System file is a large and complex piece of software that is modified continually as you use the Mac. Sometimes, a disk writing error will cause problems in the System file that don't show up immediately. If you begin having minor, intermittent problems with disk access, printing or startup, it's a good idea to replace the System file on your disk. Even if you don't begin to notice problems, replacing your System file every three months or so will help prevent them. For complete instructions see *Replacing the system software* on page 88 later in this chapter.

Avoid disk clutter.

What's good for the System Folder, System file, and desktop file is also good for your disks in general. The more files and folders you have on a disk, the larger its desktop file, and the longer it takes to display the disk's contents. Most computer users waste from ten to thirty percent of their disk space by storing old memos, letters and other data files they no longer need, or large applications they never use. Again, the principle applies: a lean Mac is a happy Mac. If you haven't used a file in several months, you can probably copy it onto a floppy disk and retrieve it when—or if—you need it again.

Defragment your hard disk.

File fragmentation is another factor that can affect your Mac's performance. When you begin storing files on a new hard disk, the files are stored side by side in concentric rings. However, when you enlarge an existing file, your Mac has to fragment, or break the file up, and store it in two or more places because the original space created for that file is now too small for it, and other files are probably stored on either side.

A fragmented file takes longer to load and store, because the disk has to read or write in two, three or more places. Fragmentation is an inevitable phenomenon on hard disks, but it doesn't usually become a performance problem until thirty percent or more of the files on a disk are fragmented.

Check for fragmentation every couple of months with a disk utility program like DiskExpress, Symantec Utilities for Macintosh, Mac Tools Deluxe or Norton Utilities for Macintosh. If the utility shows that thirty percent or more of the space on your disk is fragmented, you can defragment it using the same program. (This can be a bit risky, so be sure to back up your entire disk before you run a defragmentation program.)

A safer alternative is to make a complete backup copy of your disk, reformat the disk to erase everything on it, and then restore the backup copy. When you restore the files, they will be written to the disk in unfragmented blocks.

Repair techniques

In this section, we'll explain some specific repair techniques you'll be using in later chapters. If you're already practiced in these, you can skip ahead and just refer back to this section when you need a reminder.

Restarting the Mac and trying again

This technique should be obvious, but so many people simply freeze when a problem occurs that it's worth belaboring the point:

WHENEVER YOU GET AN ERROR MESSAGE AND YOU DON'T KNOW WHAT'S WRONG, TRY THE PROCEDURE AGAIN.

A lot of Mac problems are one-time glitches. Often, you'll get a system error message that locks up your system, forcing you to restart the machine. Once you restart, everything is fine again. If a problem doesn't recur, don't worry about it. If it does, check the specific messages and use the remedies provided in the remainder of this book.

If your Mac is locked up and won't respond to commands, you can restart it either by turning it off and on with the power switch or— on the Mac IIsi—by pressing ⌘ Control ◁ . If you have to use the power switch, wait a couple of seconds after turning the Mac off before you turn it on again.

Using another startup disk

If the system software on your hard disk (or the disk you normally use to start your Mac) becomes damaged, you'll have to start your Mac with another startup disk in order to repair the damaged disk. A Macintosh startup disk is any floppy or hard disk that contains a System Folder, which must include at least a System file and a Finder file. Make one or two startup disks like this and keep them handy. You'll need them to perform many of the repair operations covered later in this book.

If you're using System 7, it's a lot easier to make startup floppies using a version of System 6, because the standard System Folder in System 7 is too large to fit on a standard floppy disk. Even on high-density, 1.44 megabyte floppy disks, you have to eliminate lots of system software files to make a System 7 startup disk, so it's simpler just to use a System 6 startup floppy. A copy of the System 7 *Disk Tools* disk will also work for this purpose.

Checking the SCSI chain

Some problems you may have starting up or using disks can be traced to connections between various devices attached to your Mac's SCSI port. Checking the SCSI chain is one of the troubleshooting techniques we'll refer to in later chapters.

Before you attempt this procedure, be certain your Mac and all your SCSI devices are turned off. To check the SCSI chain:

1. If you have more than one device connected to your Mac's SCSI port, make sure each device has a unique address. Some devices let you see and change the address with a button or a wheel on the back panel of the device. Other devices come with special software that lets you set the address. Every externally connected SCSI device must have an address from 1 to 6, and no two can have the same address.

2. Make sure the last device in the SCSI chain is terminated. Some SCSI devices require you to insert a special terminating connector between the device and the SCSI cable, and others are self-terminating. Check the device's manual for more information. Also, make sure no terminating connectors are plugged into any other devices in the SCSI chain—only the device at the end of the chain should have a terminator.

3. Be sure all the devices are plugged in securely. If any of them use 25-pin connectors, unplug these connectors (with everything shut off, of course) and check for bent or missing pins.

4. Check the cables coming out of the back of each device to be sure they're not bent at severe angles or stretched too far as this can cause wires inside the cable to fray or break. If a cable looks like it might be damaged, try replacing it with another cable that you know works.

5. Make sure all the devices in the SCSI chain are turned on. Technically, you're supposed to be able to run properly with some devices on and others off, but in practice this setup has an adverse effect on some programs and device drivers. If you've had some devices turned off and a problem clears up once you turn everything on and restart the Mac, you'll know that this was the source of the difficulty.

6. If you have several devices connected to the SCSI port and a problem persists after you've checked their addresses and connections, looked for terminators, and turned all the devices on, there's one more thing you can try. Shut everything off and disconnect every device except the one that's not working properly (assuming this is possible—obviously, if you're running your Mac from an external hard disk and having trouble with a SCSI printer, you'll have to keep both of them connected). If the problem clears up when fewer devices are connected, the culprit is probably the SCSI circuitry in one of the devices you've unplugged.

Replacing the system software

The purpose of replacing your system software is to eliminate problems caused by a damaged System file or by related files, or to make sure such problems don't occur. When you replace the system software, you replace the entire System Folder.

If you have a complete, working System Folder on another disk, you can drag it onto the disk that's having problems and the working System Folder will replace the damaged one; however the safest and best way to replace a System Folder is to use the Installer. This procedure takes several steps; you can't simply throw away your old System Folder and install a new one. If you did, you would also toss out any custom fonts, DAs, sounds, system extensions and other files that you installed yourself. Here's the best procedure:

1. Start your Mac with a startup floppy disk.

2. Open your startup disk icon, and then open the System Folder on the hard disk.

3. Drag the System file out of the System Folder and into another folder on the disk.

4. Rename the System Folder (we'll call it *System Stuff* here).

5. Restart your Mac using the *Install 1* disk that's part of your installation package. (The disk containing the Installer will have a different name—usually *System Tools*—if you're using System 6.) The Installer will load automatically (or you may have to double-click the Installer icon to load it if you're using System 6).

6. Click the *OK* button on the Installer's welcome screen, and then click the *Easy Install* option on the main Installer screen to install a complete set of system software files.

7. Check the name of the disk drive in the upper part of the Installer dialog box to make sure it's the disk on which you want to replace the System file. If it isn't, click the *Switch Disk* button until the correct disk name appears.

8. Click the *Install* button or press ⌜Return⌝. The Installer will install a new System Folder and inform you when the installation is complete. If you're installing from floppy disks, you'll have to insert various disks as they're requested.

9. When the installation is complete, restart the Mac with the disk containing your new System Folder.

10. Open the *System Stuff* folder and copy any custom system extension files, DAs or preferences files it contains into the new System Folder by dragging them onto the new System Folder's icon. They'll automatically be installed in the proper folders within the System Folder.

11. Open the old System file that you dragged into a different folder and copy any custom fonts or sounds from it into the new System file by dragging them onto the new System Folder's icon. They'll automatically be installed in the new System file.

12. Delete the old System file and the *System Stuff* folder when you're done.

System 6 users note: System 6 users must manually install items from the old System file and the *System Stuff* folder. Under System 6, you can't double-click the System file to open it, so you must use the Font/DA Mover to copy any custom fonts or DAs from your old System file into your new one. To copy your other custom files from the *System Stuff* folder, simply drag them into the new System Folder. Once that's done, you can delete the *System Stuff* folder.

Rebuilding the desktop file

For reasons described earlier, in the maintenance section, rebuilding the desktop file can reduce the time it takes to start your Mac, or the time it takes to return to the Finder after you quit an application. Here's how to rebuild the desktop file on any disk:

1. Hold down ⌘Option as you insert the floppy disk. If you're rebuilding the desktop on a startup disk, hold these keys down as you boot from the disk. Either way, keep the keys pressed down until you see a message like this (the text of this alert is a little different under System 6):

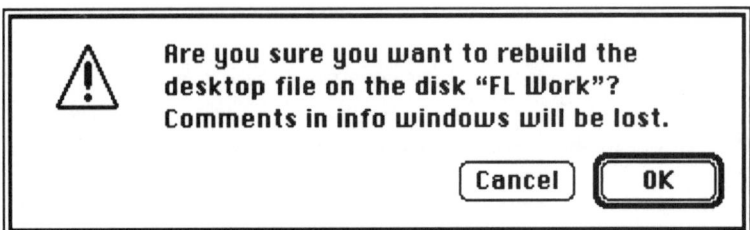

2. Click the *OK* button or press [Return] and the desktop file will be rebuilt. This operation can take anywhere from a few seconds to a few minutes, depending on how many files the disk contains.

Once the desktop file has been rebuilt, the Finder desktop will appear. The only problem with rebuilding a disk's desktop file is that doing so erases any comments you've entered in the Get Info windows for files on that disk. If you know you've used Get Info windows to store comments about certain files, you should review those comments and record any important ones before you rebuild your desktop file.

Replacing the hard disk driver

If you start your Mac from a hard disk, the file the Mac needs to recognize that disk (the hard disk driver) may become damaged over time, eventually creating problems during the startup sequence. One remedy is to reinstall the hard disk driver. Hard disk drivers come with the setup software that accompanies each hard disk; the manual for your hard disk should tell you how to install its driver.

The procedure for replacing a driver is usually the same one you used to install it in the first place—you start your Mac from the hard disk's utility software disk and then install the driver from that disk onto your hard disk. If you're using an Apple hard disk, the software for installing the driver comes on one of the system software disks and is called Apple HD SC Setup.

Using a disk repair utility

A number of disk repair utilities are available for Mac hard disks, including Disk First Aid, 1st Aid Kit, the Norton Utilities for Macintosh, MacTools Deluxe and Symantec Utilities for Macintosh. All of these perform various operations to restore damaged hard disk files so you can boot your Mac from the disk or recover data files from it. Disk First Aid is included on the Macintosh system software disks (instructions are included in Apple's system software user's guide), but it's the least effective of these programs at restoring the files your Mac needs to start from your hard disk. You're probably better off buying one of the other three programs. (For instructions on using these programs, see their manuals.)

Zapping the PRAM

As explained in Chapter 1, your Mac's parameter RAM, or PRAM, stores information about the location of the current startup disk, as well as the date, time and other information. If this portion of the Mac's memory becomes corrupted, you may have problems starting your Mac or getting it to recognize a hard disk drive once you're up and running. If your Mac's PRAM becomes corrupted, you can remedy the problem by erasing (zapping) it. There are three ways to do this: one for any Mac running under System 7; another for SEs, IIs or Portables running under System 6; and a third for Mac Plus or older machines.

If you're running under System 7, hold down Option ⌘ P R while restarting your Mac. After emitting a beep, the Mac will restart. Once the Mac begins restarting, you can let go of the keys. The PRAM will be erased and rebuilt. After that, reset the Mac's clock and calendar with the General Controls control panel.

If you have a Mac SE, Portable or II and you're running under System 6,

1. Leave your Mac running.

2. Hold down Shift Option ⌘ while you select the Control Panel DA from the menu. You'll see a dialog box explaining that you're about to zap the PRAM and asking if you really want to do so.

3. Click the *Yes* button to proceed.

4. Restart the Mac with your hard disk so the Mac can restore its PRAM with the correct information about the startup disk you want to use.

5. Reset the Mac's clock and calendar using the Control Panel DA.

If you have a Mac Plus or a 512KE, 512 or 128K model running under System 6, the only way to erase the PRAM in these machines is to physically remove the battery that maintains it. The battery is located behind a door above the power switch on the back panel of the Mac. To erase the PRAM:

1. Turn off your Mac.

2. Remove the battery and wait about a half hour. (A capacitor on the Mac logic board maintains power to the PRAM for a few minutes even if no battery is installed, so it won't be erased unless you leave the battery out for awhile.)

3. Replace the battery.

4. Restart the Mac. The correct information about your startup disk will be read into the PRAM.

5. Reset the Mac's clock and calendar using the Control Panel DA.

Now that you're up to speed on basic Mac preventive maintenance and repair techniques, you're prepared to tackle most common problems—as you'll see in the chapters that follow.

5 | Hard disk setup

What Do I Do Now

A hard disk is only a dumb piece of hardware until someone connects it to a Mac with a cable and runs the setup programs that install a device driver and Mac system software files on it. The device driver allows the Mac to recognize the disk as a standard storage device, and the system software enables the Mac to start from the disk.

Most Mac hard disks come set up and ready to use, which means the necessary software drivers and Mac system software have already been installed at the factory or dealership. In some cases, however, you may have to set up the hard disk yourself, and even after the disk is set up, you may need to use the setup software to create *partitions* (discrete storage areas) on the disk or to test its operation.

This chapter covers problems that may occur when you're setting up a hard disk so the Mac will recognize it as a storage device. Chapter 6 deals with problems that can crop up when you're running Apple's Installer program to install or replace Mac system software files on a disk. If you've already set up your hard disk and installed the necessary system software and you're having trouble starting your Mac, see Chapter 7.

Every hard disk comes with setup software provided by its manufacturer and it would be impossible to cover all the error messages for every type and brand of software here. Fortunately, the procedure for setting up a hard disk is pretty consistent for all these products, so you might encounter several common problems with any setup program.

In this chapter, some of the alert messages displayed at the tops of the pages are generic—that is, they're not genuine error messages but rather approximations of what you might see if you have problems running a hard disk setup program. In other cases, there's a description of the problem instead of an alert message at the top of the page. So when you look up a problem in this chapter, you may find a message or description that's similar, but not identical, to the one you actually see on your screen.

Some programs refer to the process of preparing a disk to store Macintosh files as *initializing,* and others call this process *formatting.* These terms are interchangeable in this chapter.

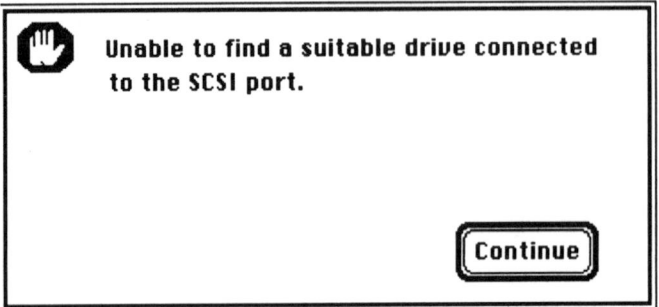

Problem:

The disk drive is either not connected, not turned on or the Mac is having trouble locating it.

Solutions:

Make sure the drive is connected and turned on. If it is and you're still getting this error message, try the solutions below:

- Turn off your Mac and check the SCSI chain (see *Checking the SCSI chain,* page 87).

- If that doesn't help, try zapping your Mac's PRAM (see *Zapping the PRAM,* page 92).

- If the problem persists, your hardware is at fault and you'll have to call your hard disk's manufacturer.

You have a hard disk connected and running, but your hard disk setup software doesn't recognize it and there's no error message.

Problem:

Many hard disk setup programs will only recognize drives that have been set up with their own drivers. For example, Apple HD SC Setup won't recognize drives set up with software from other manufacturers, even though they're connected and working properly.

Solution:

Make sure you're using the hard disk setup program that came with the disk you want to work with.

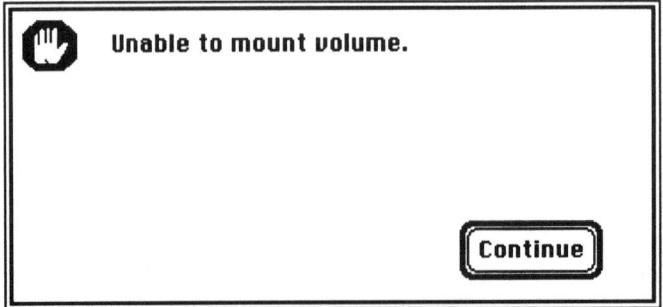

Problem:

Either the drive isn't initialized, the disk driver software is damaged or you have a hardware problem.

Solutions:

• Try the procedure again.

• Use your hard disk setup program to update the hard disk driver, and then try the procedure again.

• Restart your Mac using a startup disk that contains SUM, MacTools, Disk First Aid or another disk recovery program, and then try to mount and repair the drive. (See the disk recovery program's manual for instructions.)

• Use your hard disk setup program to reinitialize the disk. You'll erase all the data on the drive, but at least you'll get the drive working again, unless there's a hardware problem.

• If none of these solution works, call the disk's manufacturer.

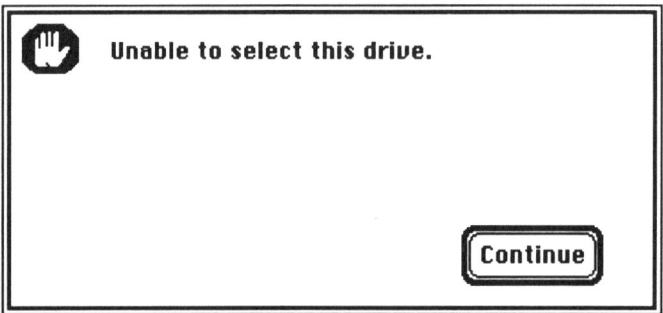

Problem:

The drive is either not connected, not turned on or the Mac is simply having trouble finding it.

Solutions:

- Turn off your Mac and check the SCSI chain (see *Checking the SCSI chain*, page 87).

- If that doesn't help, zap your Mac's PRAM (see *Zapping the PRAM*, page 92).

- If these procedures don't do the trick, you have a hardware problem. Call your hard disk's manufacturer.

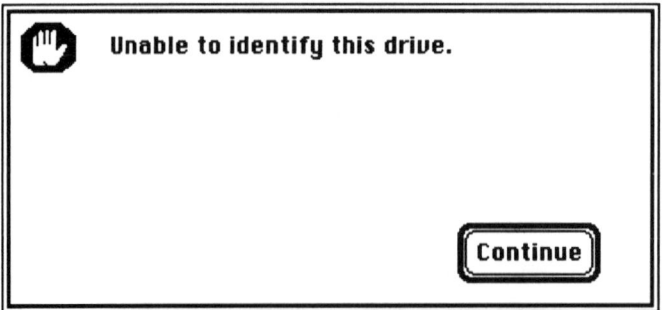

Problem:

The hard disk driver has probably become corrupted.

Solution:

Shut down first the Mac and then the hard disk. Turn on the hard disk, and start the Mac with the floppy disk that contains your hard disk setup program. Then reinstall or update the hard disk's driver using the setup program.

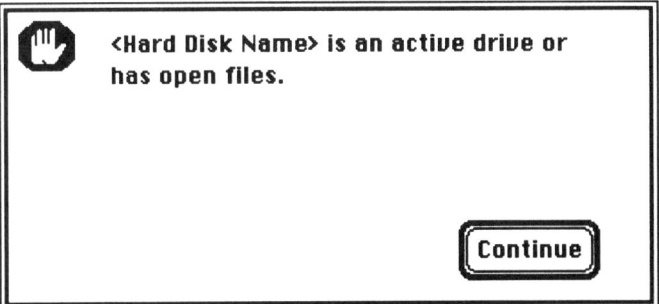

Problem:

You're trying to update the driver software or change the partitions on a disk that has files open.

Solution:

Close all the files on the drive, shut down the Mac and restart it with a different startup disk that contains the hard disk setup program. Then you'll be able to adjust the drive's partitions or update its driver.

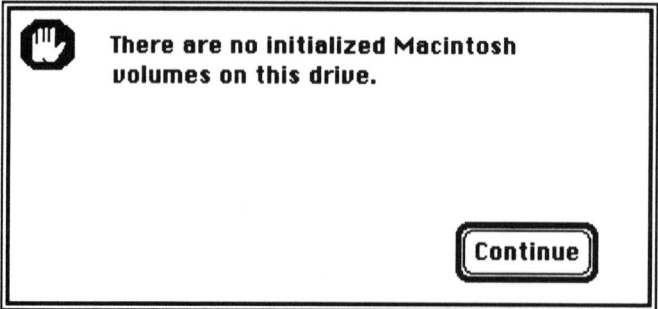

There are no initialized Macintosh volumes on this drive.

Continue

Problem:

There is no Macintosh driver software on the hard disk.

Solution:

Restart your Mac using a startup disk that contains the hard disk setup software; then initialize the hard disk and install a driver on it.

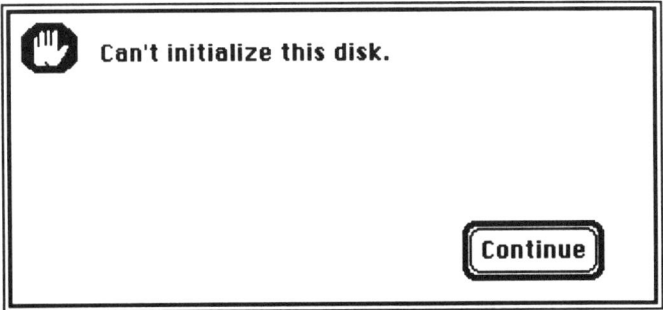

Problem:

Either your hard disk setup program has a glitch or you have a hardware problem.

Solutions:

- Restart the Macintosh with another startup disk and try initializing the disk with a different copy of the hard disk setup program.

- If that doesn't do the trick, zap your Mac's PRAM (see *Zapping the PRAM*, page 92) and try the initialization again.

- If the problem continues, restart your Mac with a startup disk that contains a disk recovery program and try initializing the disk with that program.

- If these remedies don't work, call your Apple dealer or the company that sold you the hard disk.

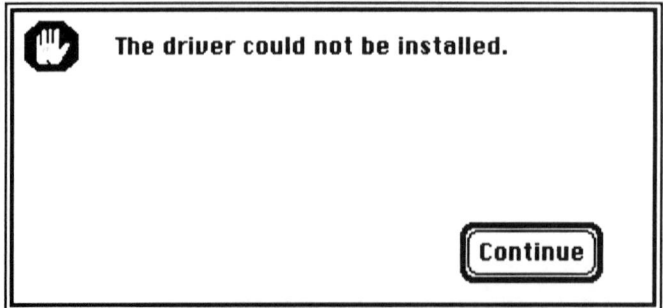

Problem:

This is a generic message that can indicate various problems.

Solutions:

- Try installing the driver a few more times.

- Check the SCSI chain (see *Checking the SCSI chain*, page 87).

- Run the setup program and initialize or format the disk; then try installing the driver again.

- If you're still having problems, call the disk's manufacturer.

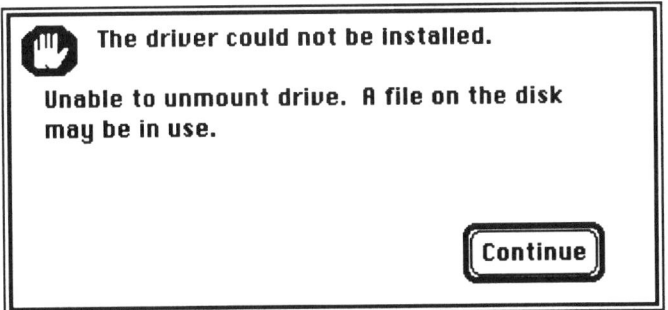

The driver could not be installed.

Unable to unmount drive. A file on the disk may be in use.

Continue

Problem:

A drive or partition must be unmounted before you can initialize it or reinstall its drivers, but you can't unmount a drive if files on that drive are open or in use. You may be trying to run the setup program from the same disk on which you're trying to install or update the driver.

Solution:

Close any files that are open and restart the Mac using a startup disk that contains your hard disk setup program; then try installing the driver again.

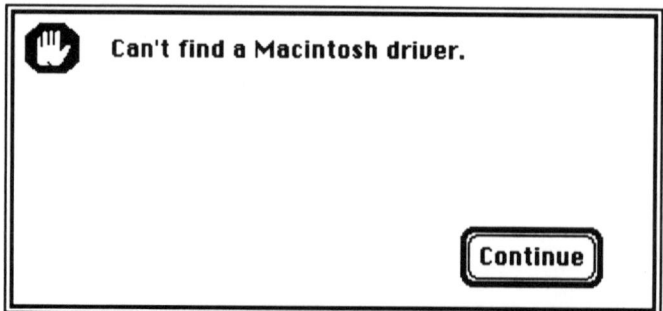

Problem:

The hard disk you've selected doesn't have a Macintosh driver on it.

Solution:

Use your hard disk's setup software to initialize the disk for use with your Mac.

Problem:

Either the disk hasn't been formatted properly or there was a minor glitch when you ran the verification routine.

Solutions:

- Try running the format verification routine again.

- Reformat the hard disk and then run the verification routine again.

- If the problem persists, the disk itself may be malfunctioning. Contact the disk's manufacturer or take it in for service.

Problem:

Your disk probably has a bad ROM; if not, something else is wrong with the disk hardware.

Solutions:

- Try the test again.

- Call the disk's manufacturer.

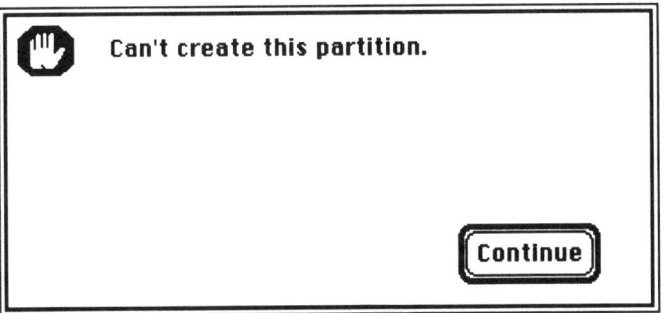

Problem:

Either there isn't enough room on your disk for the partition you want to create or you're not following the correct procedure for installing the partition.

Solutions:

- Check the manual for your setup software to be sure you're following the correct steps and observing the rules for creating the partition. Pay attention to the size of the partition you're trying to create, and check to see whether or not your setup program allows you to change the size of partitions once you've created them. Some setup programs won't let you resize existing partitions once they're created, or will let you increase, but not decrease, their size. Also, some setup programs require that a partition be empty before you change its size.

- If you've followed all the rules in the manual and you can't create the partition, you'll either have to live with the disk the way it is or reinitialize it and create a new set of partitions.

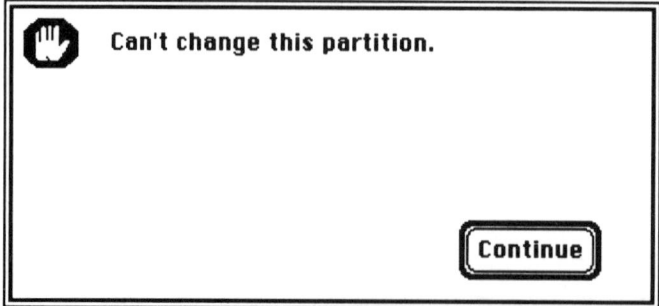

Continue

Problem:

Your setup software won't allow you to change the size or name of one or more partitions on a disk.

Solutions:

- Check the manual for your setup software to be sure you're following the correct steps and observing all the rules for creating the partition. Consider the size of the partition you're trying to create and be certain your setup program will allow you to change the size of partitions once you've created them. Some setup programs won't let you resize partitions after they're created, or will allow you to make partitions larger, but not smaller. Also, some setup programs require that a partition be empty before you can change its size.

- If you've followed all the rules in the manual and you can't change the partition, you'll either have to live with the existing partition or reinitialize the disk and create a new set of partitions.

6 | Installer problems

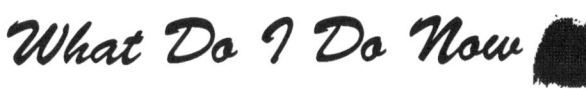

What Do I Do Now

The Installer is the program Apple gives you to install the Mac's system software files on your disks. A disk with these files installed on it—called a *startup disk*—can be used to start up your Mac. This chapter covers problems you may have while using Apple's Installer program to install, replace or remove the Mac's system software.

The Installer itself comes on a startup disk. Under System 6, this disk is called *System Tools*. Under System 7, it's called *Install 1*. For the sake of simplicity, we'll just call it the Installer disk here. Several other disks are also used for installation. We'll refer to these as the Installer disk set. Complete instructions for using the Installer are in your Mac's system software manual.

How to run the Installer

You can run the Installer from a floppy disk, a hard disk (or network server) or a CD-ROM disk. But you can't install files on the same disk you're running the Installer from—this is like changing the tires on a car while you're driving it.

If you start your Mac and then try to run the Installer program from a different floppy or hard disk than the one you started up from, the Installer will try to switch control of the Mac from your original startup disk's System Folder to the System Folder on the Installer disk. Sometimes this works and sometimes it doesn't.

To avoid this kind of problem, always use the Installer disk itself to start your Mac when you're planning to update or install system software files.

To run the Installer, double-click its icon, which looks like this:

Installer

Be sure you open the Installer program and not the script, which is called *Installer Script* in System 6 and *Install* in System 7.

When you start the Installer program, it will look for a disk other than the one it's running from on which to install system software. If the Mac finds another disk, that disk will be automatically selected as the destination for the new files. If the Mac doesn't find another disk, you'll see a message like this:

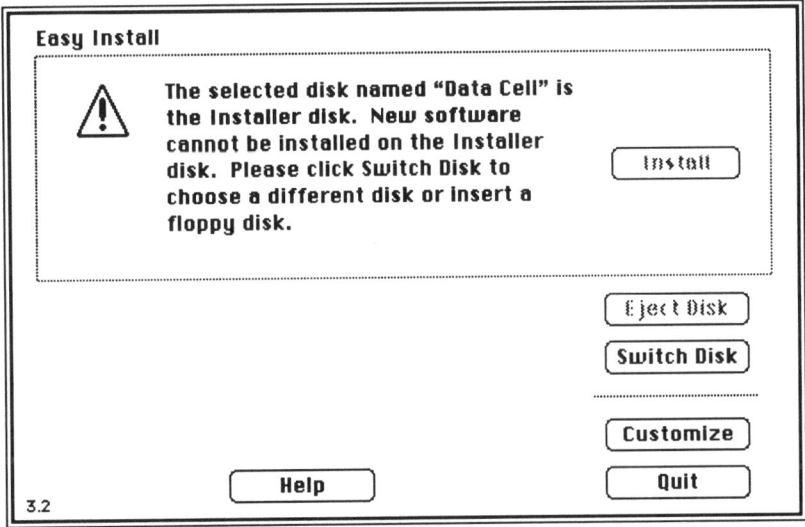

If you want the system software installed on a floppy, insert one into the Mac. If you want to install the system software on your hard disk, click the *Switch Disk* button.

Spotting Installer error messages

Many of the alerts you'll see when using the Installer appear inside the message area at the top of the Installer dialog box as shown above. Keep an eye out for these messages and when you see one, turn to the page in this chapter that shows it. To save paper, we'll only show the messages themselves, not the whole Installer dialog box.

Some Installer error messages contain specific error numbers or resource names, but we can't display every variation here. So look for the message text in this chapter that's close to what you see on the screen and don't worry if the error number or resource name isn't exactly the same—the solution to the problem will be.

Backing up your Installer disks

Many Installer problems occur because one of the files on the Installer disk or disk set is missing or has been damaged. The Installer expects to find a specific set of companion files on the disk it runs from and on other disks or folders it uses during the installation process. All those files, disks and folders must have just the right names and creation dates. If one of the files is renamed, removed or locked—or even if a new file is added—the Installer may not be able to run properly.

As a result, a lot of the solutions in this chapter involve using a different, undamaged copy of the Installer disk set. You'll save yourself a lot of trouble by making two or more backup copies of the Installer disk set. Keep these copies handy—you'll probably need them.

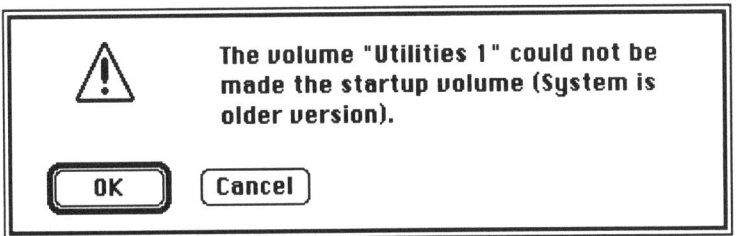

■ SYSTEM 6 ONLY

Problem:

You started your Mac with another startup disk, and your Installer disk contains an older version of the system software than your startup disk does. The Mac won't allow you to switch control from a newer version of the system software to an older version.

Solutions:

- Click the *OK* button and then eject the Installer disk. Restart the Mac with the Installer disk.

- **If you want to install an older version** of the system software than the one currently on your startup disk, delete the System file from the System Folder on your startup disk, rename the System Folder, and then run the Installer to install a new one (see *Replacing the system software* on page 88).

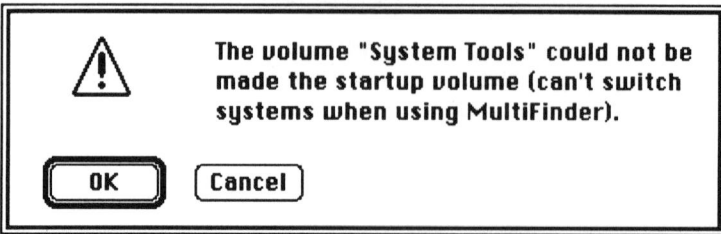

The volume "System Tools" could not be made the startup volume (can't switch systems when using MultiFinder).

OK   Cancel

■ SYSTEM 6 ONLY

Problem:

You started your Mac with another startup disk and are running under MultiFinder. Now you're trying to run the Installer. The Installer can't run properly unless the System Folder on the Installer disk is in control of the Macintosh. Your Mac can't switch control from the System Folder on the disk you started up from while running under MultiFinder.

Solution:

Click the *OK* button to return to the Finder. Then restart your Mac with the Installer disk and run the Installer program.

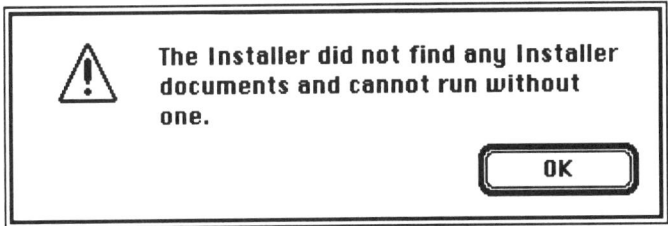

■ SYSTEM 7 VERSION

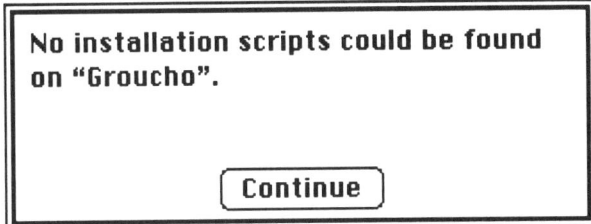

■ SYSTEM 6 VERSION

Problem:

The Installer can't find any of the scripts it needs to install your system software.

Solutions:

Click the *OK* or *Continue* button to return to the Finder. Then run the Installer from a disk that contains both the Installer and one or more Installer scripts. Any file or folder needed by the Installer must have the correct name and must be located at the same directory level on your disk as the Installer program itself. Just moving one of the folders of installation files into another folder will keep the Installer from finding it.

If you're installing from a hard disk, make sure all your Installer files and folders are inside the same folder on that hard disk. If you're installing from floppy disks, make sure all the disks in the Installer disk set have the correct names and contain all the proper files.

```
Resource error -192 opening script
file "Macintosh SE Installation (v6.0)"
on "HD20".

        ( Continue )
```

Problem:

The Installer isn't able to open an Installer script file, probably because the file is damaged.

Solutions:

- Click the *Continue* button to return to the Finder. Then restart the Mac with the same Installer disk and try the procedure again.

- If that doesn't work, use a different Installer disk to restart the Mac and then try the installation again.

```
Resource error -192 finding INIT 2 for
"Macintosh SE Installation (v6.0)".

        ( Continue )
```

Problem:

The Installer can't find one of the files it needs to install. Some of the files in your Installer disk set are missing or damaged.

Solution:

Click the *Continue* button to return to the Finder. Then restart the Mac and try the installation process again. It could be a fluke. If you get the same message again, use a different copy of the Installer disk set.

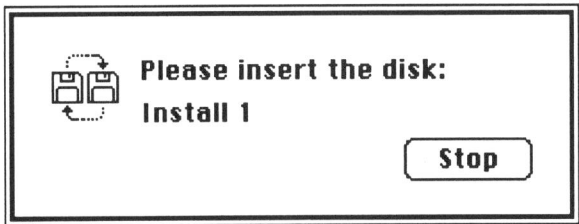

Please insert the disk:

Install 1

Stop

Problem:

If you're installing from floppy disks, this may just be a normal reminder that the Installer needs files that are on the disk named *Install 1*. (Actually, you can get this message about any of the installer disks or folders—we're just using *Install 1* as an example.) But if you've renamed the required disk or have deleted any of its files, the Installer won't recognize it anymore and will display this message.

Solutions:

- Click the *Stop* button. You'll be asked if you want to stop the installation. Click the *Stop* button again, then click the *Quit* button in the Installer dialog box to return to the Finder.

- **If you're installing from floppy disks**, insert the disk you think is *Install 1* and make sure it's really named that. If the name is right, the problem is that files are missing from the disk. You'll need to find another, complete copy of the *Install 1* disk and use it.

- **If you're installing from a hard disk**, make sure the *Install 1* folder is located inside the same folder as the Installer program itself and is named *Install 1*. If it's in a different place or has a different name, the Installer won't recognize it. If the name and the place are right, then the folder is missing some files. You'll have to replace it with a complete copy.

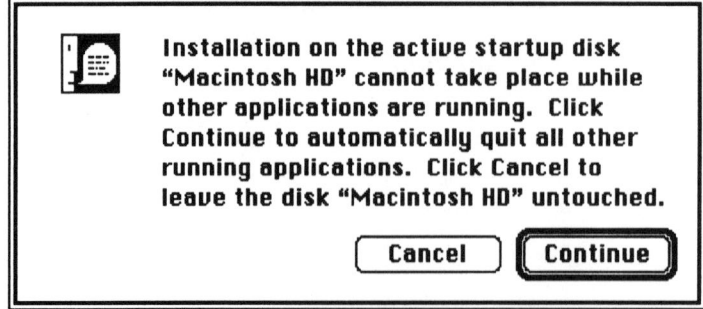

■ SYSTEM 7 ONLY

Problem:

You're trying to use the Installer to install printer extensions or device drivers, but you have another application running at the same time. The Mac can't install anything while another application (other than the Finder) is running, so it's giving you the chance to close all other programs.

Solution:

Click *Continue* to have the Mac close any open programs and complete the installation, or click *Cancel* to stop the installation.

■ SYSTEM 6 ONLY

Problem:

The System file on the destination disk contains too many desk accessories for the Installer program to transfer to the new copy of the System file it's installing. You'll get this message when the System file on the destination disk contains fifteen DAs, which is the limit.

Solution:

• Click the *OK* button to return to the Finder. Then use the Font/DA Mover program to remove at least one desk accessory from the System file on the destination disk. Once you've removed one or more DAs, try the installation process again.

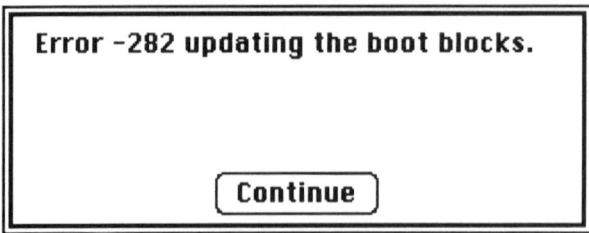

Error -282 updating the boot blocks.

Continue

Problem:

The Installer is having trouble writing information to your hard disk's boot blocks. Either there's a glitch in the Installer software or there's something wrong with that region of your hard disk.

Solutions:

- Click the *Continue* button to return to the Finder, then try running the Installer again. The glitch may be temporary.

- If you get the same message again, try using a program like Norton Utilities for Macintosh, Symantec Utilities for Macintosh or MacTools Deluxe to repair your hard disk's boot blocks.

- If you don't have a disk repair utility, use your hard disk's set-up software to reinstall the hard disk drivers. Be careful! Do not reformat the disk unless you want to erase everything from it—just choose the option in the setup software that lets you install or update the disk driver.

The selected disk named "HD20" is not large enough to accomodate the installation.

(Install)

Please click Switch Disk to choose a different disk or insert a high density (FDHD) floppy disk.

Problem:

The destination disk you've selected isn't large enough to hold all the system software files. If you're installing System 6, you need at least an 800K floppy. If you're installing System 7, you need at least a high density (1.44 MB) floppy disk or a hard disk.

Solution:

Install the software on a larger disk.

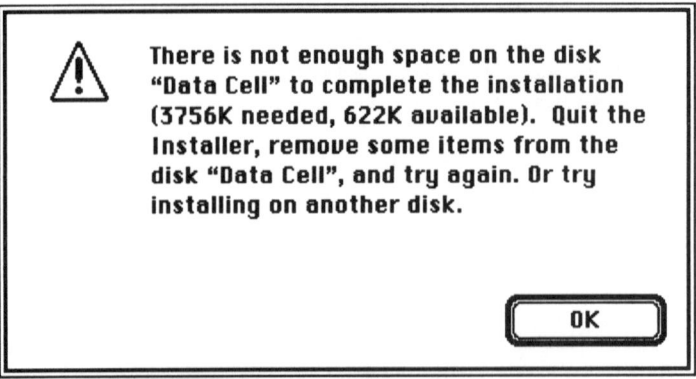

■ SYSTEM 7 VERSION

■ SYSTEM 6 VERSION

Problem:

The destination disk you've chosen is too full to hold all the system software files you're trying to install.

Note: The same problem can be indicated by the alert message, *Not enough room for file <file name> on <disk name>.*

Solution:

Click the *OK* button to return to the Finder. After that, delete enough files from the destination disk to free up the amount of space indicated in the error message—or you can just use a different destination disk. Then run the Installer program again.

The selected disk named "Startup" is locked. Click Eject Disk, unlock the disk then reinsert; or click Switch Disk to choose a different disk.

[Install]

Problem:

The disk is locked or write-protected, so the Installer can't erase or install any files on it. If you're trying to install files on a floppy disk, you may simply have the write-protect tab in the wrong position. If you get this message while trying to install onto a hard disk, then the disk has been locked either with security software or with the hard disk's own utility software.

Solutions:

- **If you're installing onto a floppy disk**, click the *Eject Disk* button, and then make sure the write-protect tab on the disk is pushed completely away from the edge of the disk so you can't see through the hole. (There are two holes on high-density, 1.44 MB floppy disks, so of course the one without the tab will stay open.)

- **If you're installing onto a hard disk**, click the *Quit* button on the Installer dialog box to quit the Installer program. If you suspect that security software or the hard disk's utility software has been used to lock the hard disk, try unlocking it with the same software.

  If the disk isn't yours, find its owner and ask about the problem. (Maybe you shouldn't be changing the system files on somebody else's disk anyway.)

  If the disk is yours and you don't know anything about security or utility software, call the company or dealer you bought it from and ask about the problem.

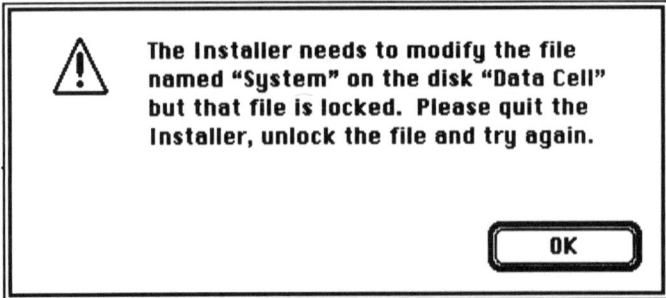

■ SYSTEM 7 VERSION

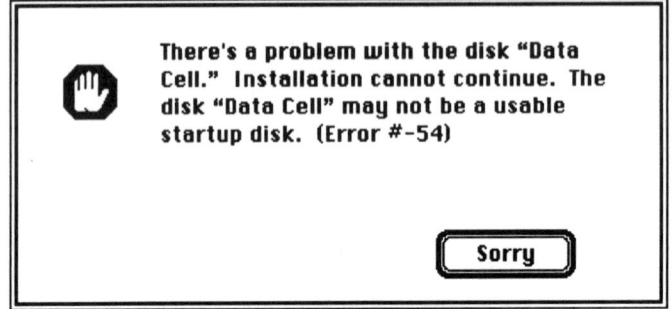

■ SYSTEM 6 VERSION

Problem:

You're trying to install a new version of the system software on a disk that already contains a System Folder. The Installer is trying to remove the old system files, but one or more of them is locked and can't be deleted. As you can see in the error messages above, System 7's Installer tells you exactly which file is locked but System 6's Installer doesn't.

Solution:

Locate the locked files in the System Folder you want to update and unlock them; then try the installation again. To unlock a file, select its icon in the Finder, press ⌘ I to choose the *Get Info* command, and then uncheck the *Locked* checkbox in the file's information window. If you're using System 6, you'll have to use the *Get Info* command on each of the files in your System Folder to find the ones that are locked and unlock them.

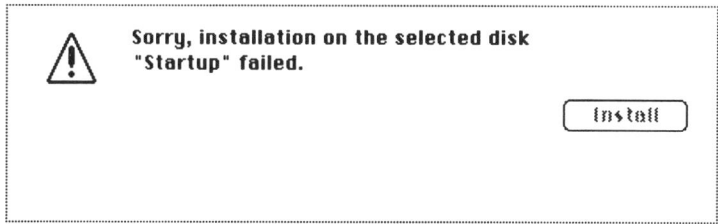

Problem:

The Installer was unable to copy files to your destination disk (which is named Startup in the example above). There could be any number of reasons for this, from a glitch in the Installer program to corrupted resource files to a problem with your hard disk.

Solutions:

- Click the *Quit* button and then restart the Mac using the floppy disk that contains the Installer program. Try the installation again. If it still doesn't work, try using another copy of the Installer program and the Installer disk set.

- If the above doesn't do the trick and you have a working System Folder on another disk, try dragging it onto the destination disk.

  If you're installing onto a floppy, try using it to start up the Mac after you've dragged the new System Folder onto it. If the Mac starts up okay, then the problem lies with the copy of the Installer program or the Installer script file you were trying to use.

  If you're installing onto a hard disk, use the Startup Disk control panel or Startup Device cdev to select it as the startup disk, then restart the Mac. If the Mac starts up okay, the problem was with your copy of the Installer or its script file.

- If dragging a System folder onto the disk doesn't work, your hard disk has a hardware problem and you'll have to call the dealer or company you bought it from.

7 | Startup problems

What Do I Do Now

This chapter covers problems you may encounter when starting up your Mac. In most cases there's a simple explanation and quick solution for these problems, but it can also be a serious hardware problem that's holding you up. You'll notice that most of the problems in this chapter aren't identified with icons or alert messages but instead are described in a heading. That's because these problems either don't cause icons or messages to appear at all, or they cause a bunch of different error messages that signify essentially the same problem.

The startup disk is ejected.

Problem:

The disk is ejected because you've tried to start up the Mac with a disk that either doesn't contain a System Folder or contains damaged system software files.

Solution:

Either insert another startup floppy disk or shut off the Mac, hook up a hard disk that contains a System Folder, turn the hard disk on and then turn the Mac on again.

A disk with a question mark appears.

Problem:

The Mac can't find a startup disk and is waiting for you to insert one. If you're starting up from a hard disk, the disk is either off or disconnected, or else its System Folder is missing, damaged or incomplete.

Solutions:

- Insert a startup floppy disk or shut off the Mac, hook up a hard disk that contains a System Folder, turn the hard disk on and then turn the Mac on again.

- If you already have a startup hard disk connected and running, then the Mac is having trouble finding it or identifying it as a startup disk. Check the SCSI chain (see *Checking the SCSI chain*, page 87).

- If the problem continues, run the hard disk's setup software and see if it recognizes the disk. If it does, update the driver on the hard disk and try restarting again. If the setup software doesn't recognize the hard disk, you probably have a problem with the hard disk. Contact the disk's manufacturer.

- If you were able to update the hard disk's driver but the Mac still doesn't start up, reinstall the system software on the disk using the Installer program.

- If the problem persists, try using the hard disk to start up a different Mac. If it starts that Mac up, there's something wrong with your Mac. If the icon still doesn't appear on a different Mac, take the hard disk in for service.

Sad Mac face

Problem:

There's a hardware problem with your Mac, either a bad memory chip or worse. The code number underneath the sad Mac face will tell a technician the general nature of the problem.

Solution:

Take the Mac to a service technician.

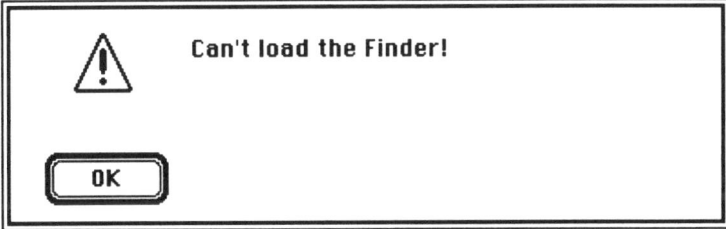

■ SYSTEM 6 ONLY

Problem:

The Finder file is either missing from your startup disk, or it's damaged.

Solution:

Start up your Mac from another startup disk and then reinstall the system software files on the problem disk using the Installer.

The Mac locks up and/or displays an error message during the startup sequence.

Problem:

Your Mac's hardware is okay but there's a problem with the software that's causing it to lock up somewhere in its startup sequence. Sometimes the Mac just locks up with the *Welcome To Macintosh* box on the screen; other times it locks up when a particular system extension or init file is loaded and its icon appears in the screen's lower left corner. Some of the alert messages you may see when your Mac locks up or crashes include:

- Sorry, a system error has occurred

- Stack collision with heap

- System file may be damaged

- Illegal instruction

- Coprocessor not installed

- Address error

But whatever the specific text of the message, the most likely causes for a problem like this are:

- incompatible system extension or init files

- too much system software (System 6 only)

- damaged or missing system software files

- damaged boot blocks on your disk

- corrupted PRAM.

Solutions:

There are several different solutions, depending on the specific problem. Before you try any of them, look through this entire section to see which solutions seem most applicable to your situation.

Whatever solution you try, the first thing you're going to have to do is restart—but since your Mac locks up or crashes on startup, you can't use the *Restart* command on the Special menu to reboot it. In fact, you need to use a different startup disk. Insert a new startup floppy disk or connect and turn on another hard disk with a working System Folder on it. Then follow one of these three startup procedures:

- If you're using a Mac IIsi or LC, press the ⌘ Control ◁ keys at the same time. If you're using a startup floppy disk, it will be ejected when you restart and you'll have to reinsert it.

- If you have a programmer's switch on the front of your Mac II model or on the side of your Mac SE, Classic, Plus or 512K model, press the front or right-hand side of the switch to restart. (The programmer's switch has two sides, and you push the side that is closest to the front of the Mac SE, Classic, Plus or 512K models or on the right on Mac II models.)

- Turn off the Mac with its power switch, wait five seconds, and then turn the Mac on again. If you're using a startup floppy disk, it will be ejected when you restart and you'll have to reinsert it.

Incompatible extensions, control panels or init files

If your System Folder contains a lot of startup files (which includes extensions and certain control panels under System 7 and inits and certain cdevs under System 6), one of them may be incompatible with the others or with the operating system. This is particularly likely if you've just added a new one to your System Folder, or if you've just upgraded to a newer version of the system software.

The best way to find out if a startup file incompatibility is the problem is to control which ones load at startup:

- **On a System 7 Mac**, you can disable all startup files by holding down the Shift key while restarting. You'll see the message *Extensions Off* in the *Welcome To Macintosh* box as the Mac starts up.

- **On a System 6 Mac,** you'll need to restart with a floppy startup disk to avoid loading the files on your regular startup disk (unless you've got a utility like InitPicker or Aask which allows you to disable inits automatically at startup).

If the Mac starts up fine without these files, you know that one of them is the problem. You can determine which one by removing them all from your system and then reloading them one at a time, restarting after you load each one.

The simplest way to remove and reload startup files is to use InitPicker or Aask. If you don't have one of these programs, drag your all non-Apple control panels (cdevs) and extensions (inits) out of your System Folder. Here's how to find them:

- **Under System 7,** these files are normally stored in the *Extensions* and *Control Panels* folders inside your System Folder, although you may also find some in the System Folder itself—they show up as *system extensions* and *control panels* in the Kind column of your System Folder's window when you view it *by Kind.*

- **Under System 6,** these files are called *startup documents* and *control panel documents* in your System Folder's Kind column.

To test the startup files you dragged out of the System folder, just drag them back to the System Folder individually, restarting the Mac after you drag each one. (Under System 7, be sure to drag them onto the System Folder's icon—not into its open window—so they'll be installed properly.) The file that's incompatible is the one that causes the Mac to lock up. If you've recently installed a new startup file, try that one first since it's the most likely culprit.

Once you've determined which file is causing the problem, restart your Mac with a startup floppy disk and then drag the offending item outside the System Folder. If the Mac starts up fine after that, you may have to live without that file. But if you really need a particular init and it seems to be causing a compatibility problem, you can try renaming it so it loads at a different time than it did before. (Since these files load in alphabetical order by name, changing a startup file's name to one that starts with a different letter will change the order in which it loads.)

Simply changing the order in which extensions, control panels and inits load sometimes clears up incompatibilities, but not always. The only surefire way to eliminate this type of problem is to eliminate the file that's causing it.

Too much system software (System 6 only)

If you're running System 6 (or an earlier system version), only a certain amount of RAM is set aside for the system software, no matter how much RAM you have installed in your Mac. (System 7 allocates RAM space for system software as it's needed.) The RAM space that's been set aside is called the *system heap*, and if you're trying to run more system software than will fit into it, you can have problems starting up or experience sudden system crashes. There are two things to check:

- **The size of your System file.** A System 6 Mac shouldn't have a System file larger than a megabyte or so. You can find out the System's size by checking its Size information in a list view window on the desktop, or by selecting the file and choosing the *Get Info* command. If your System file is too large, it's because you have too many fonts or DAs installed in it. (To remedy this problem, see *Minimize the System file* on page 80.)

- **The number and size of any inits inside your System Folder.** Any inits you load at startup increase the amount of system heap space used. Many inits are only a few kilobytes in size, but some inits for anti-virus programs or electronic mail programs can be over 150K apiece. As a rule, your system heap can't afford to spend more than a total of 150K on init files. If your inits are using more than this, you'll either have to eliminate some of them from your System Folder or increase the size of your system heap to accommodate them. To increase the size of the system heap, you'll need the HeapFixer program from CE Software in West Des Moines, Iowa.

Damaged or missing system software files

If eliminating system extension or init files doesn't work and your Mac still won't start up properly, try replacing the system software on your disk. (See *Replacing the system software*, page 88.)

Damaged boot blocks

If replacing the system software doesn't work, then the start-up instructions, or boot blocks, on your hard disk may have become damaged. If so, you can restore them:

- Start up your Mac with a startup disk that contains your hard disk setup program.

- Choose the option in the hard disk setup program that lets you reinstall or update the driver on your hard disk.

- Remove the system software files from the problem disk and reinstall new system software with the Installer program. (See *Replacing the system software*, page 88.)

- Restart the Mac with the original startup disk. If the Mac starts okay, you've solved the problem.

Corrupted PRAM

The data stored in your Mac's PRAM may have become corrupted, so your Mac can no longer identify your startup disk as the correct one. In this case, zap the PRAM (see *Zapping the PRAM*, page 92). Even after you zap the PRAM though, you should reset the startup disk with the Startup Disk control panel (under System 7) or the Startup Device cdev in the Control Panel DA (under System 6).

The hard disk icon doesn't appear on the desktop.

Problem:

In this case, your Mac seems to start up all right, but then the startup disk's icon doesn't appear on the desktop. Either your Mac's PRAM is corrupted, the desktop file needs to be rebuilt, or your hard disk has a hardware problem.

Solutions:

There are several different things you can do to try to get the icon to appear. Try the first one on the list—if that doesn't work, try the next one, and so on.

- Zap your Mac's PRAM, and then restart the Mac. (See *Zapping the PRAM*, page 92).

- Use the Startup Disk control panel or the Startup Device cdev (under System 6) to select the disk as the one you want the Mac to start up from, then restart and see if the icon appears.

- Rebuild the desktop file on the hard disk. (See *Rebuilding the desktop file*, page 90.)

- Replace the system software. (See *Replacing the system software*, page 88.)

- Update the hard disk's driver using its disk setup software.

- Check the SCSI chain. (See *Checking the SCSI chain*, page 87.)

- If possible, try using the disk to start up a different Mac. If it starts that Mac up and its icon appears there, there's something wrong with your Mac. If the icon still doesn't appear, take the hard disk in for service.

The Mac starts okay, but it doesn't respond to the mouse or the keyboard.

Problem:

Either the mouse or keyboard cables aren't properly connected, or there's a temporary software problem that prevents the Mac from recognizing them, or the Mac has a hardware problem.

Solution:

* Shut down the Mac, turn it off, and remove the mouse and keyboard cables. Look inside the cable connectors for bent pins. If a pin is bent, try straightening it with a pocket knife, a small needle-nose pliers or a small screwdriver. (If you can't straighten a bent pin, you'll have to buy a new cable.) If all the pins look straight, make sure none of them is loose. Then carefully plug all the cables back into the proper ports and make sure they're pushed in firmly. (If a loose pin breaks off inside the mouse or ADB port after you've plugged a connector into the Mac, you'll probably have to have the port replaced by a technician.) Restart the Mac.

* If the problem persists, try replacing the system software (see page 88).

* If the problem still persists, take the Mac in for service.

8 | Inserting and ejecting disks

What Do I Do Now

This chapter covers error messages or problems you may see when inserting or ejecting floppy disks or mounting hard disk volumes on a Macintosh. If you're having problems logging onto an AppleShare file server or shared disk on a System 7 Mac, see page 281.

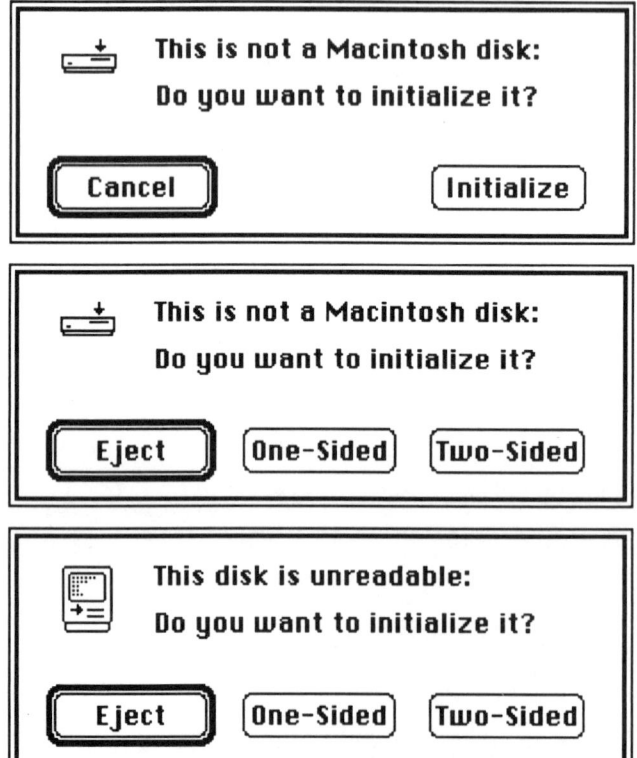

Problem:

These alerts are all essentially caused by the same problem. Which message you get depends on which Mac model you're using and whether the problem is with a hard disk or a floppy.

The error message is caused by one of four things:

- The floppy disk you've inserted (or the hard disk your Macintosh is trying to recognize) hasn't been formatted for use by the Mac. It may be unformatted, or it may have been formatted under another operating system, like DOS.

- The disk's desktop file is corrupted so the Mac doesn't recognize it.

- The disk is physically damaged.

- The floppy disk drive is dirty or out of adjustment.

Solutions:

- **If the disk has never been used,** or if you know it doesn't contain any information you want to save, click the *Initialize* or *Two-Sided* button. The Mac will then prepare the disk for use (this is called *formatting* or *initializing*). Any data on the disk will be erased as part of this process, so if you think there's something on the disk you want saved, click the *Eject* (or *Cancel)* button.

- **If the disk has already been formatted** for the Macintosh and you know it contains files, check it for physical damage. If it's a floppy, slide its metal door back and forth to make sure it moves freely. If it does or the problem is with a hard disk, try rebuilding the desktop file. (See *Rebuilding the desktop file*, page 90 for instructions.)

- **If the disk was formatted for use on a DOS computer** and you're trying to use it on the Mac, you must make sure your Mac has a high-density floppy disk drive (FDHD—Mac Classic, Portable and newer Mac SE and II models all have this drive). You also need to be running either Apple File Exchange or DOS Mounter. These are utilities that allow the Mac to read a DOS disk. (Apple File Exchange comes with your Mac system software; DOS Mounter is sold by Dayna Communications of Salt Lake City, Utah.) To work, they must be running *before* you insert the DOS disk in your Mac.

- **If none of the above remedies works and you're not trying to read a DOS disk,** then either the disk is damaged or the floppy disk drive is dirty or out of adjustment. If possible, try the disk in another Macintosh. If its icon appears on the desktop and you don't see either of the above messages, try cleaning the original Mac's disk drive with a drive cleaning kit (available from any Apple dealer or mail order house). If that doesn't work, take the drive to a service technician.

If you get the same message when you try the disk in a different Mac, you'll have to try recovering files from the disk using a disk recovery program like Disk First Aid, Symantec Utilities for Macintosh or the Norton Utilities for Macintosh (see the recovery program's manual for instructions).

Problem:

You've tried to initialize a disk but the Mac can't do it, probably because the disk is damaged.

Solution:

Click the *OK* button to eject the disk. If it's a floppy you might try repairing the disk with a disk repair utility, but the damage is probably irreparable. If it's a hard disk, call the disk's manufacturer.

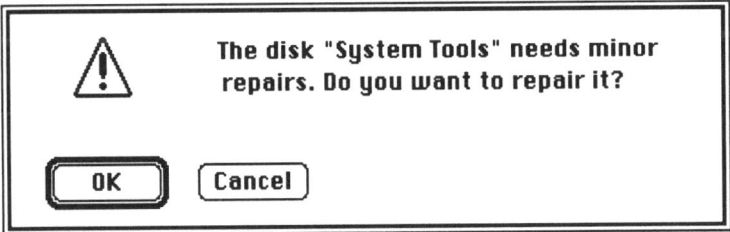

Problem:

A previous error in writing to the disk has caused a minor problem with the disk directory. Your Mac is asking for permission to repair the directory.

Solution:

Click the *OK* button to repair the disk.

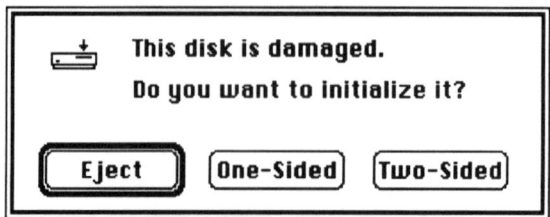

■ SYSTEM 7 VERSION

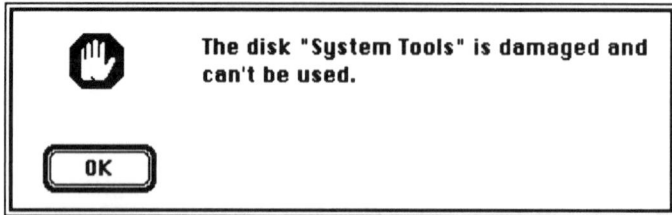

■ SYSTEM 6 VERSION

Problem:

Either the desktop file on the disk you've inserted is so damaged that the Mac doesn't think it can be repaired, or the disk's directory is damaged, or the Mac is having a temporary problem reading the desktop file. As you can see in the above alert, System 7 gives you a chance to initialize the disk anyway to see if the Mac can repair it.

Solutions:

- Click the *OK* or *Eject* button to eject the disk, and then check the metal sliding door on the floppy disk to make sure it slides freely.

- Re-insert the disk while holding down ⌘Option to rebuild the desktop file. If the file can be rebuilt, you'll see the dialog box asking you to confirm that you want the desktop file rebuilt.

- If the disk directory is damaged, rebuilding the desktop file won't work and you'll get the damaged disk alert message again. In this case, start up Disk First Aid, First Aid Kit, Symantec Utilities for Macintosh, the Norton Utilities for Macintosh or another file recovery program and then insert the disk again.

A floppy disk's icon doesn't appear on the desktop when you insert it into the floppy drive.

Problem:

Sometimes you insert a floppy disk into a drive but its icon doesn't appear on the desktop so you can't work with it. This glitch usually crops up when the Mac is so busy doing other things that it doesn't realize you've inserted a new floppy. If you have this problem with an external floppy drive, it may also be the drive's connector cable.

Solutions:

- Try ejecting the disk. If the disk is in the lower, right-hand or only internal drive, press [Shift][⌘][1]. If it's in the upper, left-hand or external drive, press [Shift][⌘][2]. If it's in a third floppy drive, press [Shift][⌘][0].

  If you've been able to eject the disk this way, switch to the Finder (you may have to save your work and quit the program you're working in first). Then insert the disk again. Usually, this clears up the problem.

- If the disk won't eject with a [Shift][⌘] keystroke sequence, close any programs you have running and save your work. Then hold down the mouse button while restarting the Mac, and keep it held down until the desktop appears. The floppy should pop out during the startup sequence. After you see the desktop, insert the floppy again. This time your Mac should recognize it.

- If these remedies don't work, shut off the Mac. Then straighten out a paperclip and poke it carefully into the small hole at the right side of the disk drive opening. Make sure you insert the paperclip straight into the hole, not at an angle. You'll feel the paperclip pressing against a lever. Gently push the paperclip against it until the disk pops out. *Be careful!* If the disk only comes a quarter inch or so out of the opening, the metal sliding door on the floppy might be caught on the retaining tabs that hold the disk drive heads in place. If this happens, yanking the disk out by brute force will damage the drive. Only take it out if it comes easily. If it doesn't, it's best to take the Mac to a service technician and have the disk removed there. It's a hassle, but an expensive disk drive repair is worse.

- If the problem continues after you've taken the above steps and you have an external floppy drive, make sure the connector cable is plugged in firmly. If it seems to be plugged in okay, shut down your Mac and then unplug the connector and check it for missing or bent pins. If a pin is bent, try straightening it with a small needle-nosed pliers. (If the pin is loose, don't plug it back into the Mac—it could break off inside the port.) If the drive still doesn't work, or if its cable is damaged, you'll need to bring it to a technician to be repaired.

■ SYSTEM 6 ONLY

Problem:

Too many applications or DAs are running, so there isn't enough memory for the Finder to read and remember the desktop file of the disk you've just inserted.

Solution:

Click the *OK* button to eject the disk, then quit one or more of the applications or DAs you have running and insert the disk again. If you have this problem a lot, you should consider expanding your Mac's memory.

■ SYSTEM 7 VERSION

■ SYSTEM 6 VERSION

Problem:

Too many applications, DAs or control panels are running, so the Mac doesn't have enough memory to display the icon or window of the disk you've just inserted. (Under System 7, the Mac will always display the disk's icon, but you may not be able to open it.)

Solutions:

Click the *OK* button. If you're running System 7, the alert message will go away and you can close some windows, programs, documents, DAs or control panels. After you've done that, you'll be able to open the disk's window. If you're running System 6, clicking the *OK* button will eject the disk. After you've quit one or more applications, control panels or DAs, insert the disk again.

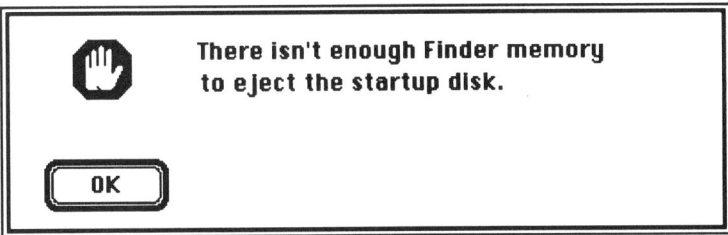

■ SYSTEM 6 ONLY

Problem:

When there's enough memory, you can eject the startup disk and the Finder will automatically store enough of its system instructions to let you work without it. In this case, you have so many applications or DAs running that the Finder can't remember the instructions it needs, so the Mac won't let you eject the disk. (Under System 7 this isn't a problem because you can't ever eject the startup disk.)

Solution:

Either forget about ejecting the startup disk, or close one or more applications or DAs to free up some memory and then try ejecting the disk again. If this is a frequent problem, you should consider expanding your Mac's memory.

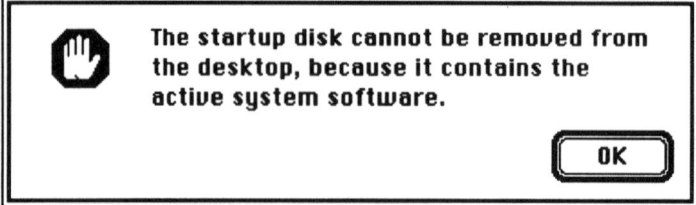

■ SYSTEM 7 ONLY

Problem:

You've tried to drag the icon of the startup disk to the Trash.

Solution:

Under System 7, you can't remove the startup disk from the desktop. Click the *OK* button to continue with your work.

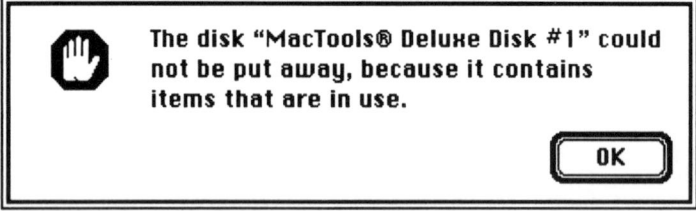

Problem:

You've tried to eject a disk by dragging its icon to the Trash while one or more of its files were open. If you use ⌘E or one of the Shift ⌘ keystrokes described on page 145, the Mac will let you eject a disk while its files are open, but it will keep a grayed-out image of the disk's icon on the desktop. If you try to drag the icon itself into the Trash, you'll see this message.

Solution:

Insert the disk again, close any files you opened from it, then eject it.

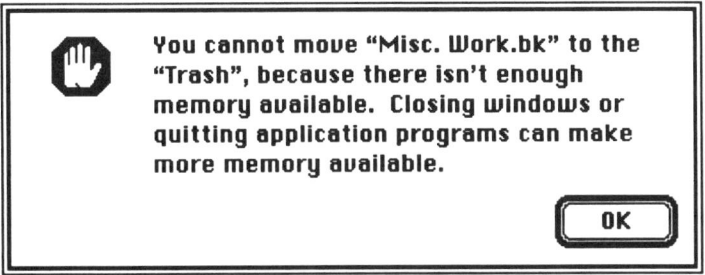

■ SYSTEM 7 ONLY

Problem:

You've tried to eject a disk by dragging its icon to the Trash, but there isn't enough memory available for the Mac to do it. (You don't have this problem under System 6 because items in the Trash aren't stored in a special folder on the disk as they are under System 7.)

Solution:

Close other applications, DAs, control panels or documents first to free up some memory, then try trashing the icon again. If you really need to eject the disk immediately and it's a floppy, use keyboard commands to eject it (press [Shift][⌃⌘][1] to eject it from the upper or right-hand internal floppy drive, [Shift][⌃⌘][2] to eject it from the lower, left-hand, or external floppy drive, or [Shift][⌃⌘][0] to eject it from a third floppy drive). The disk will be ejected, but its icon will remain grayed out on the desktop until there's enough memory available to let you delete it.

A floppy disk won't pop out of the disk drive when you eject it.

Problem:

Sometimes a floppy disk gets stuck in the disk drive so that even though you've dragged its icon into the Trash or have pressed ⌈Shift⌉⌈⌘⌉⌈3⌉, ⌈Shift⌉⌈⌘⌉⌈2⌉ or ⌈Shift⌉⌈⌘⌉⌈0⌉ to eject it, the disk doesn't pop out of the disk drive.

Solutions:

- Close everything you have running and shut down the Mac. The floppy should pop out then.

- If it doesn't, hold down the mouse button while restarting the Mac, and keep it held down until the desktop appears. The floppy should pop out during the startup sequence.

- If these remedies don't work, shut off the Mac. Then straighten out a paperclip and insert it carefully into the small hole at the right side of the disk drive opening. Make sure you insert the paperclip straight into the hole, not at an angle. You'll feel the paperclip pressing against a lever. Gently press the paperclip against it until the disk pops out. *Be careful!* If the disk only comes a quarter inch or so out of the opening, the metal sliding door on the floppy might be caught on the retaining tabs that hold the disk drive heads in place. If this happens, yanking the disk out by brute force will damage the drive. Only take it out if it comes easily. If it doesn't, it's best to take the Mac to a service technician and have the disk removed there. It's a hassle, but an expensive disk drive repair is worse.

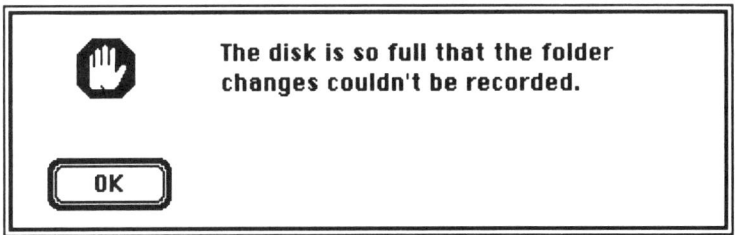

■ SYSTEM 6 ONLY

Problem:

Under System 6, whenever you eject a disk, any changes to its folders are recorded in its desktop file. In this case, the disk you're ejecting is so full that the changes can't be recorded. (System 7 doesn't have this problem because it changes the desktop file each time you make a change to a folder and it won't let you make any changes once the disk is full.)

Solution:

Click the *OK* button to eject the disk. Then insert it again and delete one or more of its files so that it has at least 1K of free space. (To see how much space is available on a disk, look at its window in icon or small icon view. The space available is shown just below the disk name.) When at least 1K of space is available on the disk, eject it and then rebuild its desktop file (see Chapter 3 for instructions). After that, it will reflect the current contents and folder organization on the disk.

9 | Opening, printing and viewing files in the Finder

What Do I Do Now

This chapter covers problems you may have when opening, printing or viewing files in the Finder. Because System 7 is far more adept at this than System 6, several of the problems in this chapter relate to System 6 only. But since the new system also offers more Finder viewing options, it has its own set of specific problems.

If you're having trouble opening files from inside a DA or application, check Chapter 13. If you're having a printing problem that isn't mentioned here, see Chapter 14. Some other problems that occur when you try to open files from a disk being shared on a network are covered in Chapter 15.

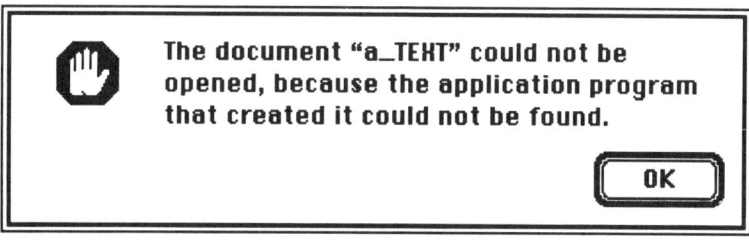

■ SYSTEM 7 VERSION

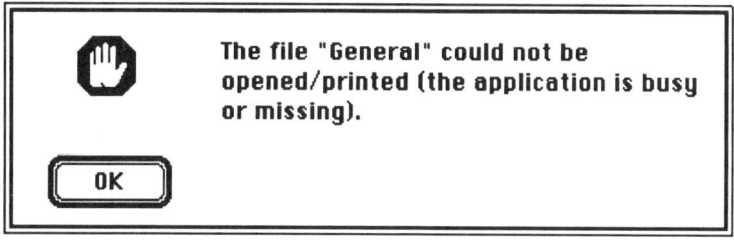

■ SYSTEM 6 VERSION

Problem:

You've double-clicked on a data file, expecting the Mac to automatically load both the file and the program needed to work with it. But the file you've clicked on is either a system-related file that can't be opened, or its document type is generic or unknown so the Mac doesn't know which application to load. It's also possible that the appropriate application isn't on your disk.

Solution:

• Open the file's application first, and then open the file you want to work with using that program's *Open...* command. (To find out which program created a document, look at the window containing it in list view. If the Kind designation is merely *file* or *document* or if it's blank, you'll have to remember on your own which program you created it with.)

• If you can't find the file's application on the disk you're working from, you're out of luck—unless you can find it somewhere else and copy it to your disk or open it from its own floppy disk.

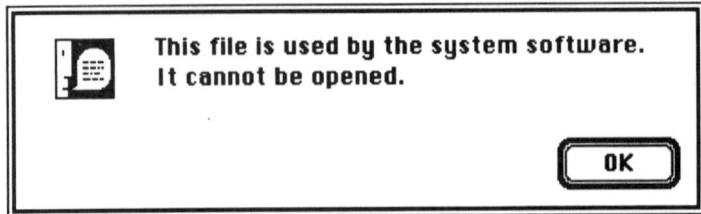

■ SYSTEM 7 VERSION

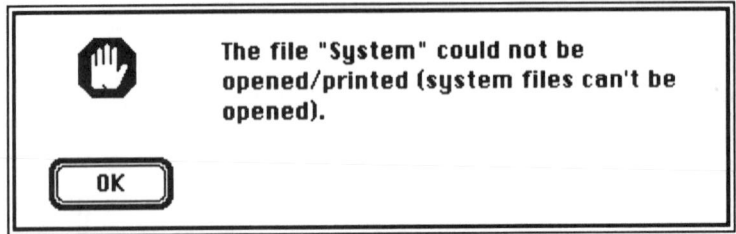

■ SYSTEM 6 VERSION

Problem:

Except for the System file itself (under System 7), system software files like the Finder, Clipboard, preferences files and Chooser extensions or device drivers can't be opened or printed. If you select one of these files and then choose the *Open* or *Print* command from the Finder's File menu, or if you double-click on such a file to open it, you'll get this message.

Solution:

Don't try opening or printing system files. You can avoid this message if you only open files whose Kind designation you recognize as belonging to a program you normally use. For example, documents created by popular programs like Microsoft Word, PageMaker and Adobe Illustrator are always identified as such in the Kind column of list view windows.

If you're trying to install fonts or DAs under System 6, you can't just double-click on the System file to open it—you need the Font/DA Mover program. Refer to your Macintosh manual if you're not sure how to use Font/DA Mover.

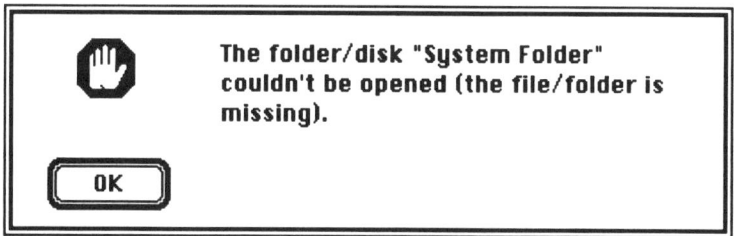

Problem:

This is a message you occasionally see when you try to open a folder in the Finder. It's usually due to a temporary problem the Mac has reading the desktop file.

Solution:

Try opening the folder again one or more times. The problem will go away.

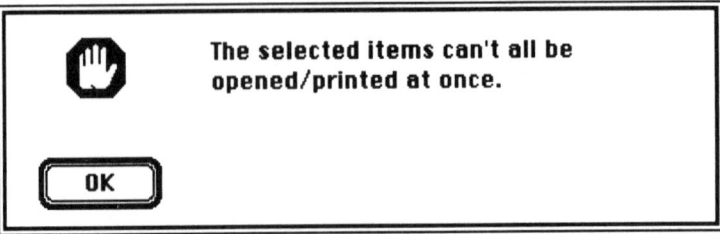

The selected items can't all be opened/printed at once.

OK

■ SYSTEM 6 ONLY

Problem:

You're running under System 6, and either you've selected files that were created by more than one application and are trying to open or print them all from the Finder at the same time, or you've simply selected too many files to be opened or printed at once. Under System 6, you can only open or print from the Finder if the files you've selected were all created by the same program. But even if you select only files that belong to one application, there's a limit to how many files you can open or print at once. It depends on how much memory the Finder has available at the time.

(Under System 7, you can select files to open or print from as many different programs as you want. The Mac will try to open them one at a time until it's out of memory. Any remaining documents or programs simply won't be opened or printed.)

Solution:

Make sure all the files you select to open or print were created by the same version of the same application. If you still get the message, choose a smaller group of files or close any open files or applications and try again.

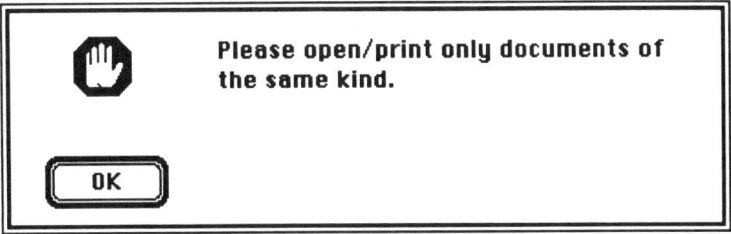

■ SYSTEM 6 ONLY

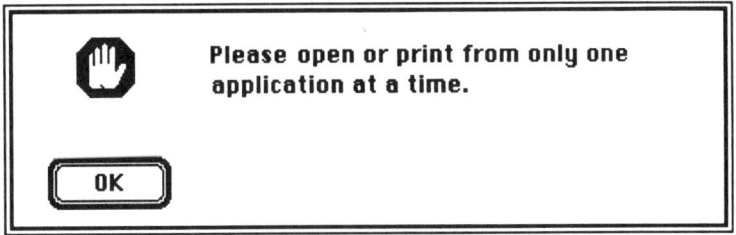

■ SYSTEM 6 ONLY

Problem:

You're running your Mac under System 6 and have selected files that were created by more than one application to open or print them from the Finder. The Mac will only let you open or print from the Finder if the files you've selected were all created by the same program. (System 7 doesn't have this restriction.)

Solution:

Select a different group of files to open or print, and make sure they were all created by the same version of the same program.

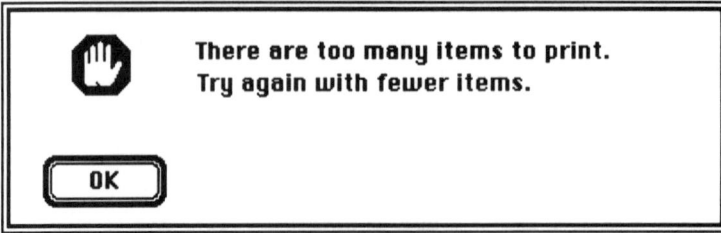

There are too many items to print.
Try again with fewer items.

[OK]

■ SYSTEM 6 ONLY

Problem:

You've selected too many files to print from the Finder at once. (System 7 won't display this message. Instead, it will try to print all the items you've selected until it runs out of memory, and then it simply won't print the remaining ones.)

Solution:

Choose a smaller group of files and try printing them again.

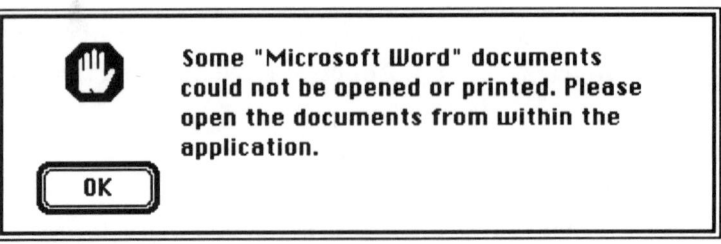

Some "Microsoft Word" documents
could not be opened or printed. Please
open the documents from within the
application.

[OK]

Problem:

You've selected one or more documents to be opened or printed from the Finder, but the Finder isn't able to open or print them.

Solution:

Go into the application you used to create the documents and then open them (and print them, if you like) from there.

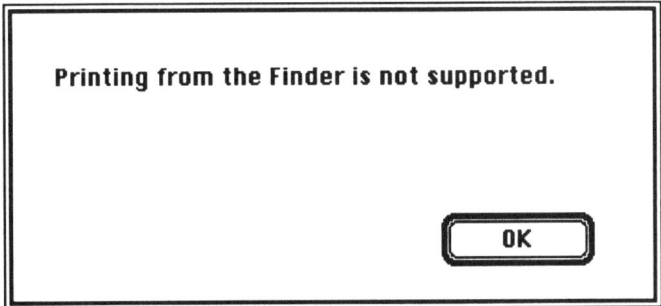

Printing from the Finder is not supported.

OK

Problem:

Some programs don't allow you to print documents from the Finder. If so, they'll display a message like this one.

Solution:

Open the program itself and then open and print the document from inside the program.

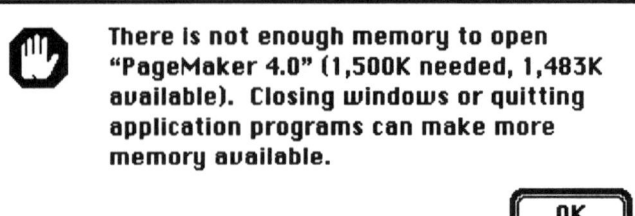

■ SYSTEM 7 VERSION

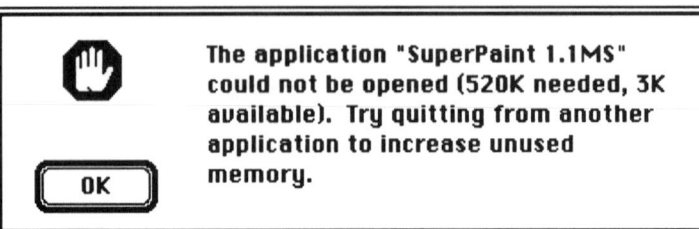

■ SYSTEM 6 VERSION

Problem:

You're either running System 7 or you're running MultiFinder in System 6, and you've tried to open an application. There isn't enough memory to run it because some other programs are already running.

Solution:

Quit one or more of the other programs you have running and then open the application again. If this doesn't work, your Mac's memory has probably become fragmented so the available RAM is broken up into a bunch of small blocks, none of which is large enough to store the program you want to load. In this case, save any work you have open, restart the Mac and then load the program.

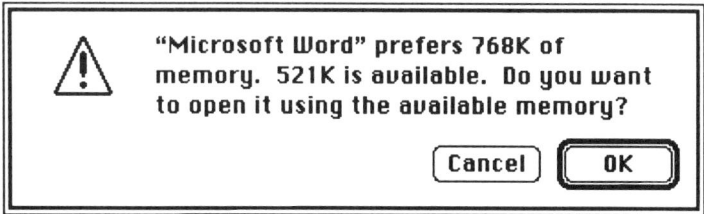

■ SYSTEM 7 VERSION

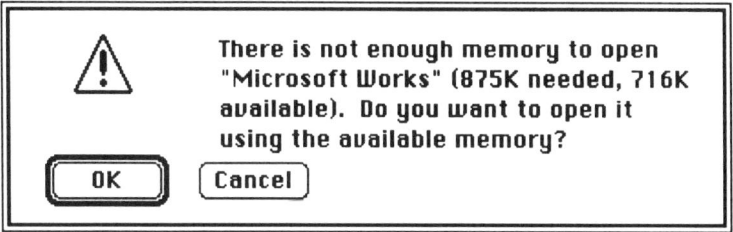

■ SYSTEM 6 VERSION

Problem:

You've tried to open an application or a file, but there isn't as much memory available as the application or file normally needs to run.

Solution:

The solution depends on whether you're running multiple programs or not.

- **If you're running multiple programs** under System 7 or with MultiFinder under System 6, click the *Cancel* button, quit another program you have running and then launch the program or open the file you originally wanted. If this doesn't work, you may need to quit all the programs you have running, restart the Mac and then load the program you want. (Your Mac's memory may have become too fragmented to assemble a large enough block of RAM to store the program you want, even though there should theoretically be enough RAM available.)

- **If you're not running multiple programs,** your Mac's memory is being used up by your system software, or else the program you ran before hasn't been completely cleared from memory. This usually happens on Macs running System 6 with one megabyte of RAM or on Macs running System 7 with two megabytes of RAM. Try restarting the Mac and then loading the program you're trying to use. If this doesn't work, you can try reducing the size of the system software by removing unneeded fonts and DAs from the System file. The best long-term solution is to expand your Mac's RAM.

    Note: You can click the *OK* button if you want to try loading the file or program, but the program may end up quitting unexpectedly some time later. If this happens you'll lose any data that's in the Mac's memory at the time. The success you have running the program with reduced memory will depend on which program it is and what else you have running.

    If your Mac has only one megabyte of RAM and you're trying to load just one program under MultiFinder, you should use the *Set Startup* command on the Special menu to restart with the Finder running, and then try loading the program. (MultiFinder itself takes up extra RAM; using the Finder instead may free up enough memory to run your program normally.)

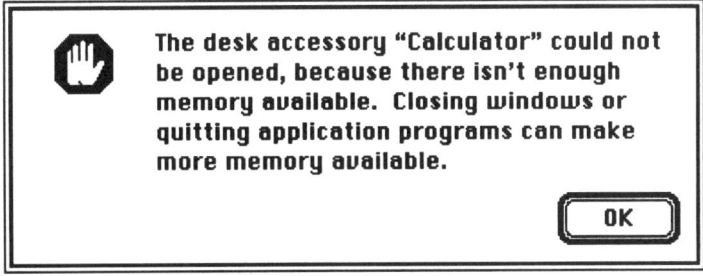

■ SYSTEM 7 VERSION

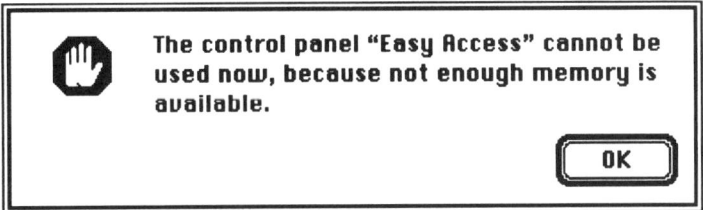

■ SYSTEM 7 VERSION

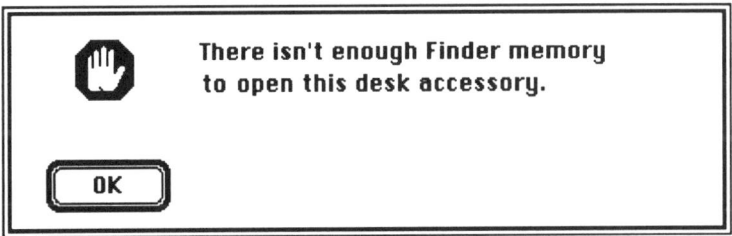

■ SYSTEM 6 VERSION

Problem:

The application (or applications, if you're running MultiFinder or System 7), DA(s) and control panels you currently have open are taking up so much of the Mac's memory that there isn't enough left to open the DA or control panel you've selected.

Solutions:

- **If you're running System 6,** try holding down the ⌥Option key while choosing the DA from the menu. The Mac will try to open the DA using memory reserved for applications. If there's enough memory available, the DA will open.

- **If that doesn't work or you're running System 7,** close one or more applications or DAs and try again until the DA opens successfully. It may be necessary to quit all the other programs and DAs you have running before you can get the new one to run. If the message persists even after you've quit everything, restart the Mac and then open the DA.

■ SYSTEM 7 VERSION

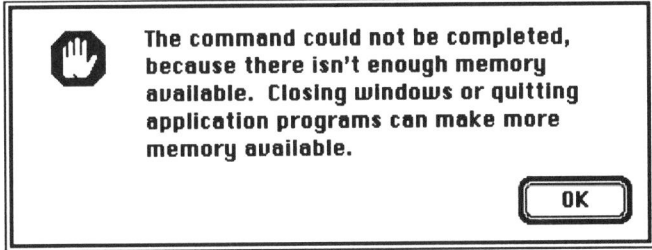

■ SYSTEM 7 VERSION

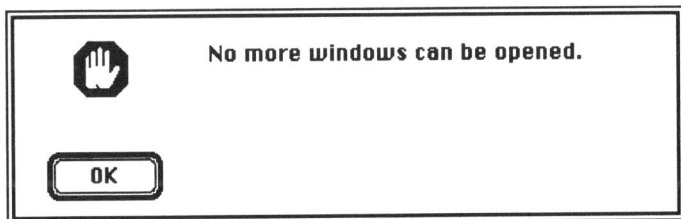

■ SYSTEM 6 VERSION

Problem:

All of these alerts signify the same problem: your Mac doesn't have enough memory available to allow you to open another window or to continue displaying all the windows you currently have open.

Solution:

Close one or more of the windows you currently have open before trying to open any others. You may have to close several windows or even an application or a couple of DAs or control panels to free up enough memory. If closing everything doesn't work, restart the Mac to clear out the memory completely and then try again.

A list view window doesn't show the categories of information you need to see.

■ SYSTEM 7 ONLY

Problem:

You're looking for a certain column of information in a list view window (such as Date, Size or Kind), but it's missing from the window.

Solution:

First try widening the window on the desktop or scrolling it to the right—the column you need to see may just be temporarily out of sight. If this doesn't work, open the Views control panel in the Control Panels folder and check the checkbox in the List Views area next to the category of information you want to see. Then close the control panel. The missing information should now be showing (although you may still need to resize or scroll the window to see it).

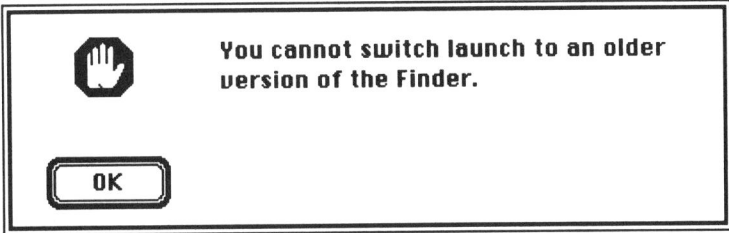

■ SYSTEM 6 ONLY

Problem:

You've tried switch-launching from the currently running Finder to another Finder under System 6, but the version you're trying to launch is older than the current one. (To switch-launch, you hold down the ⌘ and Option keys and then double-click on the Finder file on a disk. If the version of the Finder you double-click on is as new as or newer than the one you're currently running, the Mac will run the new Finder.) This problem doesn't appear under System 7, because it doesn't allow switch-launching at all.

Solution:

There really isn't one. You just can't do this. Whenever you switch-launch to another Finder, make sure it's a version as new as or newer than the one that's currently running. If you really must run your Mac under an older version of the Finder, you'll have to restart it with a disk containing that version.

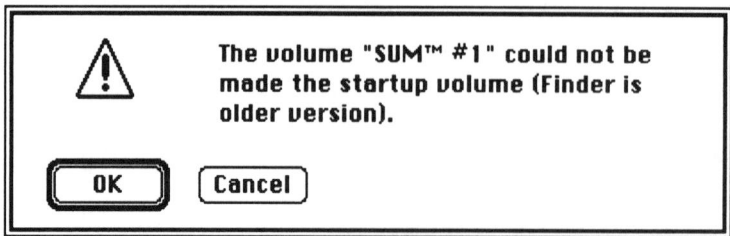

■ SYSTEM 6 ONLY

Problem:

You've tried to change the startup disk by switch-launching from the currently running System file to another System file. (To switch-launch using the System file, you hold down ⌥⌘Option and then double-click on the System file on a disk.) But the Mac won't change the current startup disk if the System file version on the new startup disk is older than the version of the System you're currently running.

Solution:

There really isn't one. You just can't do this. Whenever you switch-launch to another startup disk, make sure both the System and Finder files on the new startup disk are versions at least as new as or newer than the ones on your current startup disk.

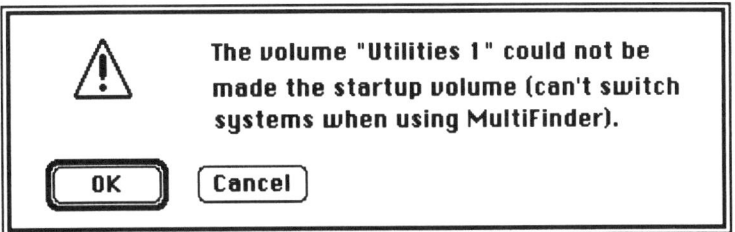

■ SYSTEM 6 ONLY

Problem:

You've tried to switch-launch to a different System file from the one you started up with, but the Mac won't let you do that when MultiFinder is running.

Solution:

If you normally start up your Mac with MultiFinder and want to keep it that way, restart while holding down the ⌘ key. This will start your Mac with the Finder only for just that one time (the *Set Startup...* options you've set won't be affected—see *System Folder operations under System 6* in Chapter 3 for more information.) With the Finder running, you can locate the alternate System file you want to use and then switch-launch to place it in control of the Mac.

To switch-launch, hold down ⌘ Option while double-clicking on the System file you want to use. For this to work, the version of the System file you want to switch-launch to must be as new as or newer than the one that's currently running.

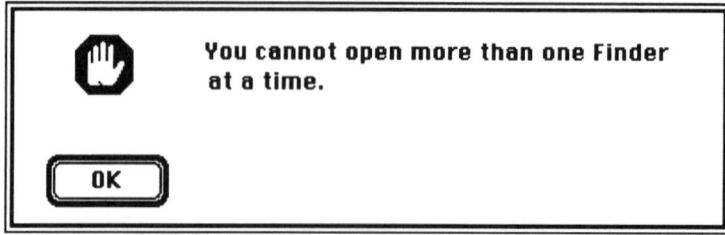

■ SYSTEM 6 ONLY

Problem:

You've double-clicked on another Finder program to open it while the Finder is running. The Mac will only let you run one Finder program at a time. (Under System 7, nothing happens when you try opening a second Finder.)

Solutions:

- **If you want to temporarily change the Finder you're running under,** you can switch-launch to a different Finder by holding down ⌘Option and double-clicking on the new Finder file. When you do this, however, the version of the Finder you're trying to launch must be as new as or newer than the one that's currently running.

- **If you want to permanently change the version of the Finder you're running under,** restart the Mac with a different startup disk. Then drag the old Finder file out of the System Folder on your normal startup disk and replace it with a different version. The next time you start from your normal startup disk, the new version of the Finder will run.

(**Note:** If the new Finder you try to run is a much older or much newer version than the corresponding System file, your Mac won't be able to run it. Rather than simply upgrading the Finder, you should upgrade all your system software at the same time. See *Replacing the system software*, page 88.)

10 | Moving and copying disks, files or folders

What Do I Do Now

This chapter covers problems you may have or alert messages you may see when moving or copying disks, files or folders in the Finder. If you're having problems copying or moving files to an AppleShare file server (or shared disk or folder under System 7) and your problem isn't explained here, look in Chapter 15.

The two disks are different types, so the contents of "90 Budgets" will be placed in a folder on "Hard Disk 20".

OK   Cancel

■ SYSTEM 6 ONLY

Problem:

This really isn't a problem. The Mac is just telling you how it will proceed with the copy operation you've started. You've dragged the icon for a source disk onto the icon for a destination disk, but the destination disk is larger than the source disk. So instead of replacing the contents of the destination disk with those of the source disk the Mac will create a folder on the destination disk and put the contents of the source disk there. (Under System 7 the Mac does this automatically, without bothering to alert you.)

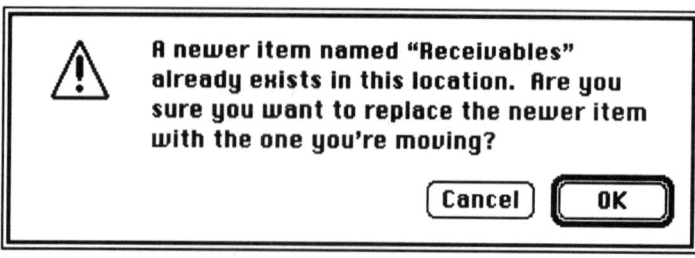

■ SYSTEM 7 VERSION

■ SYSTEM 7 VERSION

■ SYSTEM 7 VERSION

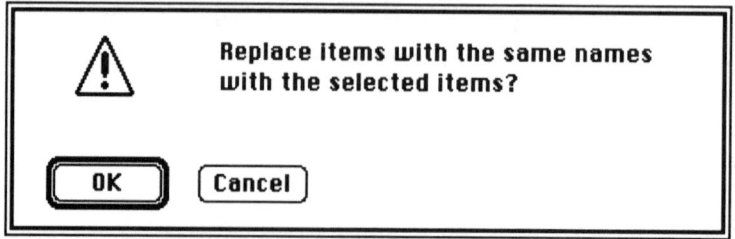

■ SYSTEM 6 VERSION

Problem:

This isn't really a problem. Whenever you copy something to a location where an item with the same name already exists, the

Mac warns you that the item you're copying will replace the item with the same name. Under System 7, the alert message will tell you if the item being replaced is older or newer than the item you're copying, based on the items' modification dates and times.

Solution:

Click the *OK* button if you want to replace the item, or click the *Cancel* button to return to the desktop. If you're not sure whether the item being replaced is older or newer than the one you're copying, click *Cancel* and then check the Date column in a list view window on the desktop. If this column isn't showing, select the file or folder you want to know about and choose the *Get Info* command. The information window will tell you the modification date.

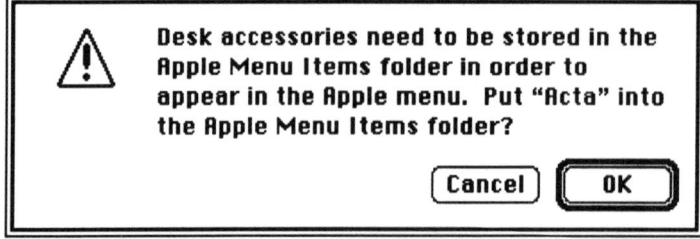

Desk accessories need to be stored in the Apple Menu Items folder in order to appear in the Apple menu. Put "Acta" into the Apple Menu Items folder?

Cancel   OK

■ SYSTEM 7 ONLY

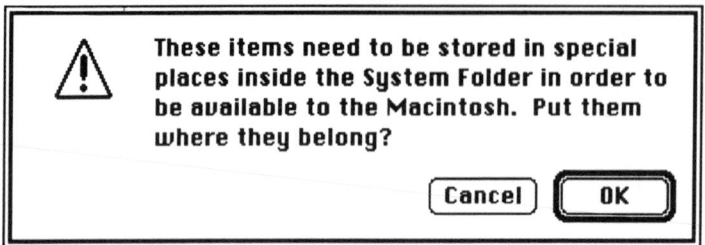

These items need to be stored in special places inside the System Folder in order to be available to the Macintosh. Put them where they belong?

Cancel   OK

■ SYSTEM 7 ONLY

Problem:

This isn't really a problem. Under System 7, there are folders within the System Folder that contain different types of system software files (see *The System Folder under System 7* in Chapter 1). When you copy files to the System Folder by dragging their icons onto the System Folder's icon, the Mac displays one of the above alerts, telling you it will automatically put the files in their proper folders inside the System Folder.

Solution:

Click the *OK* button to have the Mac put the files in their correct folders or click *Cancel* to return to the desktop. If you want to copy items into other areas of the System Folder than the ones they'd normally be stored in, open the System Folder itself and then drag the items where you want them inside its window.

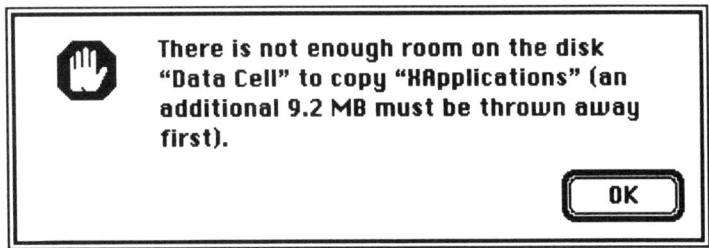

■ SYSTEM 7 VERSION

■ SYSTEM 6 VERSION

Problem:

You're trying to copy files to a disk that's too full to hold them. The alert box tells you exactly how much space you need to free up before making the copy.

Solution:

Either delete some files from the destination disk or copy fewer files to it. By viewing the files on the disk by Name, Kind, Date or Type, you can see how large each one is and then figure out just how many you need to remove from the destination disk (or from the group you're trying to copy).

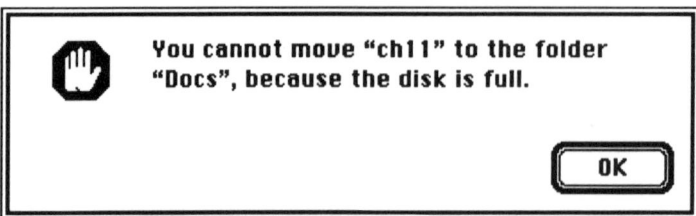

■ SYSTEM 7 VERSION

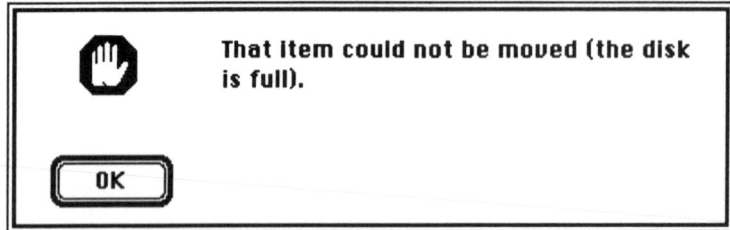

■ SYSTEM 6 VERSION

Problem:

You're trying to move a file or folder into a different folder on the disk, but the disk is too full to make the change. A disk generally has no free space available when you get this message.

Solution:

Click the *OK* button. Then either forget about moving the file or folder to a new location, or delete one or more items from the disk and then try the move operation again.

■ SYSTEM 7 ONLY

Problem:

You've tried to move a file from a disk onto the desktop, but the disk you're moving the file from is too full to record where you're moving it to. Whenever you move an item from a disk to the desktop under System 7, the new location is saved to an invisible folder called *Desktop* on the disk. But if the disk is full, there's no room for the Desktop folder and the Mac has no place to store the item's new location. When that happens, it won't let you move any files to the desktop.

Solution:

Delete some items from the disk to free up space, then move the item to the desktop. Or you can copy the item to another disk that does have room on it, and then move it to the desktop from there.

 You cannot duplicate in the folder "Control Panels", because there isn't enough memory available. Closing windows or quitting application programs can make more memory available.

OK

■ SYSTEM 7 ONLY

 You cannot copy "Outline" onto the folder "ModifyDialogs", because there isn't enough memory available. Closing windows or quitting application programs can make more memory available.

OK

■ SYSTEM 7 ONLY

Problem:

There's not enough memory available for you to duplicate or copy the selected item.

Solution:

Close some windows, DAs, or programs to free up some memory, then try the operation again. If everything's closed and you still can't duplicate or copy the item, restart the Mac and try again.

■ SYSTEM 7 VERSION

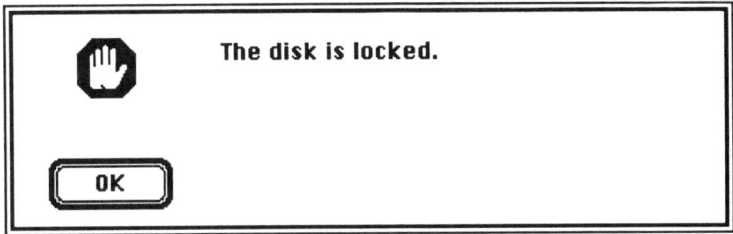

■ SYSTEM 6 VERSION

Problem:

You're trying to copy a file to a disk that is locked.

Solution:

Unlock the disk. If it's a floppy disk, eject it and slide the plastic tab on its back away from the edge (so the hole is closed). If it's a hard disk, use its own setup/utility software to unlock it. Then try copying the file again.

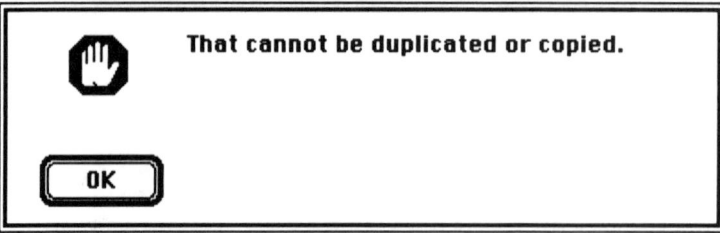

■ SYSTEM 6 ONLY

Problem:

The file or folder you've selected is either locked, busy or copy-protected. (System 7 doesn't prevent you from duplicating or copying such files.)

Solutions:

- **If the file or folder you're working with is on a disk inserted in or directly connected to your Mac**, it has probably been locked by a program that's using it. Click the *OK* button, then restart the Mac. Try copying, duplicating or moving the file again.

- **If you're working with a folder that's stored on a shared disk on a network**, click the *OK* button and then use the *Get Privileges* command to see if the folder is locked. If it is and you're its owner, you can unlock it. If you're not the folder's owner, you'll have to ask the owner to unlock it (see *Sharing files under System 6* in Chapter 15).

- If neither of the above solutions works, click the *OK* button and try restarting the Mac with another startup disk. It may be that the file is busy because it's being used by a system file on the first startup disk. If that was the case, you'll be able to copy it now.

- If that doesn't work, the file has probably been copy-protected by a software vendor. Try using a file-copying utility like Copy II Mac.

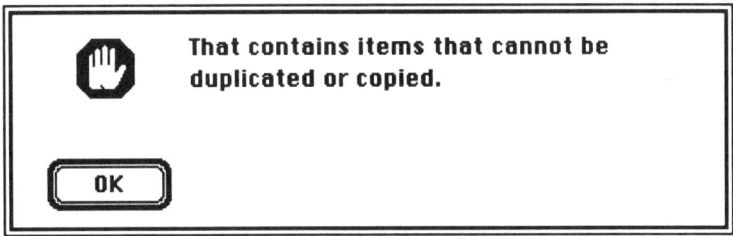

■ SYSTEM 6 ONLY

Problem:

You're trying to copy a folder that contains files that are locked, busy or copy-protected.

Solutions:

- Click the *OK* button, then copy the files inside the folder one at a time. When you try to copy the locked file, you'll get a warning message. The other files will copy properly.

- To copy the locked file, you'll have to close the file or quit the program using it first. If you still get the same message, restart the Mac and then try copying the locked file again. Usually this will unlock it. If the file is needed by the System file on your startup disk, however, you'll have to restart using a different startup disk before copying it.

- If these solutions don't work, the file has been copy-protected by a software vendor. Try using Copy II Mac or another file-copying utility. The utility may be able to overcome the copy-protection scheme.

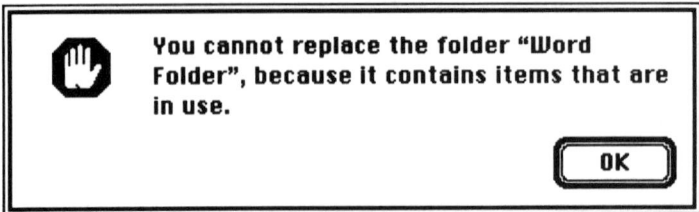

■ SYSTEM 7 VERSION

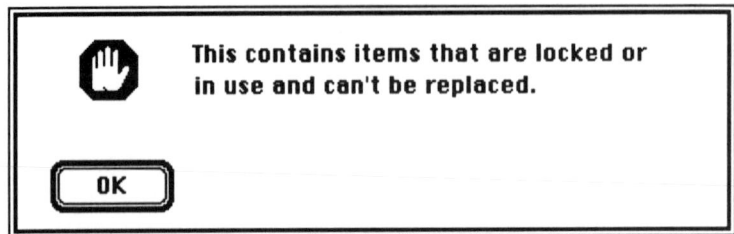

■ SYSTEM 6 VERSION

Problem:

You're trying to completely replace the contents of a disk or folder, but it contains one or more files that are either locked or in use. These may be applications, System Folder files or documents that are currently open.

Solutions:

- Click the *OK* button. Close any data files and quit any programs you have running and then try the copy operation again.

- If you get the same alert again, restart the Mac using another startup disk and then try the copy operation. When you start up from another disk, the files in the original System Folder can be replaced because they aren't active anymore.

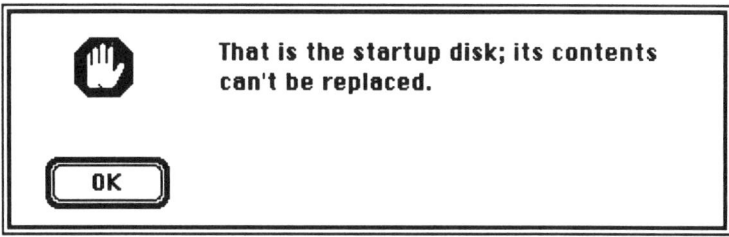

Problem:

You've selected your startup floppy disk as the destination for the contents of another disk by dragging the other disk's icon onto the startup floppy's icon. To make the copy, your Mac would have to replace the contents of the startup disk from which it's currently running, and since it needs the files on the startup disk to operate, it can't replace them. (You probably won't see this alert in System 7 because you typically use a hard disk as a startup disk, and you can't completely replace a hard disk's contents by dragging another hard disk's icon onto it.)

Solution:

You probably selected the startup disk as your copy destination by mistake. If so, try the copy procedure again with a different disk selected as the destination. If you actually do want to replace the contents of your startup disk, you'll have to restart the Mac with another startup disk first. Then your Mac won't care if you replace the contents of the first startup floppy disk.

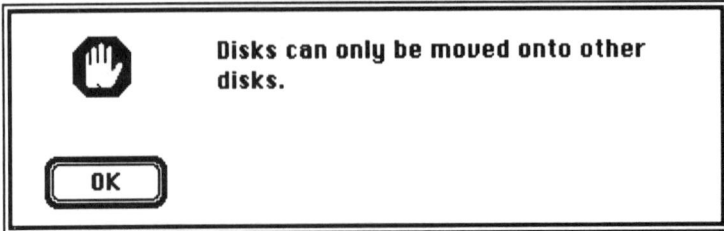

■ SYSTEM 6 ONLY

Problem:

You've dragged a disk icon onto a folder icon, and the Mac won't let you copy a disk into a folder. (System 7 will simply create a folder for the disk's contents and copy them into it.)

Solution:

* **To copy the disk onto another disk,** click the *OK* button and then drag the icon of the disk you want to copy onto another disk icon. You'll see a message saying that a folder with the source disk's name will be created on the destination disk, and the contents of the source disk put inside it.

* **If you really want to copy the disk's contents directly into the folder** you've selected, you'll have to copy the files themselves—rather than the disk icon—into the folder. The fastest way to do this is to open the disk's window so its files are showing, choose *Select All* from the Edit menu to select all the files at once and drag the selected files to the folder you want to copy them into.

    If the disk contains dozens of files, you may not be able to copy them all at one time. If so, you'll see a message saying there are too many items to copy. In that case, select smaller groups of files by shift-clicking on them—click on the first file, then hold down the [Shift] key and click on the others you want in the group.

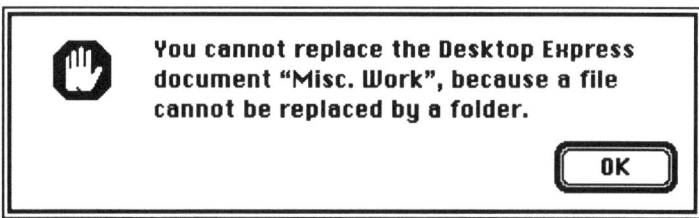

■ SYSTEM 7 VERSION

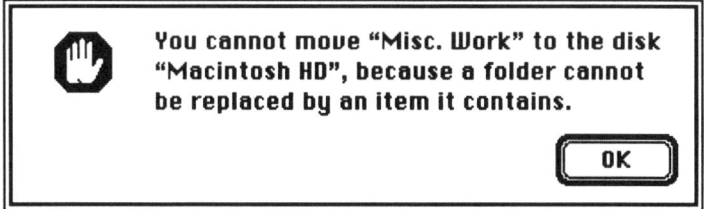

■ SYSTEM 7 VERSION

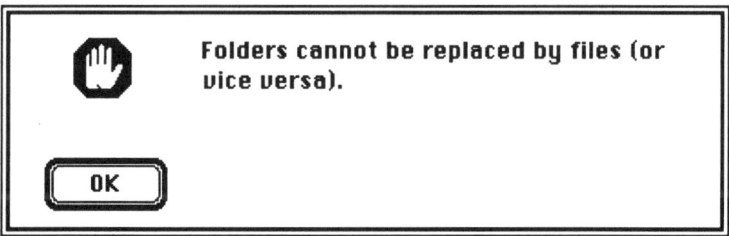

■ SYSTEM 6 VERSION

Problem:

You've tried to copy an item (a file or folder) to a location that already contains an item with the same name. The Mac won't allow you to store two items with exactly the same name in the same folder.

Solutions:

Click the *OK* button. Depending on your inclination, you can do one of two things:

- Rename either the item you're trying to copy or the item with the same name in the destination folder.

- Copy the item to a different folder on the disk.

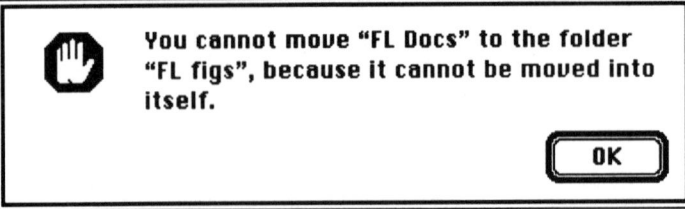

You cannot move "FL Docs" to the folder "FL figs", because it cannot be moved into itself.

OK

■ SYSTEM 7 ONLY

Problem:

You've tried to move a folder inside the folder that contains it. This is an illogical operation, and the Mac won't let you complete it.

Solution:

You probably selected the wrong destination by mistake. Just be careful about which folder you select as a destination next time.

■ SYSTEM 6 VERSION

Problem:

You have a folder that contains a folder with the same name and you've tried to drag the inner folder into the same directory where the outer folder is located. Since you can't have two items with the same name at the same directory level, you're trying to replace the outer folder with the inner folder, and the Mac won't let you do this. (If you try this under System 7, you'll see the alert from page 191, *You cannot move <file name> to the disk <disk name> because a folder cannot be replaced by an item it contains.*)

Solution:

You probably dragged the inner folder to the wrong location by mistake. Click the *OK* button to cancel the operation, and be more careful about which folder you select as the destination next time.

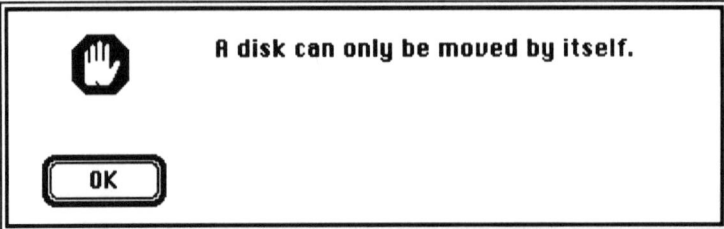

A disk can only be moved by itself.

OK

■ SYSTEM 6 ONLY

Problem:

You've selected a disk icon and a file or folder icon at the same time and are trying to move, copy or trash them. When running under System 6, the Mac won't let you work with a disk icon at the same time you're working with any other icon. (System 7 doesn't have this limitation.)

Solution:

Select the disk icon by itself and then move it.

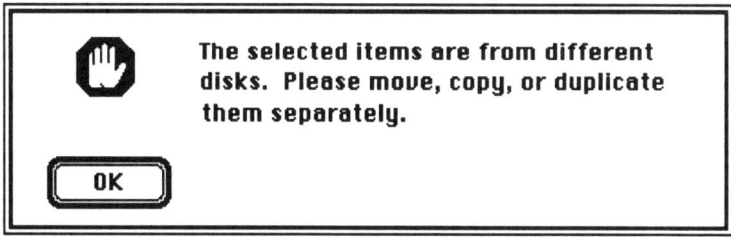

■ SYSTEM 6 ONLY

Problem:

You've selected a group of files or folders and some of them are stored on a different disk than the others. This can happen when you've moved items from two different disks onto the desktop and have selected them there. You can only copy or move items from one disk at a time. (System 7 doesn't have this restriction.)

Solution:

Copy or move items from different disks separately.

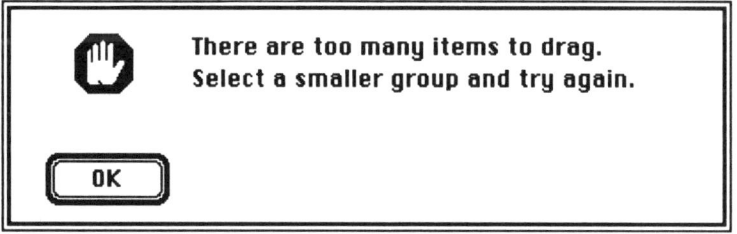

■ SYSTEM 6 ONLY

Problem:

You've selected such a large group of files to copy or move that the Mac can't keep track of them all at once. (System 7 has no practical limit on the number of items you select.)

Solution:

Click the *OK* button, then select smaller groups of files and drag the smaller groups separately.

The file "Foreign89" couldn't be written and was skipped (unknown error).

Cancel   Continue

Problem:

You've tried to copy a large group of files, or a large file by itself, and the Mac couldn't manage it.

Solutions:

- **If you're copying a group of files,** click the *Continue* button to give the Mac a chance to copy the rest of the files in the group. You may see the alert message again as the Mac tries and fails to copy other files in the group. Once the Mac has tried to copy all the files, check the destination disk and see how many were copied, and then try recopying the ones that were skipped the first time. If you're copying a particularly large group of files, try copying the files in smaller groups, or remember the names of the files that are being skipped and copy them individually.

- **If you're copying only one file,** click the *Cancel* button and then try making the copy again. You may have to try two or three times but if you persevere, the Mac will finally do it.

- If the above remedies don't work, one of the disks or the file is probably damaged. Try copying the file to a different disk. If that doesn't work, try opening the file with the application that was used to create it. Then use the *Save As* command to save a copy of it to a different disk. If you can't open the file, use a disk recovery utility to try salvaging it.

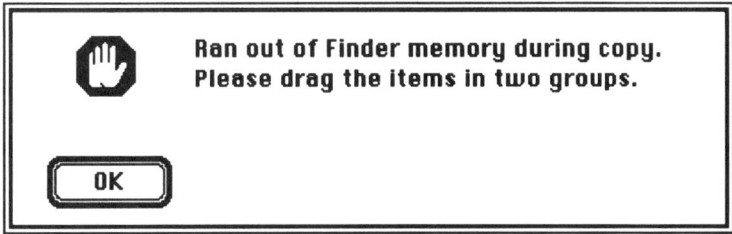

■ SYSTEM 6 ONLY

Problem:

The group of files you've selected to copy is too large for the Finder to handle all at once. (System 7 doesn't have this problem.)

Solution:

Select a smaller group of files to copy.

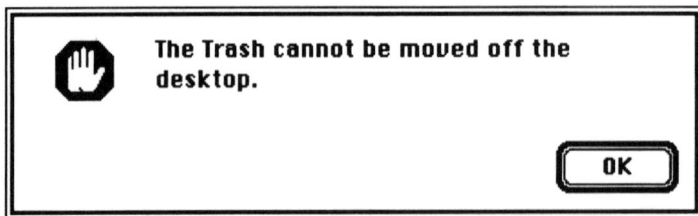

■ SYSTEM 7 VERSION

■ SYSTEM 6 VERSION

Problem:

You've selected the Trash icon and are trying to drag it into a folder or onto a disk. The Mac won't let you duplicate the Trash or move its icon off the desktop. (Under System 7, the *Duplicate* command on the File menu is unavailable when you have the Trash selected, so it's impossible to even try duplicating it.)

Solution:

Don't try duplicating the Trash or dragging it into any disk or folder. You can move it to different places on the desktop, as long as you aren't moving it into a disk or folder.

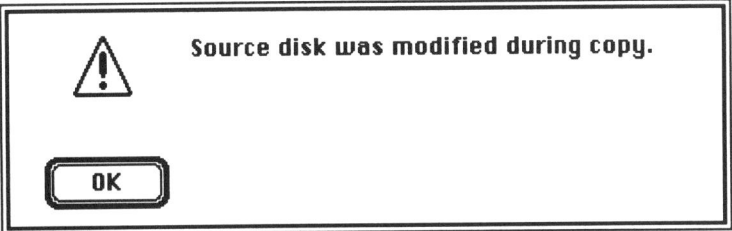

Problem:

The disk you're copying from has been modified by a software error during the copying procedure. This isn't a good sign, because it means one of the files or perhaps the disk directory was damaged.

Solution:

Select the files on the source disk one at a time and copy them to another disk. If you get a message that a file can't be read or written, try copying that file again a couple more times. If you still get the message, the file is damaged and can't be copied. In that case, try opening it with its application. If that works, use the program's *Save As* command to save the file to a different disk. If you can't open the problem file with an application, use a file-recovery utility to try recovering it and saving it onto another disk. When you've finished copying all the files on the modified source disk, don't use it again, or at least erase it completely beforehand.

11 | Renaming or erasing disks, files or folders

What Do I Do Now ❓

T his chapter covers problems you may have when renaming or erasing disks, files or folders in the Finder. If you're having problems doing these things with files or folders on an AppleShare file server or other shared folder or disk, see Chapter 15.

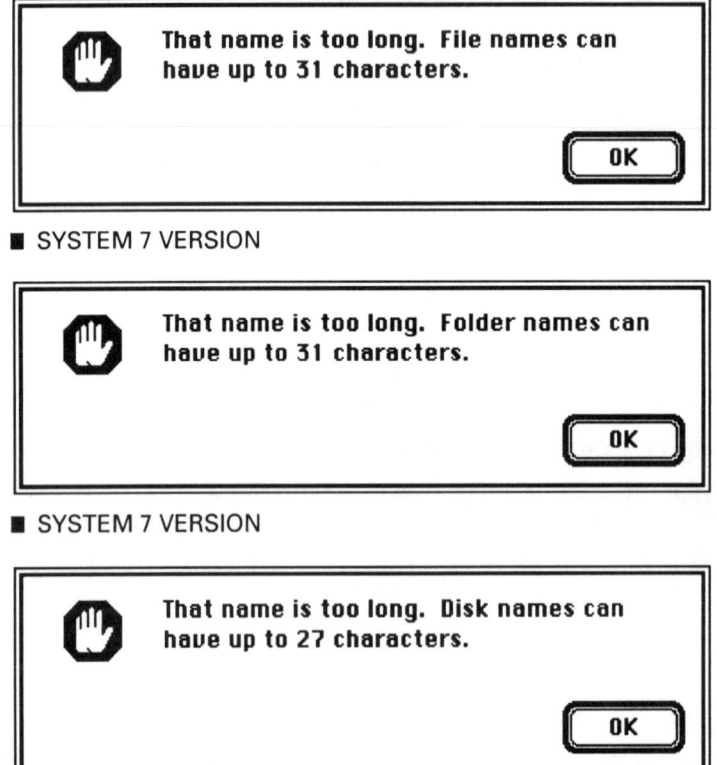

That name is too long. File names can
have up to 31 characters.

OK

■ SYSTEM 7 VERSION

That name is too long. Folder names can
have up to 31 characters.

OK

■ SYSTEM 7 VERSION

That name is too long. Disk names can
have up to 27 characters.

OK

■ SYSTEM 7 VERSION

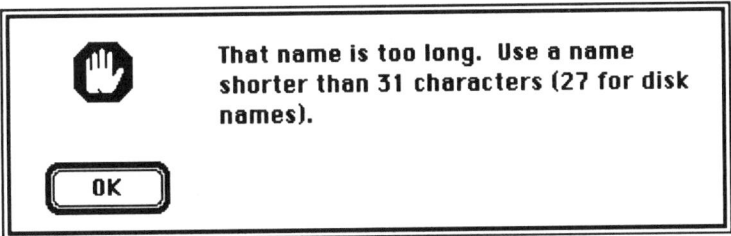

■ SYSTEM 6 VERSION

Problem:

You're trying to enter a name that's too long for the Mac to handle. The Mac's operating system won't allow disk names longer than 27 characters, or file or folder names longer than 31 characters. These limits include spaces at the beginning or end of the name and spaces between words.

Solution:

Click the *OK* button and then type a shorter name.

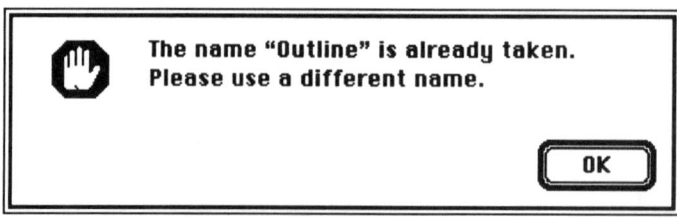

■ SYSTEM 7 VERSION

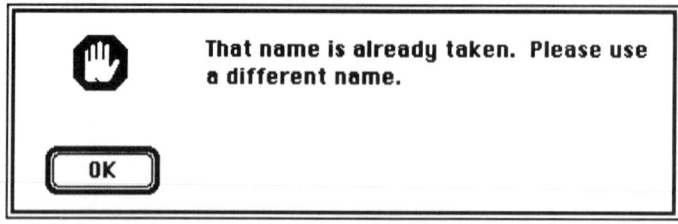

■ SYSTEM 6 VERSION

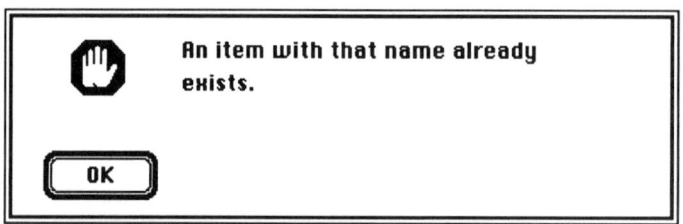

■ SYSTEM 6 VERSION

Problem:

All these alerts mean the same thing: you've tried to give a file or folder a name that's already been given to another file or folder. Each item inside a folder must have a unique name—although items inside different folders can have the same name. (Under System 6, you'll get the same message when you try to give one disk the same name as another disk on the desktop.)

Solution:

Click the *OK* button and then type a different name. Any change you make in the name will make a difference to the Mac, so if you really want to use virtually the same name as one already used for another item, just put a number or punctuation mark in front of the name.

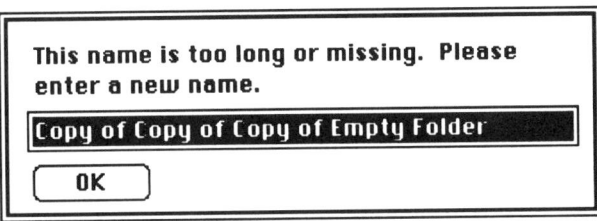

■ SYSTEM 6 ONLY

Problem:

You're trying to create a new file or folder (probably by copying an existing one) but the name is too long. The Mac wants you to enter a shorter name.

Under System 6, the Mac always puts *Copy of* in front of the existing name of any item you copy using the *Duplicate* command on the Finder's File menu. If you try to duplicate an item with a long name, adding *Copy of* to the name may push it over the Mac's limit of 31 characters. (In System 7, you'll get the same alert you get when a file name is too long—see page 202 earlier in this chapter.)

Solution:

Type a shorter name for the folder, then click the *OK* button. You won't be able to put this alert box away until you type a name shorter than 31 characters.

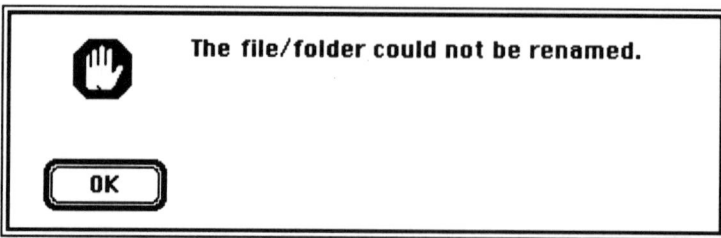

■ SYSTEM 6 ONLY

Problem:

You're trying to rename a file or folder on a disk that's locked.
Since the disk is locked, no changes can be made to it. (Under
System 7, when you try to edit the name of an item on a locked
disk, the Mac won't even let you select it.)

Solution:

Unlock the disk. If it's a floppy, eject it and slide the plastic tab
on its back toward the center of the disk so the hole is covered.
(1.44 MB floppy disks have two holes, so the one without the
tab always stays open.) If it's a hard disk, unlock it with its
setup/utility software.

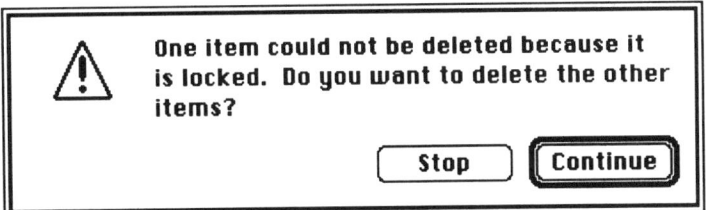

■ SYSTEM 7 VERSION

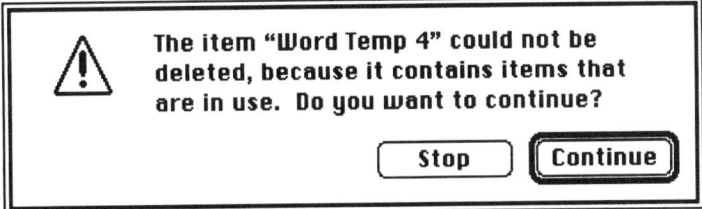

■ SYSTEM 7 VERSION

■ SYSTEM 6 VERSION

Problem:

You're trying to throw away a file that's locked or busy. If you're using System 7, you can drag such items into the Trash but you can't empty it—you'll get one of the above messages when you try. Under System 6, you'll get the above message as soon as you drag the item to the Trash.

Solutions:

- Click the *OK* button, then select the file and choose the *Get Info* command to see if it's locked. If it is, uncheck the *Locked* box in its information window (see *The Get Info command* in Chapter 3). Once the file's unlocked, you can throw it away.

Note: You can also use keystrokes to throw away locked files. If you're using System 6, hold down the (Shift), (Option), and (⌘) keys while selecting and dragging the files to the Trash. If you're using System 7, hold down the (Option) key when choosing the *Empty Trash* command.

- If the file's information window doesn't show it to be locked, it's probably been locked by a program that's using it. Restart the Mac and try throwing away the file again. If that doesn't work, restart with a different startup disk and then try the deletion again.

The System Folder cannot be put in the Trash, because it contains the active system software.

OK

■ SYSTEM 7 VERSION

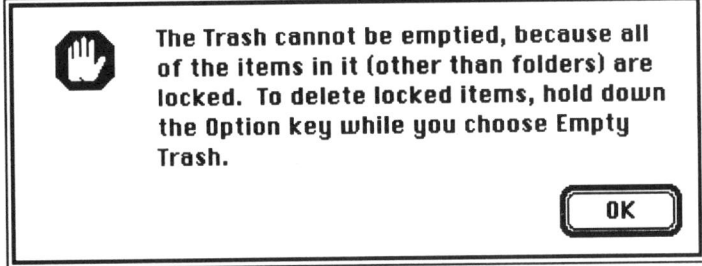

The Trash cannot be emptied, because all of the items in it (other than folders) are locked. To delete locked items, hold down the Option key while you choose Empty Trash.

OK

■ SYSTEM 7 VERSION

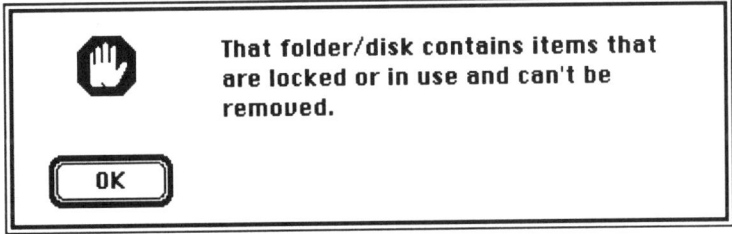

That folder/disk contains items that are locked or in use and can't be removed.

OK

■ SYSTEM 6 VERSION

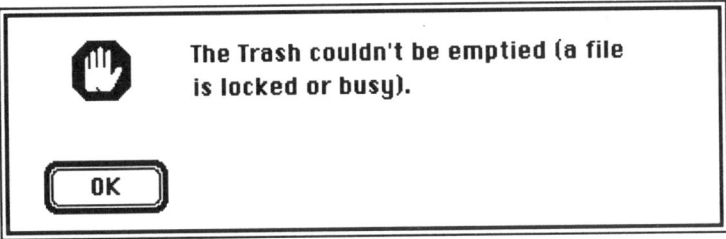

The Trash couldn't be emptied (a file is locked or busy).

OK

■ SYSTEM 6 VERSION

Problem:

You're trying to use the *Empty Trash* command but a locked or busy file is in the Trash. Or (under System 6) you're trying to throw away a folder that contains locked or busy files. You'll get this message if you try to throw away the System Folder on your startup disk for example, because it contains files that the Mac is using.

Solutions:

- Click the *OK* button to put the alert box away. Make sure you really want to throw away the disk or folder. If you do, close any files you have open. Check the information windows of the files you want to delete using the *Get Info* command (see Chapter 3)—make sure the *Locked* box is not checked. Then try deleting the items again.

- If you're using System 7, try holding down [Option] while emptying the Trash. If you're using System 6, try holding down [Shift][Option][⌥⌘] while selecting and dragging the items to the Trash.

- If you still see the alert, it's probably because the folder you're tossing out contains a system-related file that's busy. Restart the Mac with a different startup disk and then throw the item away.

- If you're working with a folder that's stored on an AppleShare server or other shared disk, use the *Get Privileges* command to view the folder's privileges and see if it's locked. If the folder's locked and you're its owner, you can unlock it. If you're not the folder's owner, you'll have to ask the owner to unlock it. (See *The Sharing command* or *Sharing files under System 6* in Chapter 15.)

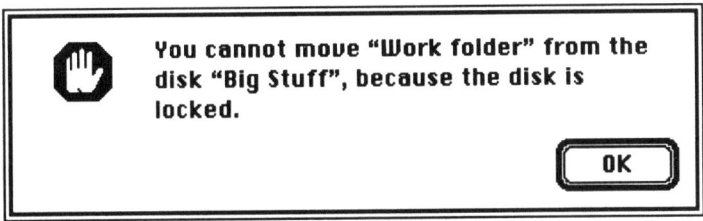

■ SYSTEM 7 VERSION

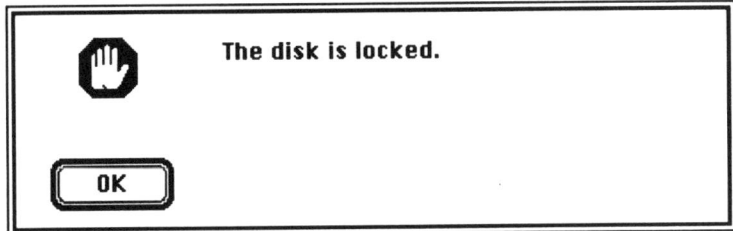

■ SYSTEM 6 VERSION

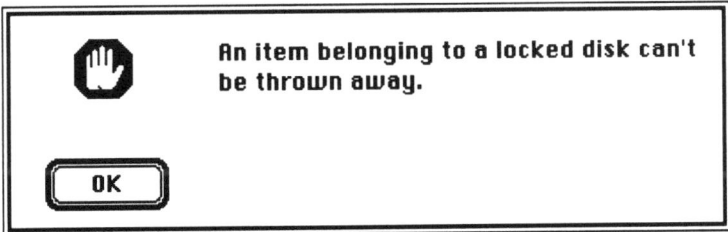

■ SYSTEM 6 VERSION

Problem:

You're trying to move or delete a file from a disk that's locked.

Solution:

Click the *OK* button, then unlock the disk. If it's a floppy disk, eject it and slide the plastic tab on its back away from the edge so the hole is closed. (1.44 MB floppy disks have two holes in them, so the hole without a tab always remains open.) If it's a hard disk, use its own setup/utility software to unlock it.

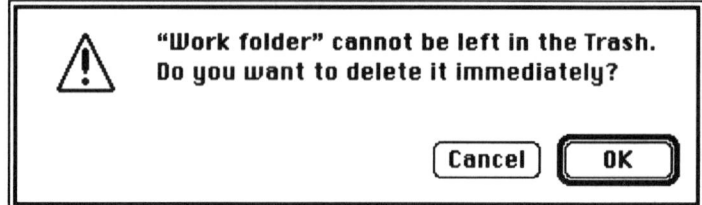

"Work folder" cannot be left in the Trash.
Do you want to delete it immediately?

Cancel   OK

■ SYSTEM 7 ONLY

Problem:

You're trying to delete a folder from a disk that's very full.
Under System 7, the Mac tries to maintain an invisible Trash
folder on every disk. When you drag items into the Trash,
they're stored in that folder. When the disk nears its capacity,
the Mac automatically deletes the Trash folder to give you more
file storage space. With the Trash folder gone, there's no place to
store items you've dragged into the Trash, and the Mac must
delete them immediately.

Solution:

Either click *OK* to delete the item immediately or click *Cancel* to
take it out of the Trash. If you want to store it in the Trash
instead of deleting it right away, you'll have to delete enough
items from the disk to make room for a new Trash folder. As
you delete the items, you'll continue to see the above message—
you'll have to keep clicking *OK* to delete them immediately
until you no longer see the alert. When you stop getting the
alert, the Trash folder has been recreated on the disk and anything you drag there will be stored until you empty it.

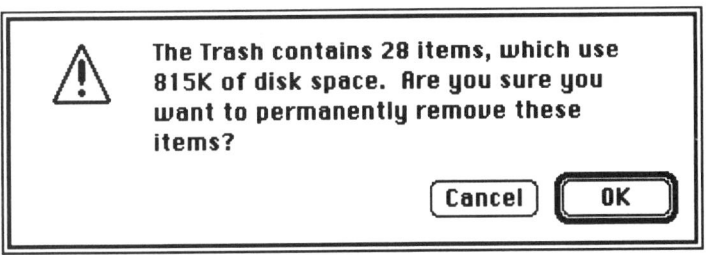

■ SYSTEM 7 ONLY

Problem:

This is the standard warning you get whenever you have items in the Trash and you choose the *Empty Trash* command from the Special menu. Under System 7, you can drag anything from an unlocked disk into the Trash. As you do, the Mac keeps track of the number of items and how much disk space they occupy. When you try to empty the Trash, you'll be warned about what you're deleting.

Solutions:

- **To empty the Trash,** click the *OK* button. Click *Cancel* to leave the items in the Trash.

- **To temporarily prevent the Mac from displaying this alert,** hold down the Option key the next time you choose the *Empty Trash* command.

- **To permanently prevent the Mac from displaying this alert,** select the Trash icon and then choose *Get Info* from the File menu. Then uncheck the *Warn before emptying* checkbox and close the information window.

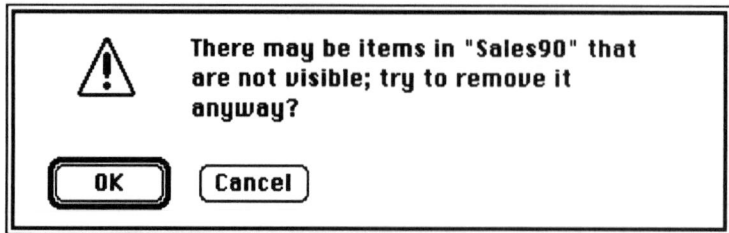

■ SYSTEM 6 ONLY

Problem:

You're trying to put a folder in the Trash and the folder may contain some invisible files. Your Mac is asking if you want to delete the folder anyway, even though you may be tossing out files you can't see. (System 7 doesn't alert you in this situation.)

Solution:

If you don't mind not knowing what you're throwing away, click the *OK* button. (Sometimes invisible files are locked or in use, though, so they can't be thrown away anyway even if you click *OK*.)

If you want to reconsider, click the *Cancel* button to take the folder back out of the Trash. If you open the folder with a utility like DiskTop, DiskTools or ResEdit, you'll be able to see any invisible items it contains and decide whether to save them.

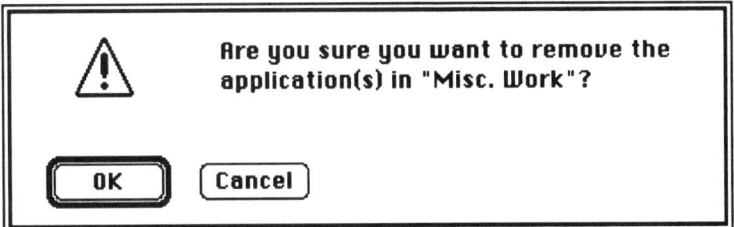

■ SYSTEM 6 ONLY

Problem:

You've dragged a folder into the Trash, and the folder contains one or more applications. Under System 6, the Mac always double-checks before letting you throw away applications. (System 7 doesn't specifically alert you about applications when you drag them to the Trash.)

Solution:

If you mean to throw the applications away, click the *OK* button. If you don't want to throw them away, click the *Cancel* button and then drag them into a different folder before throwing the original folder away.

When you want to throw away a folder containing system-related files without seeing the above alert, hold down the Option key before selecting the folder and dragging it to the Trash. But remember—you can't ever throw away system files that are in use.

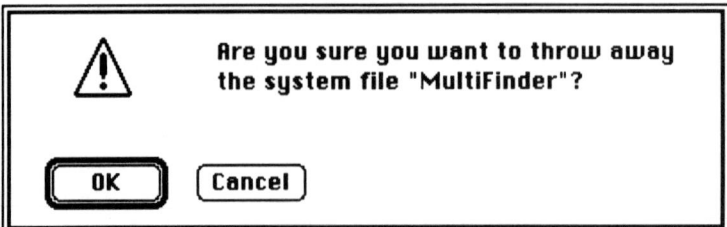

■ SYSTEM 6 ONLY

Problem:

You've dragged a folder that contains a system software file into the Trash. Under System 6, the Mac always double-checks before letting you throw away system-related files. (The Mac won't let you throw away active system software files under any version of its system software, but under System 7 the warning comes when you try to empty the Trash, not when you put the items in the Trash.)

Solution:

Click the *OK* button if you really want to throw those files away. If they aren't in use, the Mac will let you delete them. Otherwise, click the *Cancel* button and then drag the system files out of the folder you're trying to get rid of.

When you want to throw away a folder containing system-related files without seeing the above alert, hold down the (Option) key before selecting the folder and dragging it to the Trash. But remember—you can't ever throw away system files that are in use.

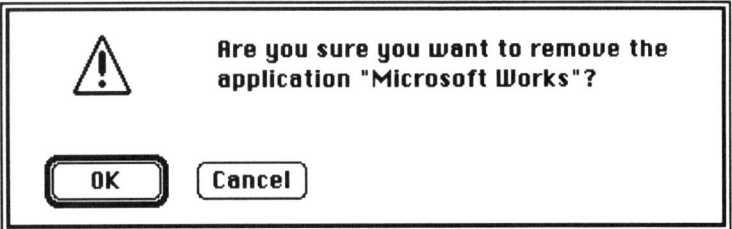

■ SYSTEM 6 ONLY

Problem:

You've dragged an application into the Trash. Under System 6, the Mac always double-checks before letting you throw away applications. (System 7 Macs don't.)

Solution:

If you really want to throw the program away, click the *OK* button. Otherwise, click the *Cancel* button.

You can avoid the above alert by holding down the Option key before selecting the application and dragging it to the Trash.

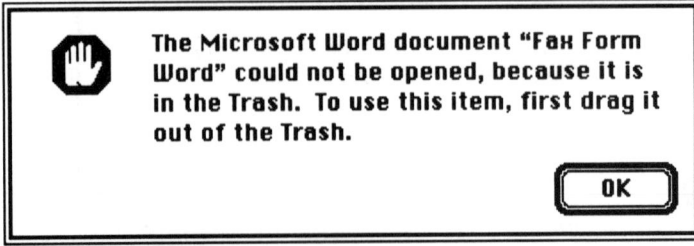

■ SYSTEM 7 VERSION

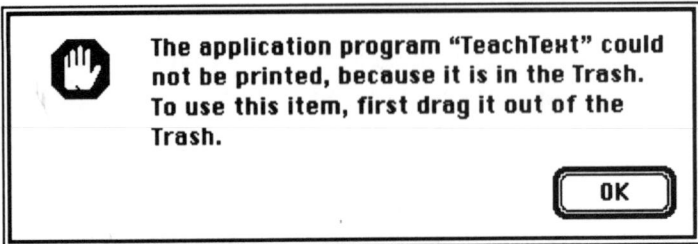

■ SYSTEM 7 VERSION

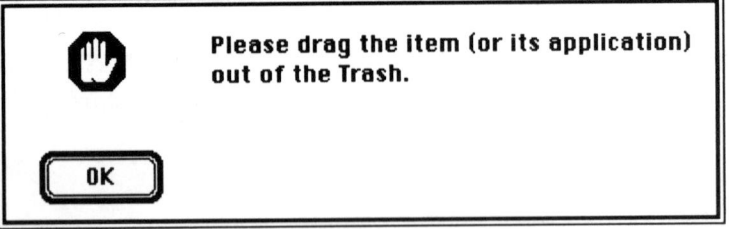

■ SYSTEM 6 VERSION

Problem:

The file you're trying to open or print is in the Trash, or else the application it requires is.

Solution:

Click the *OK* button, drag the file or its application out of the Trash, then open or print it.

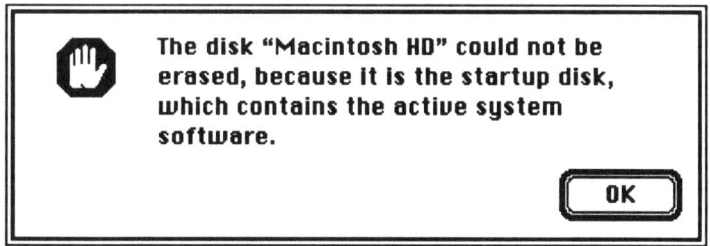

■ SYSTEM 7 VERSION

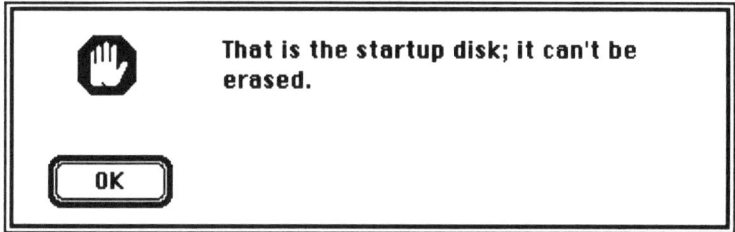

■ SYSTEM 6 VERSION

Problem:

You've tried to use the Finder's *Erase Disk* command to erase your startup disk. The Mac needs the files on the startup disk to run, so it won't let you erase them.

Solution:

Click the *OK* button to put the alert box away. You probably selected the startup disk by mistake. If so, select the disk you really want to erase and then choose the *Erase Disk* command again. If you really do want to erase your startup disk, you'll have to use another one to restart. Then you'll be free to erase the first startup disk since it won't be supplying the instructions the Mac needs.

12 | Finder commands

What Do I Do Now **?**

This chapter covers problems you might have with miscellaneous Finder operations like making aliases, making new folders or changing the amount of memory used by programs. For problems relating to the Trash or the *Empty Trash* command, see Chapter 11. For problems having to do with file sharing, see Chapter 15.

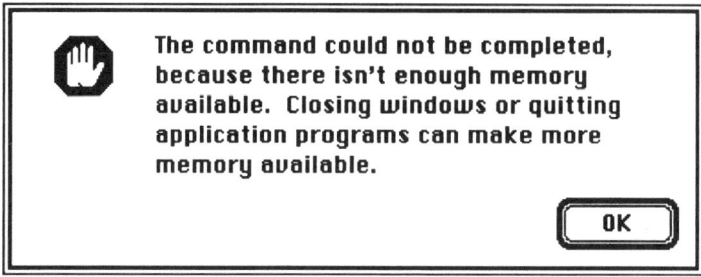

■ SYSTEM 7 VERSION

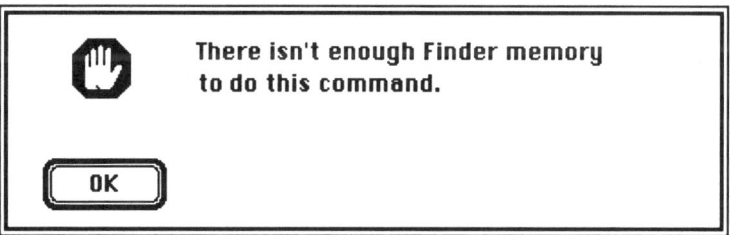

■ SYSTEM 6 VERSION

Problem:

You have too many applications, DAs or control panels running, or you have too many windows open on the desktop to allow the Finder to execute the current command.

Solution:

First click the *OK* button. Then quit one or more programs, or close some windows, and try the command again.

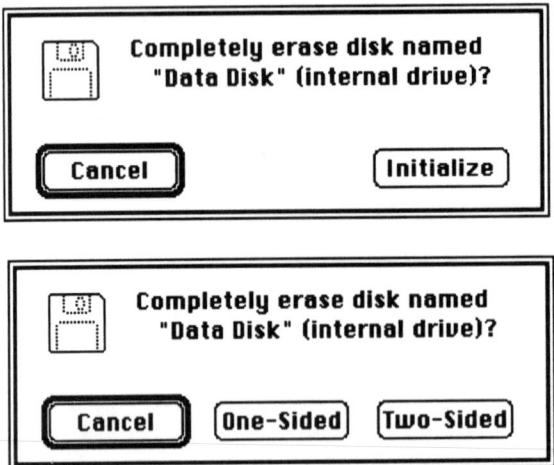

Problem:

These are messages you always see when you select a disk and then choose the *Erase Disk* command from the Special menu in the Finder. (The specific alert you see depends on whether you're trying to erase a 400K floppy, an 800K floppy, a high-density floppy or a hard disk.) The Mac is just making sure you know what you're about to do and really want to do it.

Solution:

Click the *Cancel* button if you don't want to erase the disk. If you do want to erase it, click the *Initialize* button for a hard disk or a high-density floppy, the *One-Sided* button for a single-sided (400K) floppy or the *Two-Sided* button for a double-sided (800K) floppy.

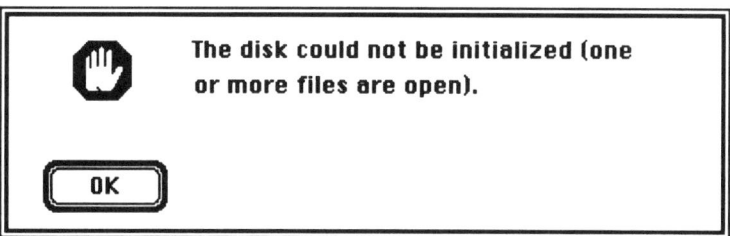

■ SYSTEM 6 ONLY

Problem:

You're trying to use the *Erase Disk* command to initialize (erase and reformat) a disk containing open files. When a disk is initialized, its contents are erased, and the Mac won't let you erase files that are open. (If you try to initialize a disk with open files under System 7, the Mac automatically closes the open files and then presents the *erase disk* warning shown in the previous section.)

Solution:

Click the *OK* button, then close all of the disk's open files. If you still get the alert, restart the Mac and try again. If that doesn't work, restart from another startup disk and then try again.

■ SYSTEM 7 VERSION

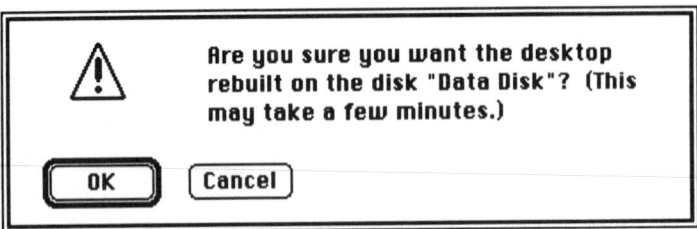

■ SYSTEM 6 VERSION

Problem:

No problem here. This is the dialog box you see when you issue the command to rebuild the desktop file on a disk. (See *Rebuilding the desktop file* on page 90.)

Solution:

Click the *OK* button to rebuild the desktop file or click the *Cancel* button to put the alert away and leave the desktop file the way it is.

■ SYSTEM 6 ONLY

■ SYSTEM 6 ONLY

Problem:

You've tried to rebuild the desktop file on a locked or damaged disk. The Mac needs to be able to write to the disk in order to rebuild the desktop file. (If you try to rebuild the desktop file on a locked disk under System 7, you won't see this warning—the disk icon will simply appear on the desktop and you won't be allowed to even try rebuilding the desktop file.)

Solution:

Click the *OK* button.

- **If the locked disk is a floppy,** it will automatically be ejected. To unlock it, slide the locking tab on the back side toward the center of the disk. Then try rebuilding the desktop file again. If it doesn't work, the disk is probably damaged and shouldn't be used.

- **If the locked disk is a hard disk,** use its setup utility software to unlock it.

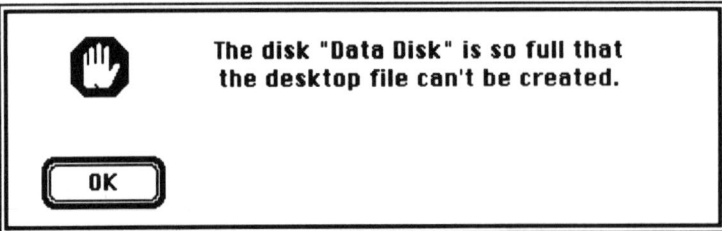

The disk "Data Disk" is so full that
the desktop file can't be created.

OK

■ SYSTEM 6 ONLY

Problem:

You're trying to rebuild the desktop file on a disk, but the disk
is too full for the Mac to do it properly. (On a System 7 Mac, you
can rebuild the desktop file even if the disk is full.)

Solution:

Click the *OK* button, then delete a file on the disk and try
rebuilding the desktop file again. If you get the same message,
delete some more files to free up more disk space, then rebuild
the desktop file.

■ SYSTEM 7 VERSION

■ SYSTEM 6 VERSION

Problem:

You've chosen the *New Folder* command from the Finder's File menu, but there isn't enough room on the disk to contain the new folder so the Mac won't let you create one.

Solution:

Click the *OK* button. Then either delete some files from the disk to make room for the new folder or select a different disk before choosing the *New Folder* command again.

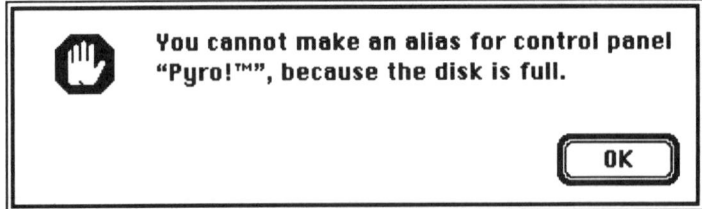

You cannot make an alias for control panel "Pyro!™", because the disk is full.

[OK]

■ SYSTEM 7 ONLY

Problem:

You've chosen the *Make Alias* command to make an alias, but there's no room for the alias because the disk is full.

Solution:

Either give up making an alias or delete an item from the disk to make room for it. Then try the command again. Aliases only take up about 2K of disk space, so you don't have to free up much space for one.

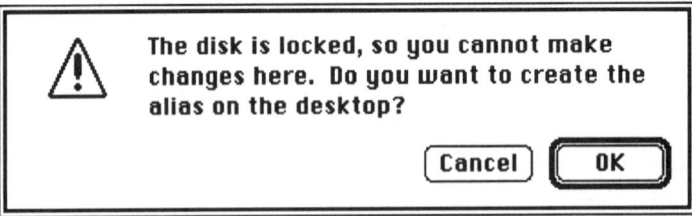

The disk is locked, so you cannot make changes here. Do you want to create the alias on the desktop?

[Cancel] [OK]

■ SYSTEM 7 ONLY

Problem:

You've tried to make an alias, but the disk is locked, so the Mac is giving you the option of putting the alias on the desktop.

Solution:

Click *OK* to create the alias and have it appear on the desktop, or click *Cancel*. If you want the alias on the disk, you'll have to unlock it first.

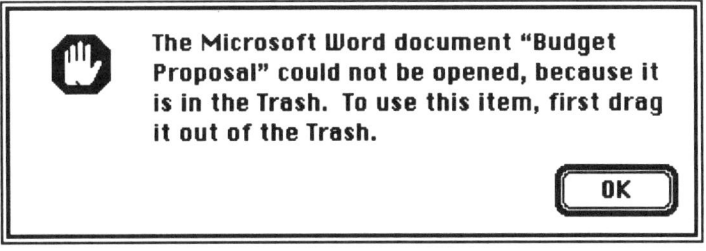

■ SYSTEM 7 ONLY

Problem:

You've tried to open the alias for an item, but the item itself is in the Trash so it can't be opened.

Solution:

Drag the item out of the Trash and try opening it again.

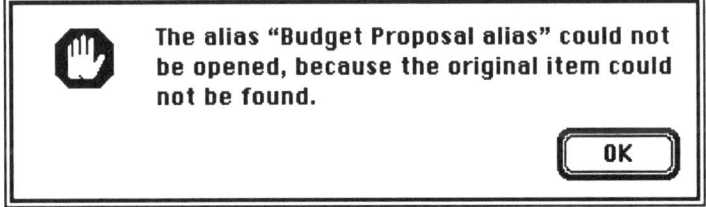

■ SYSTEM 7 ONLY

Problem:

You've tried to open an alias, but the item represented by the alias isn't on the disk.

Solution:

Select the alias and choose the *Get Info* command, then click the *Find Original* button in the information window. The Mac will try to locate the original item the alias represents. The item may have been renamed and moved into a deeply-nested folder. In most cases, however, the item is simply no longer on the disk. If that's the case, you may as well delete the alias, because it no longer serves any purpose.

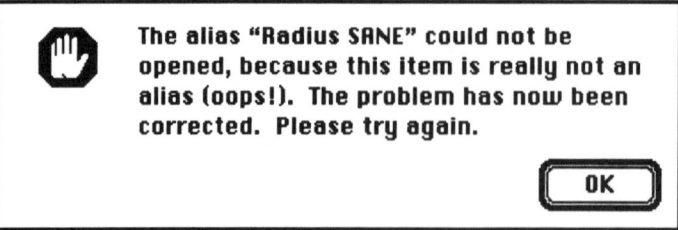

The alias "Radius SANE" could not be opened, because this item is really not an alias (oops!). The problem has now been corrected. Please try again.

OK

■ SYSTEM 7 ONLY

Problem:

You've double-clicked on an item that seems to be an alias (it has the Kind designation *alias* and its name appears in italics) but it isn't really one, so the Mac can't open it. Some startup documents that were created for System 6 are mistakenly converted to aliases when you update the System Folder on their disk to System 7.

Solution:

Click the *OK* button. The Mac will change the item's designation from alias to something else (probably *system extension*).

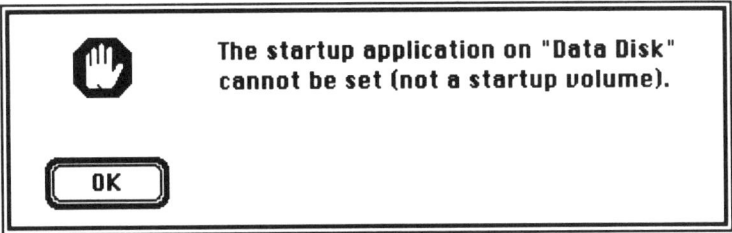

The startup application on "Data Disk" cannot be set (not a startup volume).

OK

■ SYSTEM 6 ONLY

Problem:

You've tried to set a startup application on a disk other than the one you used to start up your Mac. You can only select startup applications from among the programs stored on the startup disk you're currently using.

Solution:

Choose a startup application from the current startup disk or copy the application you want to use onto your startup disk.

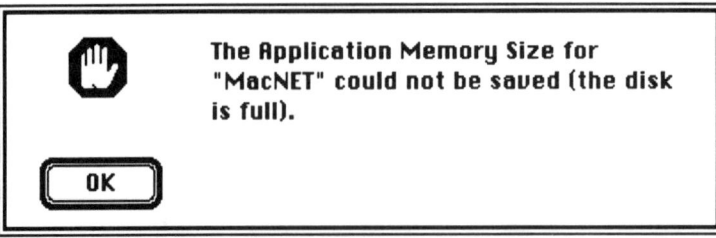

The Application Memory Size for "MacNET" could not be saved (the disk is full).

OK

■ SYSTEM 6 ONLY

Problem:

You've tried to change the application memory size for a program, but the disk where the program is stored is so full the change can't be recorded. (Under System 7, the Mac always saves enough room on the disk for you to reset a program's current memory size.)

Solution:

Delete a file from the disk where the application is stored to create some free space and then change the program's application memory size.

13 | Running programs, DAs and control panels

What Do I Do Now

This chapter covers problems you may have while running standard applications, DAs or (under System 7) control panel programs. Obviously, special problems can crop up with each specific program, but this chapter deals with problems that can occur with *any* of them (other than the Finder or MultiFinder). If you're having a program-related problem that's not covered here or in the program manual, ask someone else who has more experience with that program or call the manufacturer's technical support line.

Some of the problems covered in this chapter aren't identified by error messages. In these cases, the problem is simply described in a section heading.

A DA name doesn't appear on the menu.

Problem:

The set of DAs that appears on your menu is determined by the System Folder you started up with. So if you've started your Mac from a different disk than usual, you may not get the same DAs you're used to.

If you used your regular startup disk and still have this problem, its cause depends on which system version you're running. If you're running System 7, the simple answer is that the DA (or an alias for the DA) hasn't been placed inside the Apple Menu Items folder in the System Folder. If you're running System 6, either your Mac is running a DA manager program and you must use it to open the DA file, or the DA has been removed, corrupted or improperly installed.

Solutions:

- **If you started up from a different disk than usual,** restart your Mac with your regular startup disk. The DA you want should appear on the menu. If not, try the appropriate solution below.

- **If you're running System 7** and have started up from the disk you normally use, copy or move the DA program (or an alias for it) into the Apple Menu Items folder inside your System Folder. As soon as the DA or its alias is inside that folder, the DA name will appear on the menu.

- **If you're running System 6** and have started up from the disk you normally use, you must locate the DA file you want to use and then either install it or open it, depending on whether or not your system uses a DA manager like Suitcase, Suitcase II, Font/DA Juggler or MasterJuggler. (If you're not sure whether you're using a DA manager, check whether any of the above programs' names appear on the menu. If not, you don't have a DA manager installed in your system.)

Under System 6, DAs are stored in DA suitcase files, whose icons —when *by Icon* is selected in the Finder's View menu—look like this:

DiskTop 3.0.3

(Font suitcase files look the same except there's a letter *A* on the front of the suitcase.) DA suitcases sometimes contain more than one DA, and a suitcase's name may be different from the names of the DAs it contains. Unless you know which suitcase contains the DA you want, you'll have to open each DA suitcase to find out which one it's stored in.

If you aren't running a DA manager, use the Font/DA Mover program that came with your Mac to open suitcase files and install the DA you want once you find it. See the *Macintosh Utilities User's Guide* or *Macintosh Reference* manual for instructions on using Font/DA Mover.

If you're running a DA manager, you can use it to locate and open the suitcase file you want. Once you've done so, the program will automatically open the DA every time you start up your Mac. But if you update your System file with the Installer program, you'll have to use the DA manager again to find and open the DA suitcases. To do this, follow the instructions in the DA manager's manual.

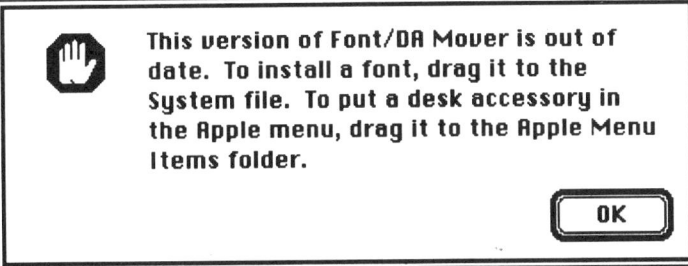

■ SYSTEM 7 ONLY

Problem:

You're trying to launch the Font/DA Mover on a Mac that's running under System 7, but you can't because you don't need it under System 7.

Solution:

To install or remove a DA on the menu, just drag it into (or out of) the Apple Menu Items folder inside the System Folder. To install or remove a font, just double-click on the System file to open it and then drag the font file into (or out of) the System file's window.

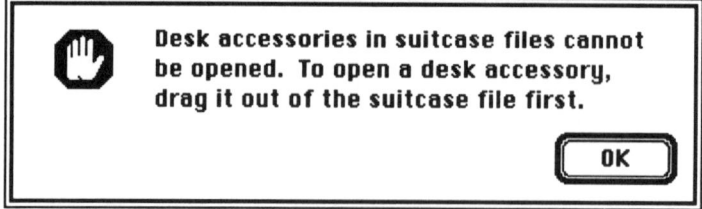

Desk accessories in suitcase files cannot
be opened. To open a desk accessory,
drag it out of the suitcase file first.

OK

■ SYSTEM 7 ONLY

Problem:

You're trying to open a DA by going into its suitcase file and
double-clicking on it, but under System 7, DAs must be taken
out of their suitcases before you can use them.

Solution:

When you double-click on a suitcase file to open it, you'll see
the DA file itself inside the suitcase file's window. To open the
DA file, drag it outside the window, then double-click on it.

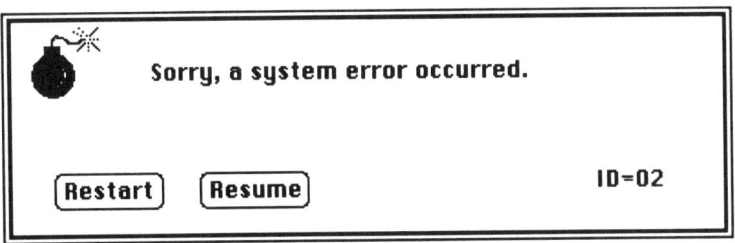

Problem:

If you get this nasty message as you try to open a DA, it's probably because there are too many other files or DAs open, and the Mac is having trouble managing all those different items in its memory. (This happens most often on Macs with only one megabyte of memory.)

If you get the message while using a control panel or application, it's probably just a temporary glitch, possibly having to do with the order in which programs were opened (if you're running more than one at a time). This message may include other text, such as *illegal instruction.*

Solutions:

- Click the *Restart* button to restart your Mac, then open the program again. Unfortunately, you'll have lost any unsaved changes you made to files that were open at the time of the system crash.

- If the problem continues, search your hard disk for multiple System files or System Folders. If you find more than one, delete the one that isn't currently in use.

  You can tell which System Folder is in use by displaying the folder in Icon view (choose *Icon* from the View menu in the Finder): if the System Folder is the one that's currently in use, it will have a small Mac icon on it. (For more information, see suggestion number nine under *Fourteen ways to avoid problems* in Chapter 4.)

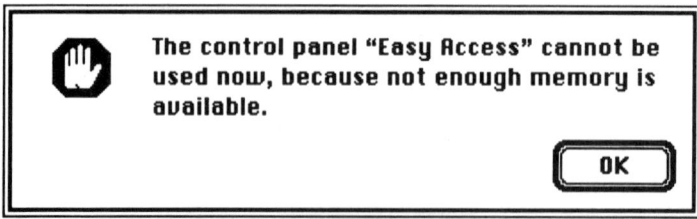

■ SYSTEM 7 ONLY

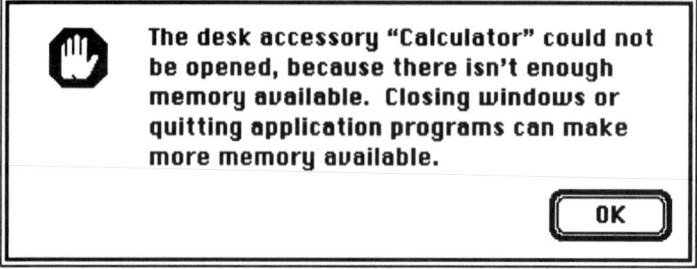

■ SYSTEM 7 VERSION

■ SYSTEM 6 VERSION

Problem:

The applications, DAs or control panels you have open are taking up so much memory that there isn't enough left to open the DA or control panel you've selected.

Solutions:

- **If you're using MultiFinder under System 6,** Click the *OK* button and then try holding down the Option key before you choose the DA from the menu. The Mac will try to use memory reserved for applications (instead of for the Finder) to open the DA.

- **If the above doesn't work or doesn't apply to you,** close one or more applications, windows, DAs or control panels and try again until the program you want opens successfully.

- If all else fails, restart the Mac and then open the item you want.

The program quits or the Mac restarts itself spontaneously while you're working.

Problem:

If too many programs, files and DAs are open at the same time, the Mac may have trouble managing them in its memory or the System file may not have enough memory to run properly. Both problems can result in a spontaneous restart, usually accompanied by an alert message saying that the program has unexpectedly quit.

The other explanation for this problem, although far less likely, is a defective or failing power supply in your Mac.

Solutions:

- Try running your Mac with fewer applications, DAs or control panels open at once. If the problem goes away, you can be sure that memory usage was the problem.

- If that doesn't work and you're running under System 6, choose *About the Finder* from the menu when the Finder is active. Look at the bar that shows the size of the System file or the system software. If it's all black, there's not enough room for your System file to operate properly.

    Use the Font/DA Mover to remove any DAs or fonts you don't use regularly, or remove your DAs and fonts from the System file and run them using a DA management program like Suitcase or MasterJuggler. If the problem continues, check to see how many inits are loading when you start up your Mac. If you have too many of them loading at once, they can cause your Mac to run low on memory. Try dragging some of the larger ones outside of the System Folder (or turning them off with an init management program like InitPicker or Aask) and then restart the Mac. If the problem goes away, you may have to live with fewer inits (or add more RAM to your Mac to accommodate them all).

- If the problem only occurs with a specific combination of programs, they may be incompatible with one another. Try running the programs one at a time. If the problem occurs while one of them is running, try re-installing it from its master disk, or ask the manufacturer if it needs to be upgraded for the version of the system software you're using.

- As a last resort, try replacing the system software (see *Replacing the system software*, page 88). You may have a defective System file.

- If, after trying all these remedies, the problem continues, you probably have a bad power supply. Take the Mac in for repairs.

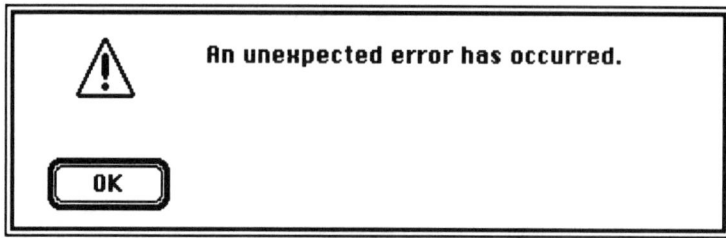

Problem:

Your Mac is having a temporary problem. It's usually an isolated event.

Solution:

Try the operation again. If you keep getting the same message, save any files you have open, close all your DAs and programs and restart the Mac. That should clear it up.

Problem:

The Mac is having a memory management problem that's preventing it from reading the Clipboard file. Usually the problem is caused by having too many programs, DAs or control panels open. More often than not, whatever you copied to the Clipboard will be lost.

Solution:

Close all the applications, DAs and control panels you have open. Then re-open the programs and documents you were using to copy and paste the data, and try it again. If this doesn't work, restart the Mac and try again.

A dialog box appears instead of the DA screen when you choose the DA name.

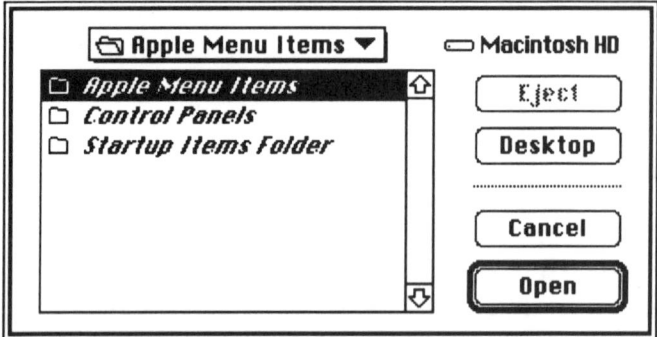

■ SYSTEM 7 VERSION

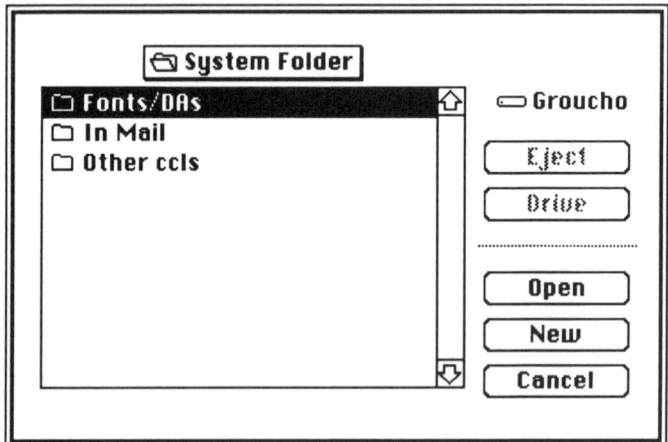

■ SYSTEM 6 VERSION

Problem:

You've chosen a desk accessory but instead of seeing the DA's screen, you see this dialog box. The DA you've chosen needs a data file, and the data file isn't where the DA expects it to be.

Solution:

Use the dialog box on the screen to locate the DA's data file, then click the *Open* button. If you can't remember the name of the data file, try files with names similar to the DA itself. For example, choosing a file named Scrapbook or New Scrapbook would be a good bet if you're using the SmartScrap DA. If you're using WordFinder, it would make sense to look for a thesaurus file. Don't be afraid to guess—if you're wrong, the DA simply won't open the file.

You're trying to open a different DA storage file, but you can't open it, or when you do, it doesn't open in the format you're used to seeing it in.

■ SYSTEM 6 ONLY

Problem:

You're probably using the wrong *Open...* command to open the DA file. Because DAs run at the same time as other programs, other program menus are still on the screen when you're working with them. (Under System 7, DA menus appear by themselves, because DAs work just like standard applications.) If the DA has file management commands of its own, they're located on a separate menu, often one with the same name as the DA, like this:

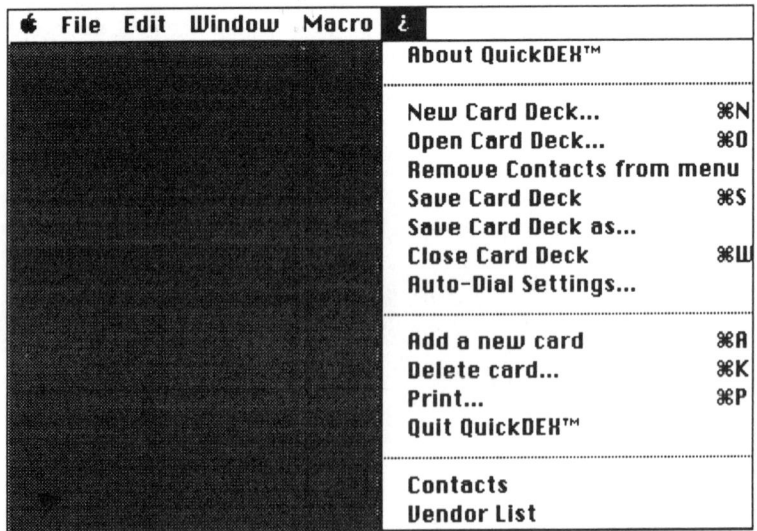

In this case, the QuickDEX menu is labeled with an upside-down question mark, rather than the program's name. Still, you can see that this menu has its own commands for opening and saving files (files are called *Card Decks* in QuickDEX). Those commands have nothing to do with the commands on the File menu, which belong to another application.

Unfortunately, the dialog box you see when you use the DA's *open* command can be almost identical to the dialog box you see when you choose the *Open...* command from another application's File menu. Sometimes you can't tell that you've made a mistake until you actually try to open the file.

In most cases, you won't be able to use a standard application's *Open...* command to open a DA storage file. If you do open the file with the wrong program, it's usually obvious. For example, if you open a QuickDEX data file with the *Open...* command on Word's File menu, the data is displayed as strings of text in an Untitled document, rather than in the QuickDEX window.

Solution:

Make sure you use the *Open...* command on the DA's menu to open files for that DA. If the file won't open, or if it opens in an unfamiliar format, you probably chose the *Open...* command from the wrong menu.

You made changes to a DA's storage file and you thought you saved them, but the changes weren't saved.

■ SYSTEM 6 ONLY

Problem:

You probably used the wrong *Save* command to save the changes. Because DAs run at the same time as other programs, other program menus are still on the screen when you're working with the DA. See the previous problem description for further discussion of this problem.

Solution:

Make sure you use the *Save* command on the DA's menu to save files for that DA.

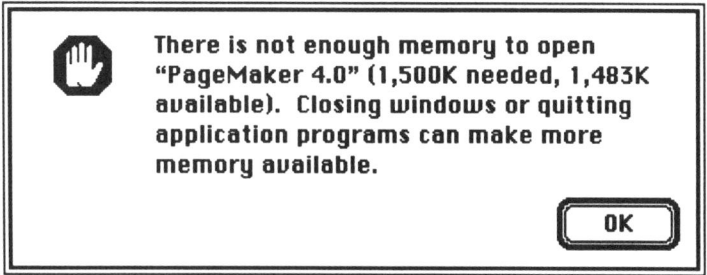

■ SYSTEM 7 VERSION

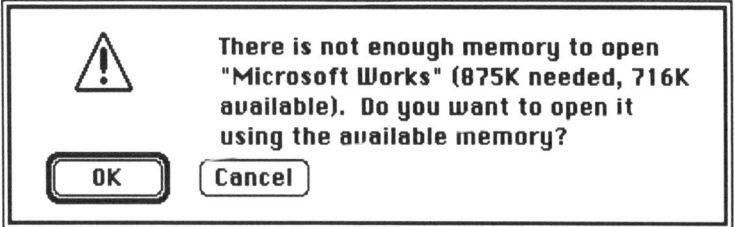

■ SYSTEM 6 VERSION

Problem:

You've tried to open an application or a file under System 7 or System 6's MultiFinder, but there isn't as much memory available as the application normally needs to run. There is enough available memory to attempt it though, and the Mac wants to know if you want to try.

Solution:

The best course of action is to click the *Cancel* button, quit another program you have running, and then launch the application or file you originally wanted. You can click the *OK* button if you want to try loading the program under reduced memory conditions, but you risk having the program quit unexpectedly later on.

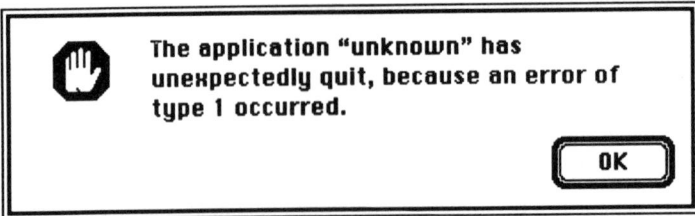

■ SYSTEM 7 VERSION

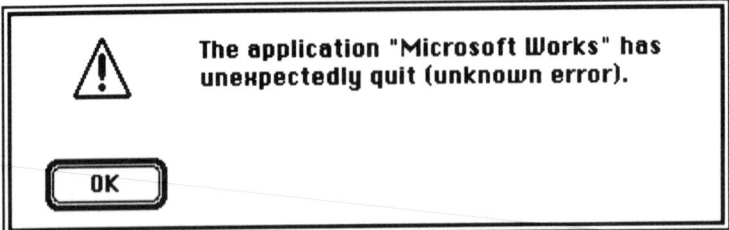

■ SYSTEM 6 VERSION

Problem:

These messages nearly always occur when you don't have enough application memory specified for the program and data file you have open, or when the Mac is having trouble managing its memory.

Solutions:

- **If you're running the program under System 7 or under MultiFinder in System 6,** click the *OK* button and then open the program's information window. Make the application memory size or current memory size at least 128K larger than it is now. (See *The Get Info command*, page 47 for instructions.)

- **If the above doesn't work, or if you're not running multiple programs,** restart the Mac and then run the program again. If it's a temporary problem, that should clear it up.

- If that doesn't do the trick, try replacing the system software (see *Replacing the system software*, page 88.) If this doesn't fix things, call the program's publisher for technical support.

You expect to see a file name in the list of files to open from within a program, but the file name isn't there.

Problem:

Either you're looking in the wrong folder or on the wrong disk, or the file isn't the program's standard type. When you use the *Open...* command with some applications or DAs, you'll only be able to see the files that were created by that particular program, or that have compatible formats, even though there may be other files inside the folder. To see other files that can be imported, you may have to select an *Import* or *All Files* option or use a separate *Import* command.

Solutions:

- Check the disk name at the right of the dialog box. If you have the wrong disk selected, click the *Desktop* or *Drive* button or insert a different floppy disk.

- Check the folder name above the list of files to see if you're looking in the right folder. If you aren't, click on the folder name and hold down the mouse button to display other folder names. Drag the pointer toward the bottom of the list to view the main disk directory, and then look in that directory for the folder you want. If you can't remember the name of the folder you need to look in, use the *Find* command (in System 7) or a file-finding DA like *Find File* to locate the file you want.

- If you know you're looking in the right folder and disk, the file may not be the program's standard type. If the dialog box has an option called *All Files, Import* or something similar, select it. If there's no such option, click *Cancel* and then look for an *Import* command on the program's File menu. You should see a list of files you can import that includes the name of the file you need. If the file name doesn't appear, it can't be opened with the program you're using.

You get an error message when you try to save a file.

Problem:

Different programs will display different error messages when there's a problem saving a file. The file could be damaged, the disk may be full or there may be a temporary glitch with the program itself. Whatever the problem is, there are a few basic remedies to try when you run into a file-saving problem.

Solutions:

- Try the save operation a couple more times. It may be a temporary glitch.

- If the problem continues, check to see whether the disk to which you're saving is full. In some programs, this information is right underneath the disk name in the dialog box that appears when you choose the *Save As...* command. If the disk is full, you obviously need to save the file to a different disk, or delete some unneeded files from the current disk to make room.

- If the disk isn't full, try saving the file under a different name—this will create a new copy of the file. If this remedy works, the original file is probably corrupted and you should delete it from the disk after saving the new copy.

- If none of these remedies works, check your SCSI chain (see *Checking the SCSI chain*, page 87).

14 | Printing problems

Spotting PrintMonitor problems   256

Printing from a Macintosh can be a complex affair, especially if you're using a program that produces PostScript files or combines PostScript commands with standard text. Printing with non-Apple printers has its own problems as well. This chapter will get you through most of the printing problems associated with basic business applications. But if you're having problems with a sophisticated graphics, CAD or desktop publishing program, you should get help from the program's publisher or the company that made the printer (if it's a non-Apple printer that requires a special printer driver).

This chapter covers problems that come from using the wrong printer driver, having the wrong printer selected on a network or not having the right font available for use by a laser printer. We'll also look at PrintMonitor error messages.

Spotting PrintMonitor problems

Note: PrintMonitor only works with printers that use one of the LaserWriter printer drivers or a recent version of the StyleWriter driver. If you're using an ImageWriter, you should skip this section.

Many of the errors discussed in this chapter appear as alert messages, just as they do in other chapters of this book. If you're running PrintMonitor, however, you may not see the messages right away.

If you've never changed PrintMonitor's preferences and you're using System 7, the Mac will notify you that there's a printing problem by displaying the message at the top of the next page:

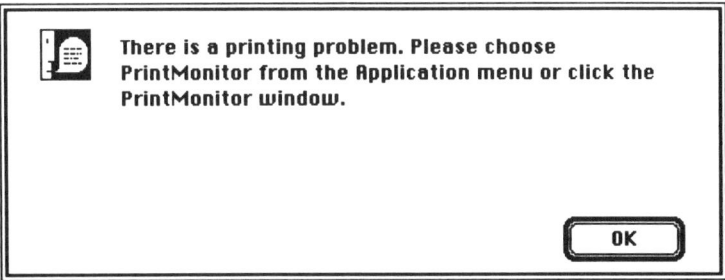

When you see this message, click the *OK* button and then choose *PrintMonitor* from the Application menu to see the error message that will tell you the specific problem.

Using PrintMonitor's preferences settings, you can have the program simply flash its icon in the menu bar to notify you of a problem. If you've set that preference, you won't see an error message until you choose PrintMonitor from the Application menu (or the ⬧ menu, under System 6).

To change PrintMonitor's preferences, double-click on the PrintMonitor icon in the Extensions folder (or the System Folder, under System 6) to open the program, and then choose *Preferences* from the File menu. You'll see a dialog box like this:

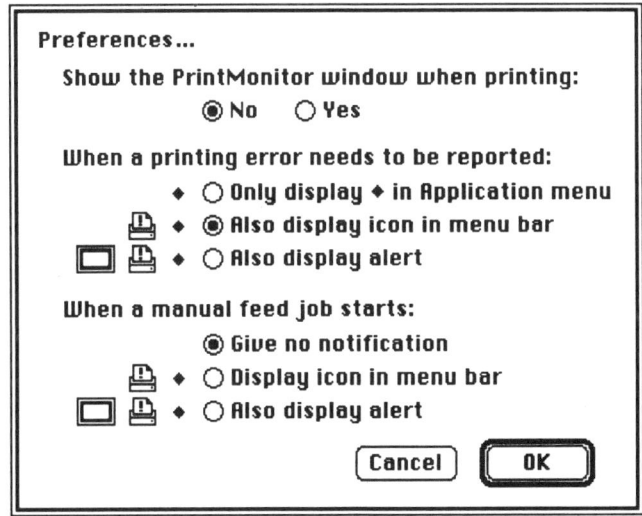

(Under System 6, the option *Only display ◆ in Application menu* reads *Only display ◆ in ⬥ menu.*)

By clicking buttons in this dialog box, you can choose whether or not to have the PrintMonitor window show immediately when you print something. You can also choose the method PrintMonitor will use to notify you of problems and decide to have it remind you to insert a sheet of paper when you choose a manual feed printing job.

Now let's get on with the common error messages and problems you might encounter while printing.

Nothing happens when you try to print a document from your program.

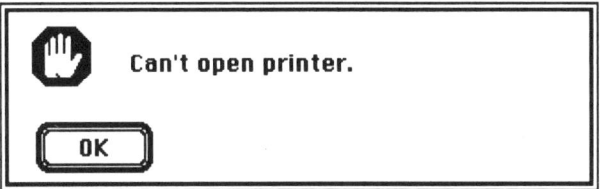

Problem:

You may or may not see the alert message above, but in any case, you don't get any results when you try to print a document. Either the printer driver you need isn't installed, you haven't chosen a printer driver for the Mac to use or you've selected the wrong printer port.

Solutions:

Select *Chooser* from the menu and see if there's an icon for the printer you want to use.

- **If there's no icon,** you'll need to install the driver for your printer. Close the Chooser window and see the instructions in the next section, *The printer icon doesn't appear in the Chooser window.*

- **If the printer icon already appears in the Chooser window** (or if you've just installed the driver so it now appears there), click on it and then (if necessary) select the specific printer of that type. If you're choosing a non-AppleTalk (cable-connected) printer, you'll also have to select the port where the printer cable is hooked up (it's probably the printer port). If you're on a network and there's more than one printer of that type connected, you'll have to tell the Mac which of the printers you want to use by clicking on the printer's name. (See *Using the Chooser DA*, page 69, for more information.)

The printer icon doesn't appear in the Chooser window.

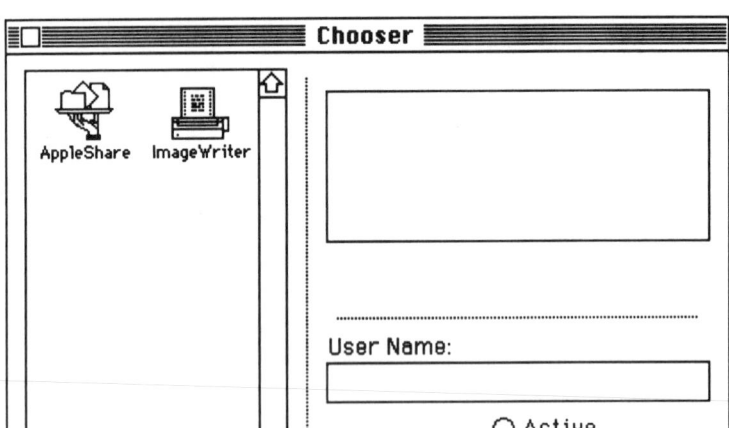

Problem:

You want to select a printer with the Chooser, but its icon doesn't appear in the Chooser window. (In the example above, the icons for a LaserWriter, StyleWriter and several other printers are missing.) The Chooser extension or driver that produces the icon isn't installed in the Extensions folder or System Folder on your Mac's startup disk.

Solution:

Close the Chooser window and quit any programs you have running to return to the Finder.

- **If you're using a non-Apple printer,** locate the disk that contains the printer driver and drag the driver file (or files) onto the System Folder's icon on your startup disk. (If you're running under System 7, you'll see a message asking if you want the items placed in the right folder; click the OK button.) The driver will then appear in the Chooser window and you can select it there.

- **If you're using an Apple printer,** use the Installer on your
  Install 1 or *System Tools* disk to install the printer software.
  Start up the Installer program from its floppy disk, click the
  OK button on the welcome screen, make sure the disk name
  is correct in the main Installer screen window (so you'll be
  installing on the correct disk), then click the *Customize* button
  on the main Installer screen. Choose the printer software
  option from the list of items you can install, then click the
  Install button. Once the installation is complete, quit the
  Installer and select the correct printer in the Chooser.
  (If you're not sure how to do this, see *Using the Chooser DA,*
  page 69.)

The printer name doesn't appear in the Chooser window.

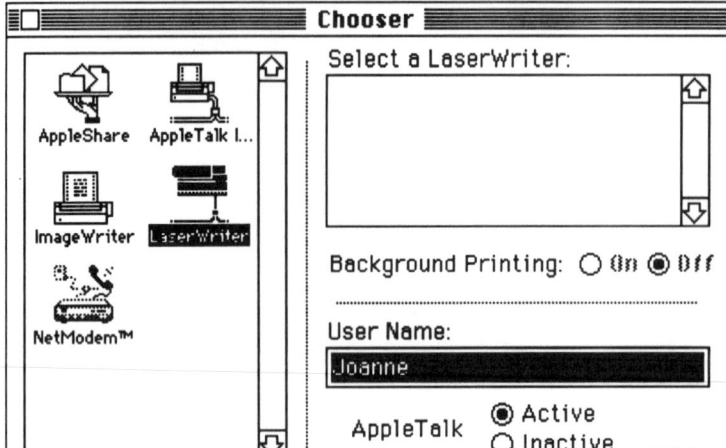

Problem:

You've tried to select a printer by clicking on its icon in the Chooser, but its name doesn't appear in the list of printers. There are four possible problems:

- The printer isn't turned on or (if it's an ImageWriter or StyleWriter) its *Select* light isn't on.

- The printer or your Mac has become unplugged from the network.

- There's some network interference that's preventing your Mac from "seeing" that printer on the network.

- There's something wrong with the printer's internal electronics.

Solutions:

- Make sure the printer is turned on and warmed up. If a laser printer was in the process of starting up, it might not have warmed up in time to appear on the network as a working printer. Once the printer is initialized (it usually prints a start-up page to let you know it's ready, or the *Ready* light stops flashing and stays lit), you can print your file.

- If that doesn't work, check the network cable at the back of the printer and the one plugged into the Mac's printer port to make sure they're plugged in firmly. If the network cable on your Mac is plugged into the phone port, move it to the printer port and make sure the *AppleTalk Active* button is selected in the Chooser window.

- If you're still having the problem, try using a different network connection cable, if you can. There may be something wrong with the one you're using. If you get the same problem with a different cable, try selecting another network device in the Chooser. If you can select and use a different device, the problem is with the connection between your Mac and that particular printer.

- If there are several other network devices (like printers or modems) plugged into the same branch of the network as the printer you want to use, heavy use on one of them may be blocking the signals that have to travel from your Mac to the printer. This is especially a problem with network modems, because using them involves transferring a lot of data over the network.

  If a network modem is daisy-chained to the same network interface as your printer, try turning it off and selecting the printer again. If the printer appears in the Chooser, select it again and try printing again. If this works, the modem is the culprit. The best solution in this case is to move the network modem to another location on the network.

- If none of the above remedies works, there's something wrong with your printer. Try restarting it. If that doesn't clear up the problem, call its manufacturer. You may need to take it in for repairs.

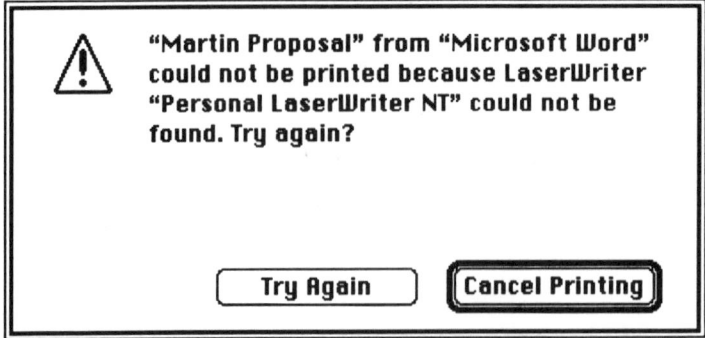

■ SYSTEM 7 VERSION

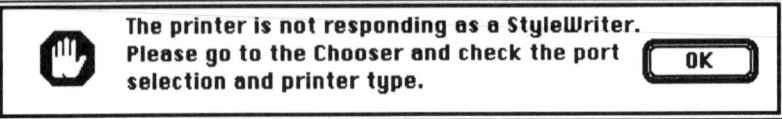

■ SYSTEM 7 VERSION

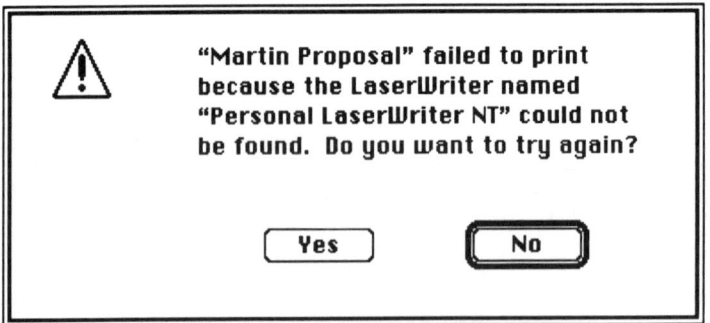

■ SYSTEM 6 VERSION

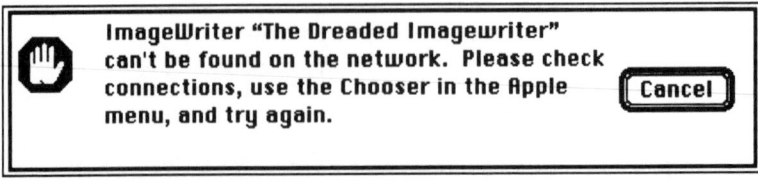

■ SYSTEM 6 VERSION

Problem:

Your Mac is expecting to print your file on a printer that's been selected with the Chooser, but the printer can't be found on the network. There are five possible causes for this:

- You've selected the wrong type of printer with the Chooser, so the Mac can't find the one you've specified.
- The printer isn't turned on or its *Select* light isn't on.
- The printer or your Mac has become unplugged from the network.
- There's some network interference that's blocking the Mac's electronic access to that printer.
- There's something wrong with the printer's internal electronics.

Solutions:

- Click the *Cancel Printing* or *Cancel* button. Then open the Chooser and select the printer driver for the type of printer you're using.
- Try the solutions offered for the preceding problem (starting on page 262).

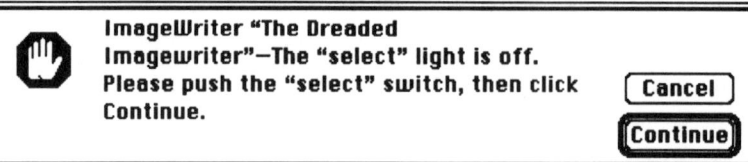

ImageWriter "The Dreaded
Imagewriter"—The "select" light is off.
Please push the "select" switch, then click
Continue.

Cancel

Continue

Problem:

You're trying to print a file to an ImageWriter or other printer that's directly connected to your printer port (as opposed to being connected over an AppleTalk network). You've chosen the printer with the Chooser, but the printer either isn't connected properly, isn't selected or isn't turned on.

Solution:

Check the cable connecting your Mac and the printer to make sure it's plugged in firmly at both ends. Be sure the printer cable is plugged into the printer port on your Mac and not into the modem port (see Chapter 1).

Check that the printer is on and has paper. Then make sure the printer's *Select* or *Ready* light is lit. If the light isn't on, press the *Select* button, then click *Continue* to finish printing the file.

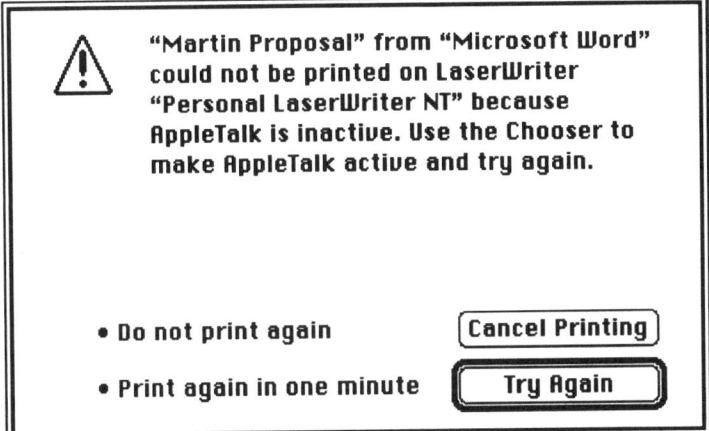

■ SYSTEM 7 VERSION

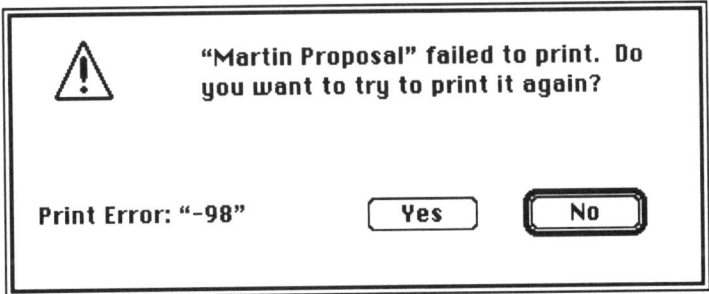

■ SYSTEM 6 VERSION

Problem:

You're trying to print to a network printer, but you have AppleTalk set to *Inactive* in the Chooser window.

Solution:

Open the Chooser DA and click the *Active* button next to the word *AppleTalk* in the lower right corner. If you don't see these buttons, select the LaserWriter or network printer's icon first to make them appear.

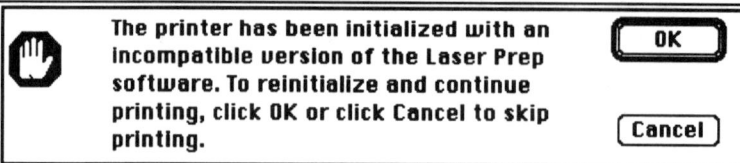

The printer has been initialized with an incompatible version of the Laser Prep software. To reinitialize and continue printing, click OK or click Cancel to skip printing.

OK

Cancel

Problem:

You're printing to a laser printer on a network, and someone else on the network is using a different version of the Laser Prep file than you have. Laser Prep is a file in your System Folder that the Mac uses to prepare a laser printer for each printing job.

Once a laser printer is initialized with a Laser Prep file, it expects every print job to be sent from a Mac with the same version of the Laser Prep file installed. If your Mac has a different version, you'll be given the above option to reinitialize the printer (which takes a couple of minutes) before the file can be printed.

Solution:

If you're in a hurry, click the *OK* button and the printer will be reinitialized for your version of the Laser Prep file; then your file will be printed. But when someone who's using a different version of the Laser Prep file tries to print, they'll get this message too and will have to initialize the printer again.

The best solution to this problem is to make sure everyone on the network is using the same (and hopefully the latest) version of the Laser Prep file and the LaserWriter printer driver. You can find out the version number of each of these files by selecting them and then using the *Get Info* command on the Finder's file menu. (Under System 7, the files are in the Extensions folder inside the System Folder; under System 6 they're just in the System Folder itself.)

Once you've determined which of the Laser Prep and LaserWriter files is the newest version on your network, copy that version into the Extensions folder inside the System Folder (under System 7) or into the System Folder (under System 6) on the startup disk of each Mac on the network. Even if two Macs on the network are using different versions of the system software, they both can use the same version of the Laser Prep and LaserWriter files.

The laser printer stalls in the *preparing data* sequence.

Problem:

You're trying to print to a laser printer, but the *preparing data* message on your screen (or in the PrintMonitor dialog box) doesn't go away. Some print jobs, particularly those that use lots of graphics or different fonts, require several minutes to prepare on a laser printer. But sometimes the printer can become stalled in this sequence.

Solution:

Hold down ⌘. to cancel the printing job. It will probably take a few minutes. If the job doesn't cancel, or if you get impatient, shut off the laser printer and then turn it on again to clear its memory buffer. Then press ⌘. again. Once the laser printer is ready to go, try printing again.

Your document prints on the wrong printer.

Problem:

You've selected the wrong printer with the Chooser. Remember, the Chooser indicates which printer will be used for any printing job you send from your Mac, so if you chose a different printer for another program or file you were printing, that printer will continue to be used for all future print jobs until you select another printer.

Solution:

Select the Chooser from the menu, click on the icon representing the type of printer you want to use, and then (if necessary) select the specific printer of that type (if you're on a network and there is more than one printer of that type connected). (See *Using the Chooser DA*, page 69, for more information.)

Your document prints with the wrong font.

Problem:

If your document includes fonts that aren't built into the LaserWriter and you've selected the *Font Substitution* option in the LaserWriter's Page Setup dialog box, the LaserWriter will substitute some of its built-in fonts for the ones that were in your document. If your document contains the Geneva font, for example, the LaserWriter will substitute Helvetica. If your document contains the New York font, the LaserWriter will substitute Times.

If the LaserWriter can't come up with a suitable substitute, or if you haven't chosen the *Font Substitution* option, it will print a bit map of the font you're sending from your Mac. Bit-mapped fonts don't look as good as the built-in ones from your LaserWriter.

There are also times when the font you specify has the same font number as a different font stored in your System Folder. The LaserWriter selects fonts by number, so if the numbers are the same, the LaserWriter will download the font from your System Folder and use it, even if it isn't the one you specified.

Solution:

Make sure you have a copy of the printer font you want to use in the System Folder of your startup disk. That way, the LaserWriter can download it and use it if necessary. If you don't want any font substitutions, deselect the *Font Substitution* option in the LaserWriter Page Setup dialog box.

15 | Sharing files on a network

What Do I Do Now

If you're connected to an AppleTalk network and are working with files stored on network servers, you may run into some problems specific to accessing or using files on these shared disks. In this chapter, we'll discuss file sharing in general, see how you can use the Mac's system software to access shared files on a network, and then look at the most common problems you might have when doing so.

File sharing basics

Sharing files on an AppleTalk network means being able to access disks connected to other Macs on the same network. Those disks may be connected to an AppleShare file server (a Mac specifically set up to share files) or to a Mac running System 7 whose owner has decided to share files. When you're connected to a remote disk, its icon appears on your desktop just like a disk that's directly connected to your Mac.

Each Mac on a network must have a unique identity or name so that users can distinguish between them. A Mac is given a name when it's first set up to share files (see *Setting up your Mac for file sharing* on page 281.) Disks connected to these Macs must also have unique names so you can tell which is which from your remote location on the network.

The person who controls each file-sharing Mac is called the Mac's *owner* or, if the Mac is an AppleShare file server, the *AppleShare administrator*. AppleShare disks are always available on the network as long as the AppleShare server is running. Under System 7, a Mac's owner must specifically make disks available for sharing on the network. If you're using System 6, you can't make your own disks available for sharing.

Even if a disk is available on the network, though, you can't necessarily access it. Before you can access a Mac's disks, its owner must grant access privileges to you.

In addition to the Macs themselves, each folder on a shared disk has an owner—the person who created that folder or copied it to the shared disk. On most disks shared under System 7, the Mac's owner owns the majority of folders because he or she created them before deciding to share the disk. Once the disk has been shared, however, other network users who have access to it may create folders on it, which they then own.

The owner of any shared folder can control access to it by assigning it specific *access privileges.* In some folders you may grant full access (so other users can open or modify any existing file or create new ones); in other folders you might grant more restricted access (the ability to see files but not to create new ones, for example) or no access at all.

If you're an AppleShare administrator or the owner of a Mac running System 7, you give individual network users access to your disks either by making them *registered users* of that Mac, or by allowing them to connect as *guests*. A privilege assigned to a specific user only applies to that user, while one assigned to guests applies to anyone who connects to that Mac as a guest; thus the privileges you have depend on which name you use to connect to a particular Mac.

These are the basics of file sharing on the Mac. Now, let's look at how you connect to a network file server.

Choosing a network file server

When choosing a network file server, you have to enter a user name and sometimes a password to connect to the remote disk. This is true whether you're using System 6 or System 7, and whether you're connecting to an AppleShare file server or to a disk being shared from a System 7 Mac. If you're using a different type of networking software such as TOPS, the procedure is entirely different. Consult the software's manual for more information.

To choose a network file server:

1. Open the Chooser window by selecting its name from the ⬢ menu.

2. Click on the AppleShare icon. The names of all Apple-Share servers and individual Macs that are currently sharing files will appear at the right, like this:

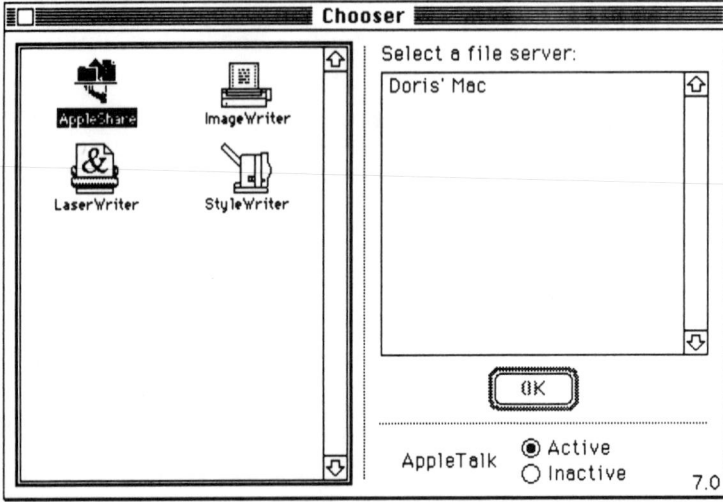

If you don't see an AppleShare icon, your Mac hasn't been set up for use with AppleShare. In this case, ask your network administrator for help.

3. Click on the name of the file server to which you want to connect. You'll see a dialog box where you can register as a user of that file server, like the one at the top of the next page:

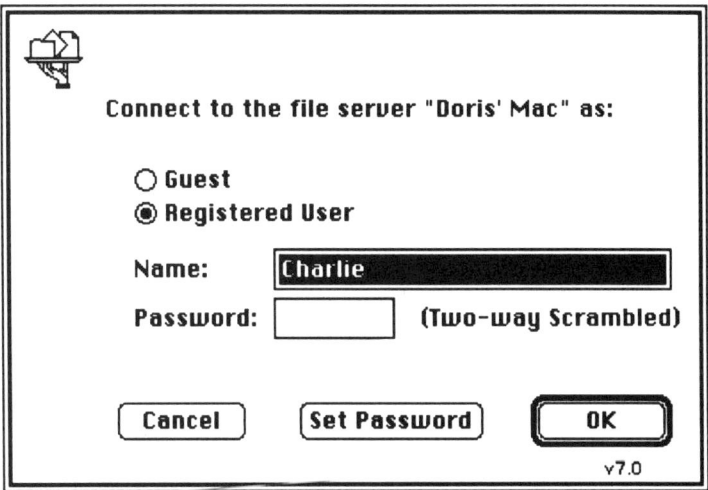

If you're a registered user of the file server, type your name (and password, if necessary). Otherwise, click the *Guest* button to register as a guest. (If you're not sure whether you're registered or if you have a password, ask the remote Mac's owner or your AppleShare administrator.)

4. Click the *OK* button to connect to the server you've selected. A list of all the disks or shared folders currently connected to the server will appear. If only one disk is connected, it will be selected automatically, as in the example at the top of the next page:

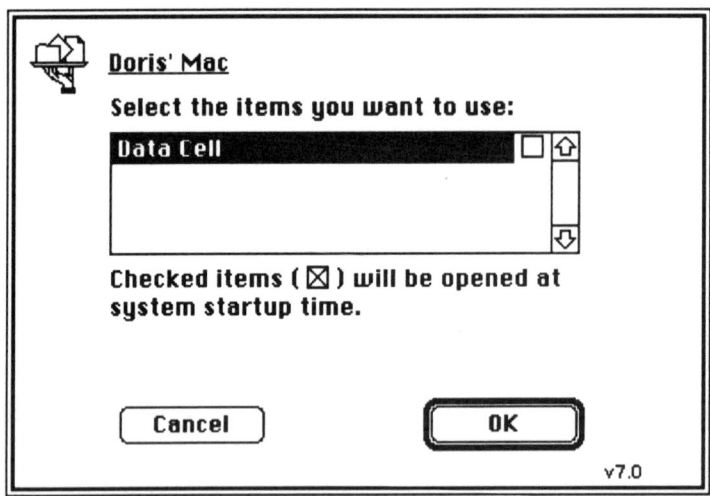

5. Select the disk or folder you want to access, and then click the *OK* button. The item's icon will appear on your desktop and you'll be returned to the Chooser window, which you can then close.

   Note: The checkbox following the item name gives you the option of connecting to the remote disk automatically each time you start your Mac. Once you've checked the checkbox, you'll see options for storing your user name and password so they're supplied automatically at startup when your Mac connects to the remote disk. For a full explanation of these options, consult a general System 7 or System 7 file sharing user's guide, or—if you're using System 6—an AppleShare user's guide.

Once you've connected to a remote disk or folder, you can access it as if it were directly connected to your own Mac; however, your ability to open files or make new folders on the shared item may be restricted, depending on how you registered as a user and which access privileges are assigned to that user name.

As a registered user, you can create folders of your own on the shared disk or folder and then control who can access them by setting access privileges. If you connect to a remote Mac as a guest, you can still create folders on the remote disk, but you can't control access to them.

Although the method for connecting to a remote server is the same under both systems, the specifics of sharing files and setting access privileges differ significantly, depending on whether you're using System 7 or System 6. In the two sections that follow, we'll cover the two versions separately.

System 7 file sharing

If you're running System 7 and you're on a network, you can make any hard disk or CD-ROM disk on your Mac available to other people on the network. (You can't share floppy disks because it takes too long to access them.) With System 7's built-in file sharing capabilities, you can share an entire disk or just the folders you specify.

Sharing files from your Mac involves five types of activities:

- setting up your Mac for file sharing
- registering users (to specify who can connect to your Mac)
- sharing disks or folders (specifying which disks or folders you want to share)
- setting access privileges (to restrict access to shared items)
- managing connected users (seeing who's connected and/or disconnecting people)

Setting up your Mac for file sharing

To set up your Mac for file sharing and turn file sharing on, the first tool you use is the Sharing Setup control panel, which looks like the one at the top of the next page:

The *Network Identity* section is where you type your name (in the Owner Name box), your password (in the Owner Password box), and a name for your Macintosh (in the Macintosh Name box). To turn on file sharing, you must enter at least your name and the name of a Mac. The password is optional, but it's a good idea to make one up and enter it here because it prevents other people from changing your Mac's file sharing options.

To turn on file sharing, click the *Start* button in the File Sharing area. After a few seconds, the button name will change to *Stop* and the Status area will report that file sharing is on.

The *Program Linking* area of the Sharing Setup control panel turns on System 7's program linking feature. This feature must be implemented by individual applications before you can take advantage of it. At this writing, no programs have incorporated program linking, but when they do, you'll have to turn the feature on here.

Registering users

If you want to share your Mac's files with specific people on your network and assign different access privileges to those people, you need to register them by name. For this purpose, you use the Users & Groups control panel, which looks like this:

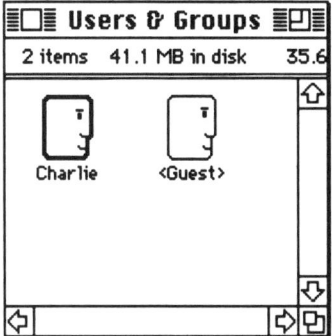

When this control panel is open, commands called *New User* and *New Group* appear on the File menu.

To register a new user, choose the *New User* command or press ⌘N. A new user icon will appear in the control panel with the name *New User*. You can then change the icon's name to one that identifies the person you're registering.

To give a user a password, double-click on his or her icon. A dialog box will appear in which you can either enter a password or click a checkbox that will prevent the user from connecting to your Mac.

Groups are collections of users who all have the same access privileges for a given shared item. Granting privileges to a group gives more than one user, but not all users, access to an item. For example, everyone in a group called *Marketing* might have access to a folder called *Sales,* while users who weren't in that group would not.

To register a new group, choose the *New Groups* command from the File menu. A *New Group* icon will appear in the Users & Groups control panel. You can rename the icon if you like. To add users to a group, just drag their icons onto the group icon.

To delete users from a group, double-click on the group icon to open it and then drag the user icons from the group's window into the Trash. To delete an entire group, just drag its icon to the Trash.

Once you've registered users or groups, you can assign them specific access privileges with the *Sharing...* command.

Sharing disks or folders

As we've mentioned, System 7 lets you share individual folders or whole disks, but before you can share disks or folders from your own Mac, you must turn on file sharing using the Sharing Setup control panel (see *Setting up your Mac for file sharing* on page 281). Once file sharing is on, follow these steps to share an item from your Mac:

1. Select the item by clicking on its name or icon.

2. Choose the *Sharing...* command from the File menu in the Finder. You'll see a window like this one:

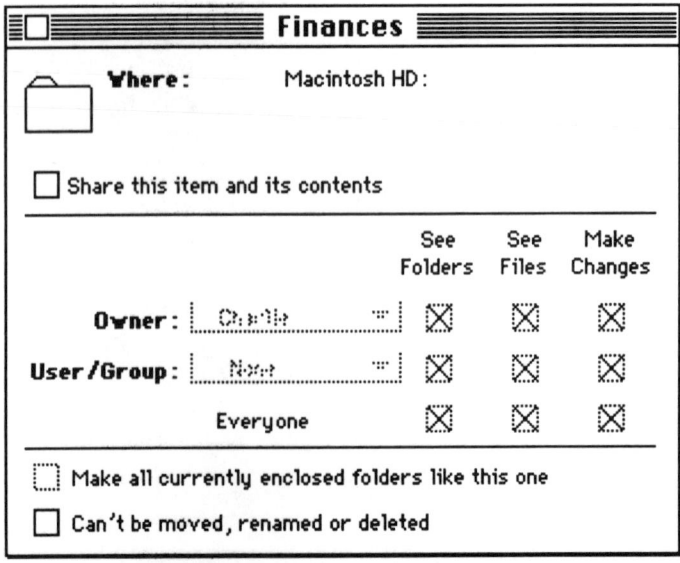

The sharing window has the name of the folder or disk you selected. The item's type is indicated by an icon at the top left corner of the window (in this case, a folder).

3. Click the *Share this item and its contents* checkbox. The access privileges options in the middle of the window become active, and you can change them if you like. (See *Setting access privileges* below.)

4. If you want all the folders within the current folder to have the same access privileges it had, check the *Make all currently enclosed folders like this one* checkbox. Otherwise, items inside the current folder will retain whatever privileges were originally assigned to them.

5. Check the *Can't be moved, renamed or deleted* checkbox if you want to lock the folder or disk so other users can't rearrange or rename it or throw it away. It's a good idea to check this box so that you're the only person who can make such changes.

6. Once the access privileges and other checkboxes are the way you want them, close the sharing window. You'll see an alert asking you to confirm changes to the folder's access privileges, like this:

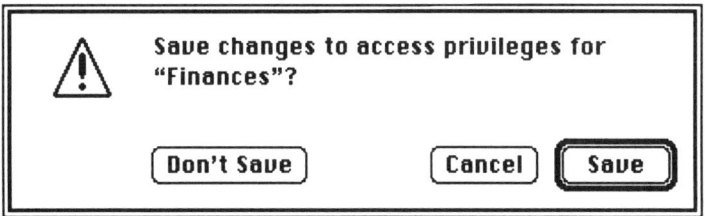

7. Click the *Save* button. The folder will now be available to other users on the network.

Setting access privileges

As mentioned in step three above, clicking the checkbox to share an item activates the access privileges options in the middle of the sharing window, as shown here:

```
┌──────────────────────────────────────────────────┐
│ ▤□▤▤▤▤▤▤ Shared Stuff ▤▤▤▤▤▤▤▤▤ │
│ ┌────────────────────────────────────────────────┐│
│ │ ┌───┐  Where :      Macintosh HD : Shared Stuff ││
│ │ │   │                                           ││
│ │ └───┘                                           ││
│ │                                                 ││
│ │ ☒ Share this item and its contents              ││
│ │                                                 ││
│ │                       See    See    Make        ││
│ │                     Folders  Files  Changes     ││
│ │   Owner : │ Charlie      ▼│  ☒     ☒     ☒      ││
│ │ User/Group : │ <None>     ▼│  ☒    ☒     ☒       ││
│ │               Everyone      ☒     ☒     ☒        ││
│ │ ┌─────────────────────────────────────────────┐ ││
│ │ │ ☐ Make all enclosed folders like this one   │ ││
│ │ │ ☐ Can't be moved, renamed or deleted        │ ││
│ └─────────────────────────────────────────────────┘│
└──────────────────────────────────────────────────┘
```

You can set separate privileges for the item's owner (yourself), for a particular user or group name you've registered, and for Everyone (for anyone who connects to your Mac, either as a registered user or as a guest). When someone connects to your Mac over the network and selects this item to share, the privileges they have will depend on how the checkboxes are set and what name they've used. Select the name of the user or group whose privileges you want to set from the User/Group pop-up menu.

The checkboxes in the See Folders, See Files and Make Changes columns of the sharing window grant different types of access to the shared item. The See Folders level allows others to see any folders contained in the current folder. The See Files level allows others to view, open and copy data files and applications in the folder. The Make Changes level allows others to change files in the folder, create new ones or make new folders.

You can use the checkboxes in any combination. When a box is checked, that privilege is granted; when it is unchecked, the privilege is withheld.

For example, if only the *Make Changes* boxes are checked, others on the network will be able to save new files to the folder, but they won't be able to open the folder and see its contents. (You might use this setup when you want others to save new files to a folder that contains private items.) If you check only the *See Files* boxes, others will be able to see and open files in the folder but they won't be allowed to save new files to it. (You could use this option if your folder contained standard documents that you wanted others on the network to use, but not change.)

In the sharing window shown above everything is checked, so anyone who shares this item can do anything with it. These options are set this way by default when you first share an item; to restrict access, you must uncheck some of the boxes.

Make sure you uncheck boxes in the Everyone row if you're going to uncheck them in the User/Group row. If you only uncheck boxes in the User/Group row, everyone on the network will still have access, because the Everyone boxes are checked.

Viewing sharing information

You can also use the *Sharing...* command to view a shared item's status at any time, whether the shared item is on your own disk or on one you're connected to over the network. To see a shared item's information, select it on the desktop and choose the *Sharing...* command. If you own the shared item, you'll see a sharing window like the one in the previous section. If someone else owns the item and it's located elsewhere on the network, its sharing window will look something like the one at the top of the next page:

This window shows you where the shared item is located (in this case, on the *Data Cell* disk connected to *Doris' Mac*); the user name you've used to connect to that Mac (in this case you're connected as a guest); and the access privileges you have for that item. Because you don't own the item, all the access options in the middle and bottom of the window are dimmed, and you can't change them. Also, there are no checkboxes for sharing or locking the item because only the item's owner can set these options.

Managing connected users

To find out which other network users are connected to your Mac, or to disconnect a user, use the File Sharing Monitor control panel, which looks like the one at the top of the next page:

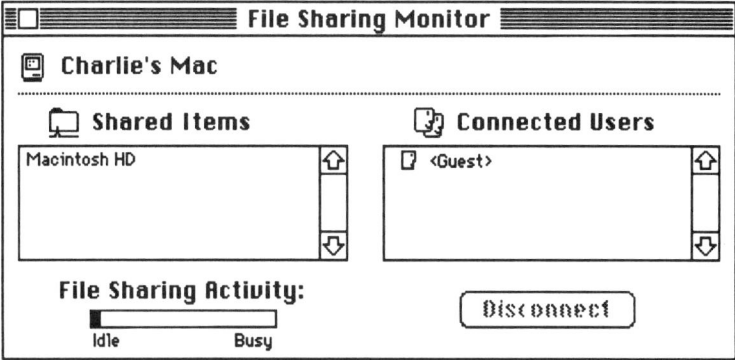

If other users are connected to your Mac, their names will appear in the Connected Users list on the right. (In this example, the only user who is currently connected has registered as a guest.)

In addition to seeing who's connected to your Mac, you can use this control panel to disconnect users. Just select the user's name in the Connected User list and click the *Disconnect* button in the lower-right corner. Before this change takes effect, you'll be given a chance to notify users that they're about to be disconnected.

System 6 file sharing

Under System 6, you can't share files from your own disk on the network. You can connect to remote file servers, but your Mac must have AppleShare workstation software installed. This software comes with system versions 6.0.4 and later, and with the AppleShare server software package. It adds the Access Privileges DA to the menu and the *Get Privileges* command to the File menu in the Finder. It also puts the AppleShare driver in the System Folder so you can select it in the Chooser window.

Once your Mac has been set up as an AppleShare work-station, you can connect to AppleShare file servers or to disks or folders that have been shared on the network by System 7 Macs. If you connect to a shared disk as a registered user, any folders you create on that disk will be available only to you—no user on the network will be able to open these folders or change their contents except for the administrator of the AppleShare server or the owner of the System 7 Mac that's sharing the disk. (These people have full access privileges for your folders and can even reassign ownership of them to someone else.) If you connect as a guest, folders you create will be available to anyone on the network and you won't be able to restrict access to them.

To make a folder you create on a shared disk available to others, you must change its access privileges using either the *Get Privileges* command or the Access Privileges DA. If you're using MultiFinder, you'll only be able to use the *Get Privileges* command; if you're using the Finder, you can use the Access Privileges DA so you can view or change privileges without quitting the program you're running.

Using the Get Privileges command

To view a folder or disk's privileges, select it and then choose *Get Privileges* from the File menu. Provided you're the folder's owner, you'll see a dialog box like the one at the top of the next page:

```
┌──────────────────────────────────────────┐
│ ▤□▤▤▤▤▤▤  Access Privileges ▤▤▤▤▤▤▤▤ │
├──────────────────────────────────────────┤
│                          Locked ☐        │
│    ┌──┐                                   │
│    │  │    Charlie                        │
│    └──┘                                   │
│    Where: The Server, File Server: Water  │
│           Fountain                        │
│                                           │
│  Logged on as: Charlie                    │
│     Privileges: See Folders, See Files,   │
│                 Make Changes              │
│  ......................................   │
│     Owner: [Charlie              ]        │
│                                           │
│     Group: [                     ]        │
│  ......................................   │
│                Owner  Group Everyone      │
│   See Folders:   ☒     ☐     ☐           │
│     See Files:   ☒     ☐     ☐           │
│  Make Changes:   ☒     ☐     ☐           │
│     Change All Enclosed Folders: ☐        │
│  ......................................   │
│    ┌───────────┐   ┌───────────────┐      │
│    │   Undo    │   │    Save       │      │
│    └───────────┘   └───────────────┘      │
└──────────────────────────────────────────┘
```

This example shows the privileges settings for an item that has just been created on a shared disk. Notice that only the item's owner (Charlie) has access to it. You can click the other checkboxes to assign privileges to a particular group of users or to everyone on the network.

If you don't own the folder, the *Get Privileges* command displays this smaller dialog box, which doesn't allow you to view or change any privileges:

```
┌──────────────────────────────────────────┐
│ ▤□▤▤▤▤  Access Privileges ▤▤▤▤▤▤▤▤▤▤ │
├──────────────────────────────────────────┤
│                          Locked ☐        │
│    ┌──┐                                   │
│    │  │    Consul agreements/Props        │
│    └──┘                                   │
│    Where: The Server, File Server: Water  │
│           Fountain                        │
│                                           │
│  Logged on as: Lucinda                    │
│     Privileges: No Privileges             │
│  ......................................   │
│                                           │
│     Owner:  Kim                           │
│                                           │
│     Group:                                │
│                                           │
└──────────────────────────────────────────┘
```

This dialog box tells you whether the folder is locked, where it is located, what guest or user you're logged on as, what your access privileges are, who the folder's owner is and which group of users, if any, has access to it.

The options for locking folders and setting access privileges in the Get Privileges dialog box are the same as those described for the *Sharing...* command under System 7. See *Sharing disks or folders* on page 284 and *Setting access privileges* on page 286 of this chapter for more information on these options.

If you're a folder's owner and you want to change its access privileges, reset them by clicking the checkboxes in the lower part of the dialog box. To reset the access privileges for any folders contained inside the current folder, click the *Change All Enclosed Folders* checkbox at the bottom of the dialog box. Then all folders inside the current one will have the same privileges it has.

When you're finished, click the *Save* button to reset the folder privileges and click the close box to put away the Get Privileges dialog box. The changes you've made will take effect immediately.

As you work with an AppleShare file server or other shared disk, you'll probably use the *Get Privileges* command a lot. Every new folder you create on an AppleShare server is only available to you, and every new folder you create on a disk that's connected to a Mac running System 7 is available only to you and the shared disk's owner until you use *Get Privileges* to make them available to other users on the network.

Using the Access Privileges DA

If your Mac is set up to use AppleShare, you also have an Access Privileges DA on your menu. This DA serves the same purpose as the *Get Privileges* command—it lets you change user access to folders on an AppleShare file server. The main difference between the two is that the Access Privileges DA only works under the Finder—you can't use it with MultiFinder. When you're using MultiFinder, you must switch to the Finder from whatever other program you're running and use the *Get Privileges* command.

To use the Access Privileges DA:

1. Choose *Access Privileges* from the menu. The Mac displays a file navigation box that lets you select the folder whose privileges you want to view, like this:

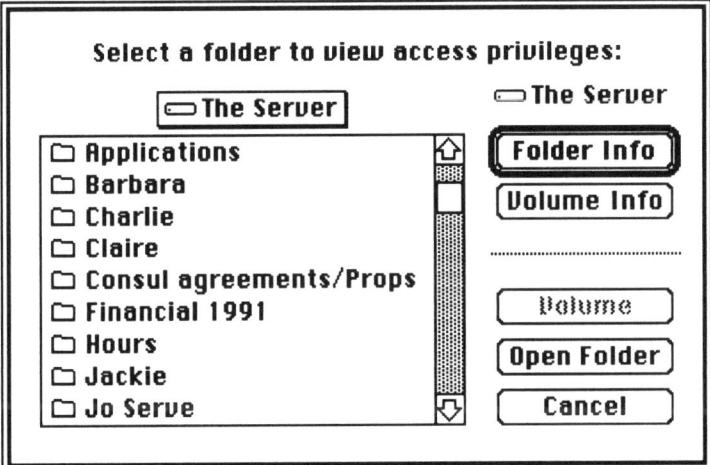

2. From the list in the box, select the folder whose privileges you want to view.

3. Click the *Folder Info* button to view or change the folder's privileges. The Mac displays a dialog box like the one at the top of the next page:

```
┌──────────────────────────────────────────────────────────┐
│ □              Access Privileges                          │
│  ┌──┐                                              v2.0.1 │
│  │  │  Financial 1991                                      │
│  └──┘      On volume:  The Server                          │
│        Logged in as:  Charlie                              │
│   Your privileges are:  See Folders, See Files, Make Changes │
│  ......................................................... │
│  □ Locked   Owner:  ┌────────────────────────────────────┐│
│                     │ Charlie                            │ │
│                     └────────────────────────────────────┘│
│            Group:   ┌────────────────────────────────────┐│
│                     │                                    │ │
│                     └────────────────────────────────────┘│
│     See Folders:  ⊠ Owner    □ Group    □ Everyone        │
│       See Files:  ⊠ Owner    □ Group    □ Everyone        │
│    Make Changes:  ⊠ Owner    □ Group    □ Everyone        │
│  ......................................................... │
│   ┌──────────┐    ┌──────────┐    ┌────────────────┐       │
│   │  Undo    │    │   Save   │    │  View Another  │       │
│   └──────────┘    └──────────┘    └────────────────┘       │
└──────────────────────────────────────────────────────────┘
```

(If you aren't the folder's owner, you'll see a smaller dialog box that won't let you reset the access privileges.)

4. Reset the folder's access privileges by clicking the options you want to change, and then click the *Save* button to save the changes.

5. Click the *View Another* button to view or change the privileges on another folder, or click the close box to close this dialog box.

As with the *Get Privileges* command, any changes you make with the Access Privileges DA occur immediately.

You may have noticed that there isn't a *Change All Enclosed Folders* option in this dialog box as there is in the Get Privileges dialog box. Instead, you have to change the privileges for each folder individually. If you want to reset the privileges for a whole group of folders contained inside another folder, it's easier to switch to the Finder and use the *Get Privileges* command to change them all at once.

Now that we've covered the Mac's software tools and options for working with shared files, let's look at some common error messages or problems you're likely to encounter as you use shared files on a network.

Solving common networking problems

■ SYSTEM 7 ONLY

Problem:

You've chosen the *Sharing...* command in order to share a selected disk or folder, but you haven't turned on file sharing with the Sharing Setup control panel. Before you can share anything you must turn on file sharing, so the Mac is giving you a chance to do so.

Solution:

Click the *OK* button to open the Sharing Setup control panel so you can turn file sharing on or click *Cancel* to give up trying to share the item.

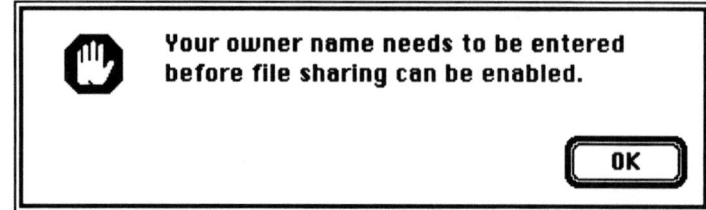

Your owner name needs to be entered before file sharing can be enabled.

OK

■ SYSTEM 7 ONLY

Problem:

You've clicked the *Start* button to turn on file sharing in the Sharing Setup control panel, but you haven't entered a Macintosh Name and Owner Name in the Network Identity area of the dialog box.

Solution:

Click the *OK* button, type names in the Macintosh Name and Owner Name boxes and then click *Start* to turn on file sharing.

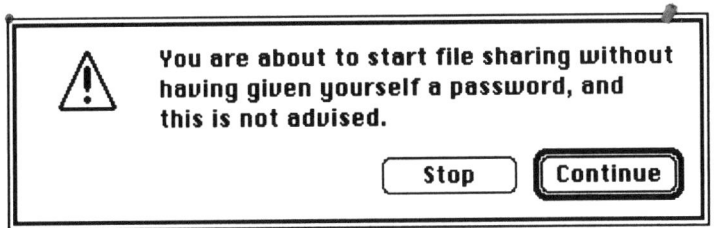

■ SYSTEM 7 ONLY

Problem:

You've entered a Macintosh Name and Owner Name in the boxes in the Sharing Setup control panel and have clicked the *Start* button to turn on File Sharing, but you haven't entered a password in the Password box, and the Mac is letting you know this.

Solution:

A password isn't required for you to start up file sharing. Click the *Continue* button to turn on file sharing without a password, or click *Stop* to go back and enter a password in the Password box. The password protects your Mac so nobody else can share disks or folders when you're not there (they'll need a password before they can turn on file sharing). If you don't care about this, you don't need a password.

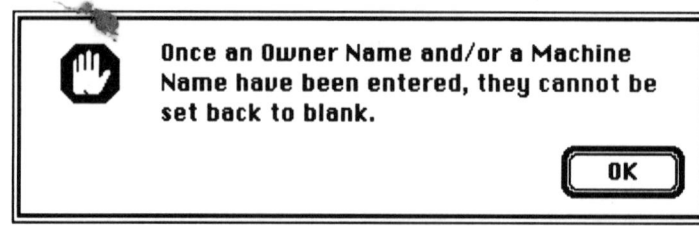

Once an Owner Name and/or a Machine Name have been entered, they cannot be set back to blank.

[OK]

■ SYSTEM 7 ONLY

Problem:

You've deleted the Owner Name and/or Mac Name from the Sharing Setup control panel and now you're trying to close it. Once you've entered a Mac Name and Owner Name, the names can only be changed—they can't be eliminated.

Solution:

Click the *OK* button and type a name of some sort in the Owner Name and Macintosh Name boxes; then close the control panel.

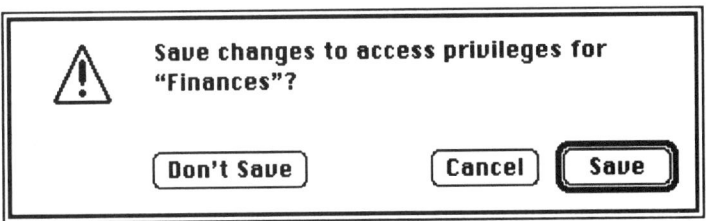

■ SYSTEM 7 VERSION

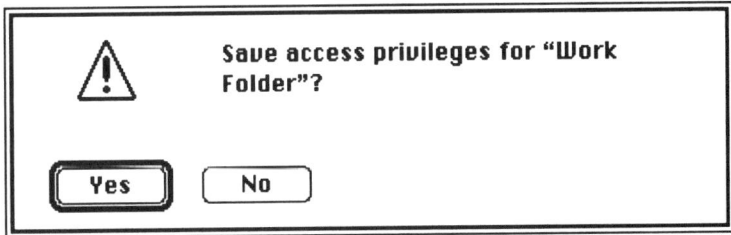

■ SYSTEM 6 VERSION

Problem:

You've made a change to the access privileges for a shared folder or disk, and you're trying to close the sharing window (in System 7) or the access privileges dialog box (in System 6). The Mac is asking if you want to save the changes you've made.

Solution:

If you want to save the changes you've made, click *Save* or press Return. If you want to close the dialog box or window and return to the desktop without making any changes in the item's access privileges, click *Don't Save* or *No*. If you want to return to the access privileges dialog box or window to view the current settings or make more changes, click *Cancel*.

You've set access privileges to prevent a certain user or group from accessing a folder or disk, but that user or group still has access.

Problem:

When you set access privileges to restrict access to a shared item, denying privileges to one particular user or group doesn't do any good unless you also deny them to Everyone in the access privileges window. Here's an example:

```
┌─────────────────────── Finances ═══════════════════════╗
│                                                          │
│   ┌──┐    Where:        Macintosh HD:                    │
│   │  │                                                   │
│   └──┘                                                   │
│          Inside:        Macintosh HD                     │
│   ─────────────────────────────────────────────────     │
│   ☐ Same as enclosing folder        See    See    Make   │
│                                    Folders  Files Changes │
│                                                           │
│     Owner: [ Charlie      ▼]        ☒      ☒      ☒       │
│  User/Group: [ Doris      ▼]        ☐      ☐      ☐       │
│              Everyone               ☒      ☒      ☒       │
│   ─────────────────────────────────────────────────     │
│   ☐ Make all currently enclosed folders like this one    │
│   ☐ Can't be moved, renamed or deleted                   │
└──────────────────────────────────────────────────────────┘
```

In this sharing window, none of the access boxes is checked for the user named Doris. At first glance, you might think that Doris wouldn't have any access to this folder. But since all the access options are checked for Everyone, Doris can access the folder just like anyone else. The Everyone category of privileges is the lowest common denominator, so these privileges must be at least as restrictive as those for any user or group whose access you want to limit.

Solution:

When using the sharing or access privileges window to restrict the access of a particular user or group, make sure you also restrict the privileges for the Everyone category.

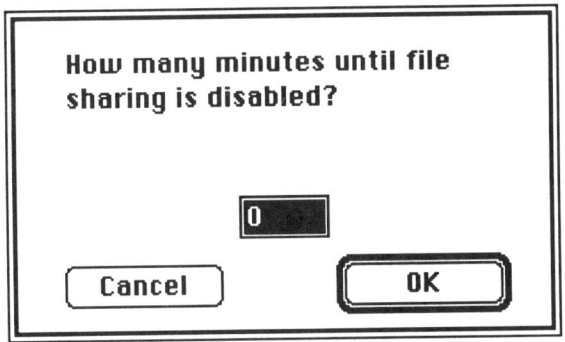

■ SYSTEM 7 ONLY

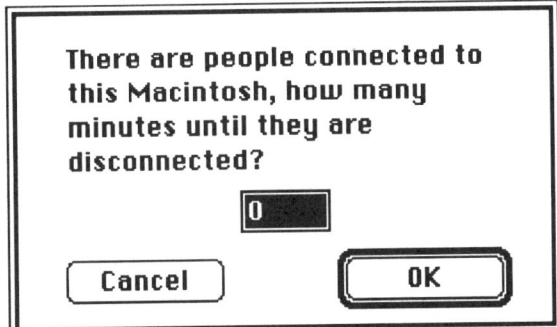

■ SYSTEM 7 ONLY

Problem:

You've shared disks or folders from your Mac, and now you're trying to shut down, turn off file sharing, or disconnect users. These dialog boxes give you the chance to warn other users on the network that your Mac is about to become disconnected as a server.

Solution:

Type in the number of minutes you want to elapse before your Mac shuts down and then click the *OK* button—or click the *Cancel* button to discontinue the operation. When you type in a number and click *OK*, other users on the network will see a message on their screens telling them that your Mac is about to shut down. Once your Mac or its file sharing feature actually turns off, the other users will see a message saying that this has happened.

As a matter of network courtesy, you should give other users at least a minute's warning before you disconnect them, shut off file sharing or shut down your Mac. That way, they can save any open files they're using and remove any shared items from their desktops by dragging those items into the Trash.

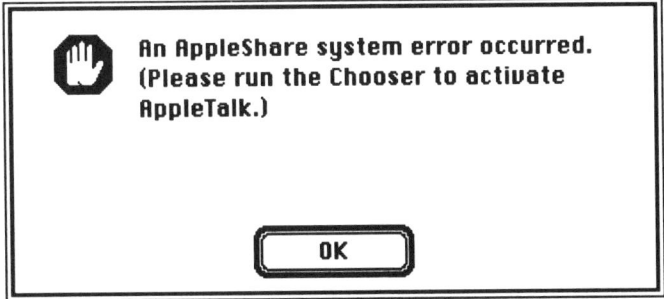

■ SYSTEM 7 VERSION

■ SYSTEM 6 VERSION

Problem:

Basically, you're trying to access an AppleTalk device but you don't have AppleTalk set to *Active* in the Chooser window. On System 7 Macs, you can get the above message during start up if the Mac is connected to an AppleTalk network but AppleTalk has been turned off in the Chooser window. Under System 6, you can get the message when you click on the AppleShare icon or a networked LaserWriter icon in the Chooser window, but you haven't made AppleTalk active by clicking the AppleTalk *Active* button. Finally, you can get one of these messages when you've clicked the AppleTalk *Active* button in the Chooser but you have something other than a network cable (like a StyleWriter cable) connected to your printer port, so the Mac won't let you activate AppleTalk.

Note: Some communications devices that allow remote connections to an AppleTalk network over telephone lines, such as the Shiva NetModem or Hayes Interbridge, come with software that fools the Mac into thinking its printer port is connected to AppleTalk when it actually isn't. Sometimes, the Mac gets really confused by this software.

Solutions:

First click the *OK* button. If you're not returned to the Chooser window, open the Chooser and then click the AppleTalk *Active* button to turn on AppleTalk. If you still get the error message, try one of the following:

- **If you're not trying to connect to a shared device from a remote location** via a modem and telephone line, make sure you have an AppleTalk network cable or the interface cable for an AppleTalk network device firmly plugged into your printer port.

- **If you're trying to log onto an AppleTalk network from a remote location via a modem and telephone line,** make sure the software for the AppleTalk network bridge is correctly installed in your System Folder. If it is, disconnect anything that is currently connected to your printer port, restart the Mac, open the Chooser and then choose the AppleTalk *Active* option again.

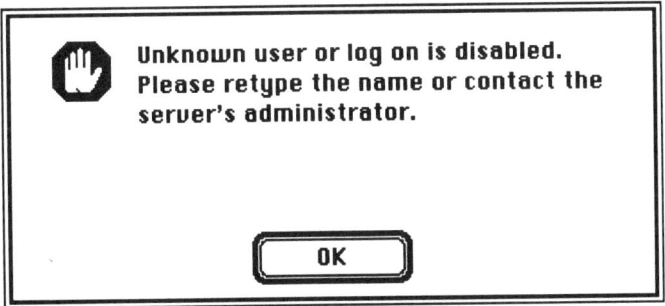

Problem:

You've tried to log onto a shared disk with a user name that isn't registered on that server or file-sharing Mac.

Solution:

Click the *OK* button.

- **If you know you're a registered user** of the network, try typing the name again. Make sure you don't add any extra spaces or punctuation—the Mac is particular about these things.

- **If you don't have a registered user name,** choose the option to connect as a guest. You'll be able to create folders and save files to the server, but you won't be able to restrict access to folders you create.

Problem:

You've typed an incorrect password while trying to connect to a shared disk.

Solution:

Click the *OK* button.

- **If you know the password,** be sure you type it exactly as it was given to you. Don't add any extra spaces or punctuation —the Mac is particular about these things. Also, make sure you're using the correct password for the user name that appears above the Password box on the screen.

- **If you've forgotten the password,** ask the AppleShare server's administrator or the owner of the Mac that's sharing the item to tell you what it is.

- **If you don't know the password** and nobody will tell you what it is, you can log onto the shared disk as a guest. You'll be able to create folders and save files to the server, but you won't be able to restrict access to folders you create.

- **If you set the password yourself** and you don't remember it, you'll have to ask the AppleShare administrator or the owner of the Mac that's sharing the item to delete your user name and then register you as a user again, so you can enter a new password.

  When you delete your user name from the AppleShare server or file-sharing Mac, the ownership of any folders you created on those shared disks will be reassigned to the AppleShare administrator or Mac owner. That means that once you are reregistered as a user (so you can set a new password for yourself), you'll have to ask the AppleShare administrator or shared Mac's owner to transfer ownership of those folders back to you. Obviously, all of this is a real pain in the neck, so the moral is: *don't forget your password!*

The shared disk's icon doesn't appear on your desktop.

Problem:

You haven't connected to the shared disk from your Mac. To have access to a shared disk, you must first connect to it (see *Choosing a network file server* on page 277).

Solution:

Follow the instructions on page 277, or ask your AppleShare administrator or the local network guru to show you how to connect.

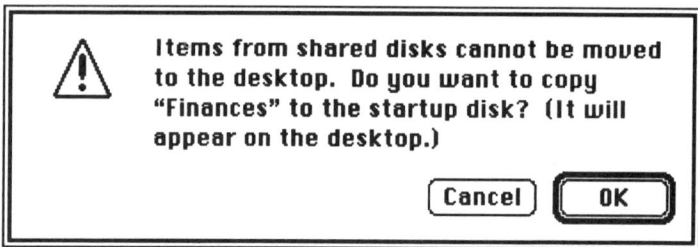

■ SYSTEM 7 VERSION

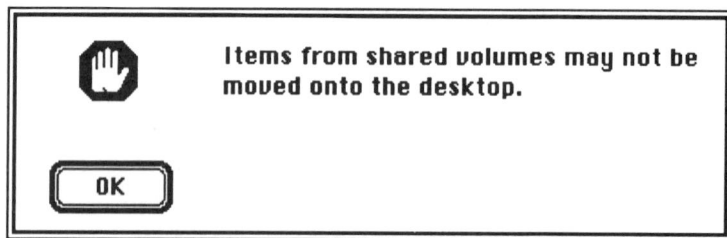

■ SYSTEM 6 VERSION

Problem:

You're trying to drag a folder or file from a shared disk's window onto your desktop. The Mac doesn't allow you to do this. If you're using System 7, the Mac will offer to copy the item to your startup disk.

Solution:

Click the *OK* button. If you want to put a file or folder from a shared disk onto your desktop, you must first copy that file or folder to a disk directly connected to your Mac. (Clicking the *OK* button under System 7 automatically copies the item to your startup disk.)

If the Mac won't let you copy the file or folder, it's because you don't have the access privileges required to do so. In that case, select the file or folder, choose the *Sharing...* command (in System 7) or the *Get Privileges* command (in System 6) to find out who owns the file or folder, and then ask that person to change the privileges so you can copy it.

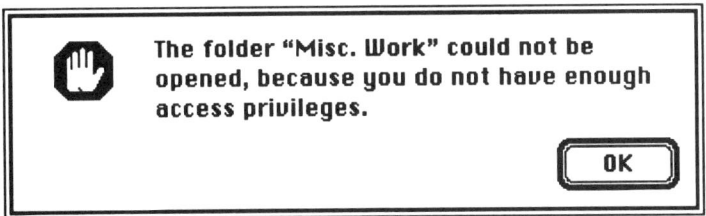

■ SYSTEM 7 VERSION

■ SYSTEM 6 VERSION

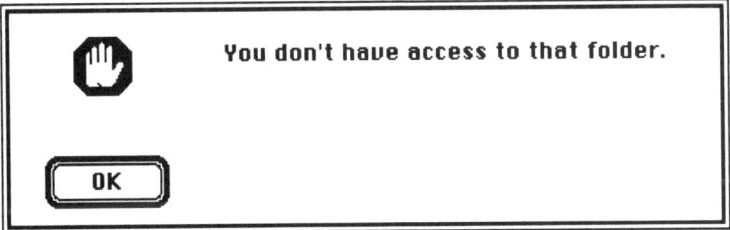

■ SYSTEM 6 VERSION

Problem:

All these messages mean you're trying to open a folder or disk, and you don't have the See Folders or See Files privileges that you need to open it.

Solution:

Ask the folder's owner, the file-sharing Mac's owner, or the AppleShare server's administrator to change the disk or folder's access privileges so you can open it. You can see who owns the item by selecting it and then choosing the *Sharing...* command (in System 7) or the *Get Privileges* command (in System 6) from the File menu in the Finder.

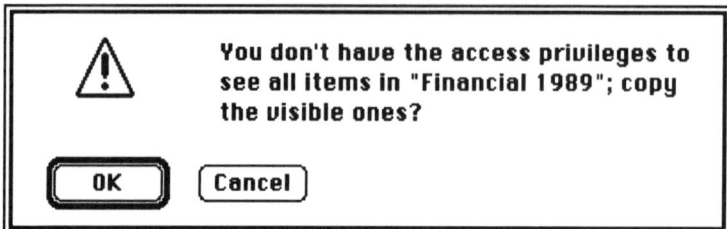

Problem:

You're trying to copy a shared folder for which you have only See Folders privileges. With these privileges, you can't see the files stored within the folder. The Mac won't let you copy files that you aren't allowed to see (because copying them to your own disk would enable you to see them and thus violate the security of the access privileges), so it's asking you if you want to copy only the folders you can see.

Solution:

Click the *OK* button to copy the folders you're allowed to see, or click the *Cancel* button to cancel the copy operation.

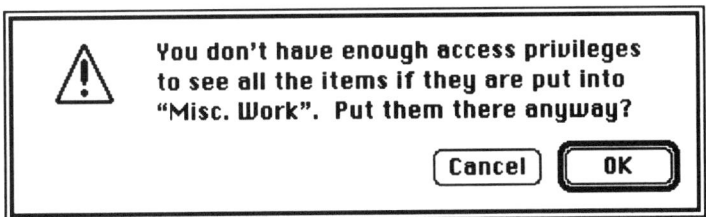

■ SYSTEM 7 VERSION

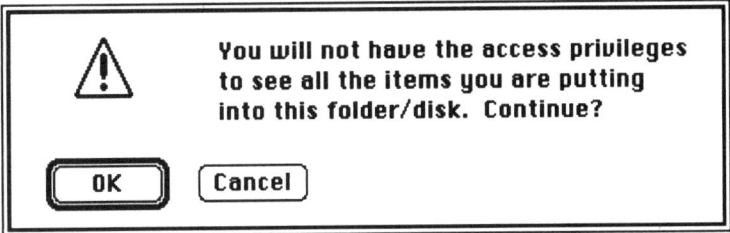

■ SYSTEM 6 VERSION

Problem:

You're saving some folders and files to a shared folder for which you don't have See Files privileges. Without these privileges, you won't be able to see the files you save. (See the sections on file sharing at the beginning of this chapter.)

Solution:

If you don't care that you can't see the files you save to that folder, click the *OK* button. If you want to be able to see the files, click the *Cancel* button to return to the desktop, and then ask the folder's owner to change your access privileges to See Files.

You cannot duplicate in the folder
"Finances", because you do not have the
privilege to make changes.

OK

■ SYSTEM 7 VERSION

 You cannot copy "Budget 91" onto the
folder "Financial Tools", because you do
not have the privilege to make changes.

OK

■ SYSTEM 7 VERSION

 You cannot move "Budget 91" from the
folder "Finances", because you do not
have the privilege to make changes.

OK

■ SYSTEM 7 VERSION

 You do not have the access privileges
to make changes to that disk/folder.

OK

■ SYSTEM 6 VERSION

■ SYSTEM 6 VERSION

Problem:

All these messages indicate the same thing: you're trying to make changes to a shared folder or disk for which you don't have Make Changes privileges. Any of the above operations, such as duplicating items, moving items, or saving new items to a folder would change the folder you're working in, and you don't have the privileges you need to do this.

Solution:

Click the *OK* button, and either give up the operation or ask the folder's owner to change its privileges so you can make changes. You can find out who owns the folder by selecting the folder and choosing the *Sharing...* command (under System 7) or the *Get Privileges* command (under System 6). (See the beginning of this chapter for more information.)

■ SYSTEM 6 ONLY

Problem:

You're trying to save a file to a folder on a shared disk, and the folder already contains a file with the same name as the one you're trying to save, but you don't have permission to replace the existing file. (You probably don't have See Files or Make Changes privileges.) See the beginning of this chapter for more information.

Solution:

Click the *OK* button, and either change the name of the file you're trying to save or have the folder's owner change the access privileges so you can replace it.

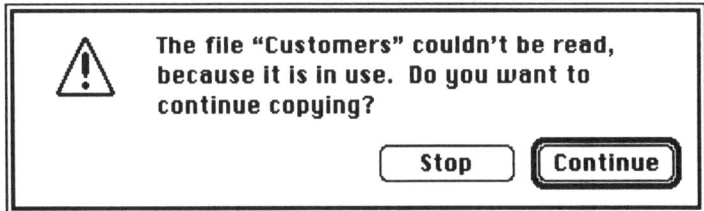

■ SYSTEM 7 VERSION

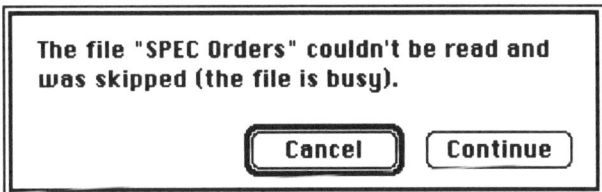

■ SYSTEM 6 VERSION

Problem:

You've tried to copy a file from a shared disk, but the file is in use and the Mac can't copy it. This problem will occur with files that lock themselves upon being opened to prevent more than one user from using them at a time.

Solution:

If you're only copying one file, click the *Stop* or *Cancel* button, wait until the file is closed by whoever's using it, and then copy it. If you know who's using the file, ask him or her to close it. If you're copying a group of files, click the *Continue* button to copy the other files in the group, and wait until later to copy the file that's busy.

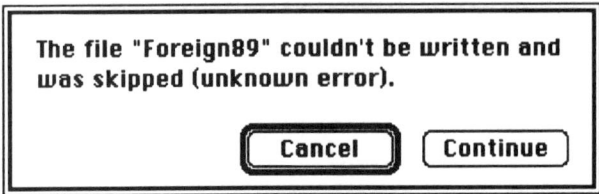

Problem:

You've tried to copy a file from a shared disk but for some rea-son, the Mac can't manage the copy. This usually happens when you're copying a particularly large file (or a large group of files) over a busy network. It's a temporary problem.

Solution:

If you're copying a group of files, click the *Continue* button to give the Mac a chance to copy the rest of the files in the group. You may see the alert message again as the Mac tries and fails to copy other files in the group. Once the Mac has tried to copy all the files in the group, check the destination disk and see how many of them were copied; then try copying those that were skipped. If you're copying a particularly large group of files, try copying them in smaller groups, or remember the names of the files that are being skipped and copy them individually.

If you're only copying one file, click the *Cancel* button and then try the copy again. You may have to try it two or three times, but if you persevere, the Mac will finally make the copy.

■ SYSTEM 6 ONLY

Problem:

You have selected the Access Privileges DA, but you aren't connected to an AppleShare file server. Since the only use for the Access Privileges DA is to view or change the access privileges for folders on an AppleShare server, you must be connected to a server to use it.

Solution:

Click the *OK* button, and then use the Chooser DA to locate and log onto an AppleShare file server. (See *Choosing a network file server* on page 277 for more information.)

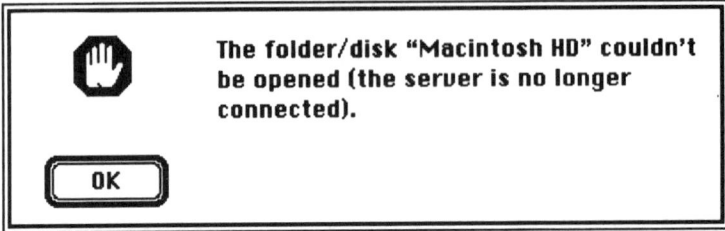

■ SYSTEM 7 VERSION

■ SYSTEM 6 VERSION

Problem:

You were connected to a shared disk, but the disk has become disconnected. There are several possibilities—the Mac's network cable may have come loose, the file-sharing Mac's owner may have turned off file sharing or has disconnected you as a user, or the file-sharing Mac or AppleShare server may have been shut off.

Solution:

Click the *OK* button, and report the problem to the owner of the file-sharing Mac or the AppleShare server administrator. If you want to try fixing it yourself, check the cable connecting your Mac to the network and make sure both ends are plugged in securely. The network cable for your Mac should be plugged into your Mac's printer port. If you still can't see the shared disk when you click on the AppleShare icon in the Chooser window, ask the shared disk's owner or administrator to check its connections and operation, to make sure you're allowed to connect to that Mac, and—if it's a file-sharing Mac under System 7—to verify that file sharing is on.

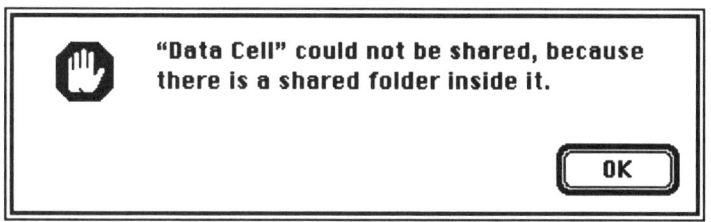

■ SYSTEM 7 ONLY

Problem:

You're trying to share an entire disk with System 7's *Sharing...*
command, but you've already shared a folder inside that disk.

Solution:

Select the folder inside the disk that's currently being shared,
choose the *Sharing...* command and uncheck the *Share this item
and its contents* checkbox in the Sharing window. Then select the
disk icon itself and share it. (See *Sharing disks or folders* on page
284.) If you're not sure which folder on the disk is being shared,
you'll have to check them out individually by selecting them
one at a time and then choosing the *Sharing...* command.

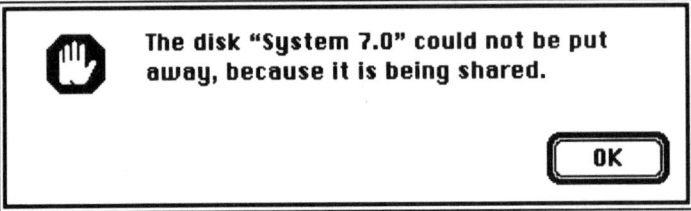

■ SYSTEM 7 ONLY

Problem:

You're trying to drag a disk icon into the Trash while the disk or a folder inside it is currently being shared.

Solution:

Select the folder inside the disk that's being shared, choose the *Sharing...* command, and uncheck the *Share this item and its contents* checkbox in the Sharing window. Then, drag the disk icon into the Trash.

Note that this technique doesn't always work for CD-ROM disks. If it fails, try turning file sharing off completely with the Sharing Setup control panel. If this doesn't work, you'll have to restart the Mac before you can eject the disk.

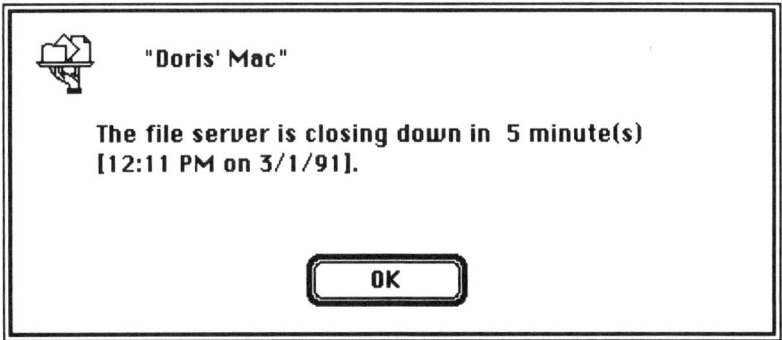

Problem:

You'll see this message on your Mac when another Mac that's sharing files on the network (either a System 7 Mac or an AppleShare server) is about to disconnect or shut down.

Solution:

Click the *OK* button to make the message go away, then save or close any files from the shared disk that you have open and drag the shared disk's icon into the Trash to break the connection from your end.

Problem:

This message just lets you know that this particular server or file-sharing Mac has closed down, and you've been disconnected from its disk(s).

Solution:

Click the *OK* button to put the message away.

Alert message locator

Page numbers followed by [6] or [7] refer to material pertaining only to System 6 or System 7 respectively.

Index

Page numbers followed by [6] or [7] refer to material pertaining only to System 6 or System 7 respectively.

32-bit addressing,   66

A

Aask,   134
Access Privileges DA
  problems using,   317 [6]
  using,   292–294 [6]
ADB. *See* Apple desktop bus
alert boxes described, 44–45
  For specific alert boxes consult the Alert message locator,   323
aliases
  explained,   52–53 [7]
  information windows,   52 [7]
  making,   54–55 [7], 228 [7]
  maximum number,   55 [7]
  memory used by,   228 [7]
  removing,   55 [7]
  renaming,   55 [7]
Apple desktop bus,   17
Apple File Exchange,   141
Apple Menu Items folder
  contents under System 7,   23

AppleShare
  administrators,   276–277
  file server,   276
  icon absent from Chooser,   278
AppleTalk
  activation for printing,   39
  activation lacking problems,   303–304
  port for connection to,   18, 318
applications
  data files missing from Open dialog box,   253
  information windows,   48–51
  managing multiple
    System 6,   36 [6], 38–39 [6]
    System 7,   36–38 [7]
  memory size resetting,   50–51, 252
  memory use current,   49
  memory use suggested,   49
  opening,   31–33
  quitting spontaneously,   50, 242, 252
  startup, setting,   72–73
application software
  explained,   19

B

backups,   82–83

Macintosh® Bible products

The Mac Bible, Third Edition. It's the best-selling Mac book ever, with 591,000 copies in print (including six foreign translations). The Third Edition has **1,115 pages**, with a 90-page index and a 68-page glossary. At 2.5¢ a page for the best—and most clearly written—Mac information available, how can you go wrong? **$28.**

The Mac Bible Guide to FileMaker Pro. "A must for every FileMaker Pro user," as Dennis Marshall, Claris's FileMaker Pro product manager put it, this is the first comprehensive guide to the Mac's leading database program. With dozens of step-by-step procedures, shortcuts and troubleshooting tips, it will save hours of your time. **$18.**

The Mac Bible Guide to System 7. System 7 represents the most dramatic changes ever made to the Mac's basic system software, and sets the stage for all future system improvements. Our crystal-clear, accessible and affordable guide, by veteran Mac author Charles Rubin, gets you up to speed with System 7 in no time. **$12.**

The Mac Bible Software Disks, Third Edition. This companion to *The Mac Bible* is full of great public-domain software, shareware, templates, fonts and art. Painstakingly gleaned from literally thousands of programs, these disks offer you *la crème de la crème.* Over 1.5 megabytes of software on two 800K disks. **$20.**

The Mac Bible "What Do I Do Now?" Book, Second Edition. Completely updated through System 7, this bestseller covers just about every sort of basic problem a Mac user can encounter—from the wrong fonts appearing in a printout to the mouse not responding. Easy to understand, it's an essential resource for beginners and experienced users alike. **$15.**

The Dead Mac Scrolls. Now any Mac owner—from the novice to the expert—can keep repair costs down. In this unique and encyclopedic guide, Macintosh guru Larry Pina diagnoses hundreds of hardware problems, shows you the simplest and cheapest way to fix them, and tells you how much the repairs should cost. **$32.**

System 7 package. Save $5 when you buy *The Mac Bible* and our *Guide to System 7* together. **$35.**
Bible/software combo. Save $10 when you buy *The Mac Bible* and the *Bible* disks together. **$38.**
Super combo. Save $13 by buying *The Mac Bible*, the *Bible* disks and *"What Do I Do Now?" Book.* **$48.**
Ultra combo. Save $15 by buying *The Mac Bible* with the *Bible* disks, the *"What Do I Do Now?" Book* and the *Guide to System 7.* **$58.**

The Macintosh Bible T-shirt. Our T-shirts are striking—bright magenta lettering on your choice of black or white. Here's a little picture of the front. The back says: **Easy is hard** *(The second commandment from The Macintosh Bible).* These are high-quality, preshrunk, 100% cotton shirts; they're thick, well-made and run large. **$9.**

How to Order:

To order any of these products, just fill out the form on the next page and send it with your payment to **Peachpit Press, 2414 Sixth Street, Berkeley, CA 94710.** You can also order by phone with Visa or MasterCard. Call us at 510/548-4393 or 800/283-9444, or fax your order to us at 510/548-5991.

Satisfaction is unconditionally guaranteed or your money will be cheerfully refunded!

Order form for Macintosh® Bible products

Please send me:

_____ copies of *The Macintosh Bible, 3 ed.*	@ $28 =	$_____
_____ copies of *The Macintosh Bible Guide to FileMaker Pro*	@ $18 =	$_____
_____ copies of *The Macintosh Bible Guide to System 7*	@ $12 =	$_____
_____ copies of *The Macintosh Bible Software Disks, 3 ed.*	@ $20 =	$_____
_____ copies of *The Macintosh Bible "What Do I Do Now?" Book, 2 ed.*	@ $15 =	$_____
_____ copies of *The Dead Mac Scrolls*	@ $32 =	$_____
_____ copies of *The Dead Mac Scrolls disk*	@ $32 =	$_____
_____ copies of the System 7 package	@ $35 =	$_____
_____ copies of the *Bible*/software combination	@ $38 =	$_____
_____ copies of the super combo	@ $48 =	$_____
_____ copies of the ultra combo	@ $58 =	$_____
_____ *Macintosh Bible* T-shirts	@ $ 9 =	$_____

(in black:___S ___M ___L ___XL; in white:___S ___M ___L ___XL)

Tax of 8.25% applies to California residents only.
UPS ground shipping: $4 first item, $1 each additional.
UPS 2nd day air: $7 for first item, $2 each additional.
Air mail to Canada: $6 first item, $4 each additional.
Air mail overseas: $14 each item.

shipping, handling and tax (if any): $_____

TOTAL: $_____

☐ I'm enclosing a check for the total shown above. *(Customers outside the US: checks must be in US funds and payable through a US bank. You can also pay with an international postal money order, but not a Eurocheque. It's easiest if you pay by credit card.)*

☐ Please charge my charge card for the total amount shown above:

VISA/MasterCard # _____ exp. date _____

cardholder signature _____

Ship this order to: *(PLEASE PRINT CLEARLY)*

_____
name

_____
address (please give us a street address so we can ship via UPS)

_____
city, state, zip (or city, postal code, country)

_____
daytime phone number (with area code)

Peachpit Press, 2414 Sixth Street, Berkeley, CA 94710
510/548-4393 or 800/283-9444 • Fax: 510/548-5991